59.95

D1518127

AMBIGUITY, COPING, AND GOVERNANCE

ISRAELI EXPERIENCES IN POLITICS, RELIGION, AND POLICYMAKING

Ira Sharkansky

Westport, Connecticut
London

Library of Congress Cataloging-in-Publication Data

Sharkansky, Ira.
    Ambiguity, coping, and governance : Israeli experiences in
politics, religion, and policymaking / Ira Sharkansky.
      p.   cm.
    Includes bibliographical references (p.   ) and index.
    ISBN 0–275–96718–2 (alk. paper)
    1. Political planning—Israel.   2. Israel—Politics and
government.   3. Religion and politics—Israel.   4. Ambiguity.
I. Title.
JQ1830.A56P647   1999
320′.6′095694—dc21   99–14850

British Library Cataloguing in Publication Data is available.

Library of Congress Catalog Card Number: 99–14850
ISBN: 0–275–96718–2

First published in 1999

Praeger Publishers, 88 Post Road West, Westport, CT 06881
An imprint of Greenwood Publishing Group, Inc.
www.praeger.com

Printed in the United States of America

The paper used in this book complies with the
Permanent Paper Standard issued by the National
Information Standards Organization (Z39.48–1984).

10 9 8 7 6 5 4 3 2 1

Contents

Preface   ix

1.   Difficult and Interesting Problems   1

    Coping   5

    Politics   19

    Governance   20

    Rational Decision Making   21

    The Supremacy of Politics in Governance   22

    Coping Is Humane as Well as Inevitable   23

2.   Why Israel?   27

    National Security   28

    Immigration   29

    Jewish Majorities   29

    A Cumbersome Giant   31

    Limits to Israel's Power   33

    Moving Towards Normality   46

3.   Ambiguity in Religion as Well as Politics   53

    Ambiguity in Religion   54

    The Positive and Negative Sides of Ambiguity   60

    Religion and Politics in the Jewish State   61

Religion and Politics in Utah   67
On the Nature of Religion(s)   76

**4. A Typology of Ambiguity in Policymaking and
Administration**   79
Who, Where, When, How, Why, and with
What Effects?   79

5. Which Jerusalem?   93
Synonyms for Jerusalem   96
Which Locale of Jerusalem?   97
The Political Significance of Numerous
"Jerusalems"   103
A Proposal That Could Work, but that Politicians
Cannot Articulate   106
On the Advantages of Coping and Ambiguity in
Jerusalem   107
Jewish Ambiguities in Jerusalem   109
A Name   110

6. Assessing Israel   111
Allegations and Assessment   115
Testing the Claims   118
Is the Glass Half Empty or Half Full?   126

7. Ambiguities of the Peace Process   129
Multiple Disputes   131
Ambiguities   137
Coping with Our Neighbors and Ourselves   141
Finality, Like Consistency, Is the Preoccupation
of Small Minds   145

**8. If Social Science Is Ambiguous, Can Governance
Be Different?**   149
Points in the Historical Record   151
The Outer Reaches of Policy Analysis:
James S. Coleman and Others   154
On the Basic Assumptions in Policy Analysis:
What Does It All Mean?   158

9.   Coping with the Downside of Coping   163

          The Downside of Coping   163

          Political Perspectives and the Judgment of Coping   166

          Coping with the Problems of Coping   168

          When is Coping Worth the Costs?   170

Notes   173

For Further Reading   195

Index   199

Preface

This book combines description and advocacy. It describes ambiguity and other forms of coping for dealing with difficult public problems, and portrays the benefits as well as the costs of these less-than-perfect ways of policymaking. It is written in the context of Israel's conflict with the Palestinians and other Arabs, and Israel's even more ancient conflict within itself about Judaism.

There is both optimism and pessimism. The bright side is that ambiguity works. The dark side is not so much its disadvantages as the realization that many commentators and practitioners of the craft seem unwilling to recognize its advantages and unwilling to promote its use for difficult problems. The irony is that officials who have shown considerable skill as creators and exploiters of ambiguity demand clear and fulsome solutions. Pragmatists thereby become demagogues.

Shimon Peres and his Labor Party colleagues had done well in obfuscating the emotional problems of Jerusalem until they seemed to shy away from their own reality in the 1996 election campaign. They insisted that they would not grant the workaday concessions that they had, in fact, already allowed the Palestinians. The detailed issue of the moment was perhaps minor: the use of Orient House as a symbolic site of Palestinian government in East Jerusalem. The minister of internal security promised not to allow the Palestine Authority to use the building for meeting foreign dignitaries. He thereby lost an opportunity to lead the voters in the realization that ceremonial sites need not threaten an entire city. An American example is that the United Nations' sovereignty over its headquarters in New

York does not threaten the United States. By their fright over the voters' emotions about Jerusalem, Labor politicians also lost an even larger opportunity to educate the people that "Jerusalem" has numerous meanings, and some of them could be used to the mutual benefit of Israelis and Palestinians.

Intellectuals also have trouble recognizing that ambiguity works and may be better than clear solutions. Several of my Israeli political science colleagues challenge the notions of coping and ambiguity. "What is your solution?" is the refrain. The whole point is that there is no clear solution to vexatious problems, as when there are contradictory claims about small and overlapping spaces. Politicians and academics will continue to search for the elusive solutions. They will criticize this description of what works, and say that it offers no clear and final settlement. True.

Ambiguity and other forms of coping do not offer magic solutions for all problems. They assume a mutual desire for accommodation. In this respect, it is not clear that the situation surrounding this book is one of optimism or pessimism. The peace process has not collapsed, but neither does it show clear signs of producing the kind of peace that now prevails among the countries of western Europe. Each side may have extended the maximum accommodations that are possible in the eyes of fearful leaders concerned about the reliability of their adversaries and worried about their political standing. For a political scientist, it is risky to write about conflicts that are ongoing, and where violence may flare up in place of muddling through. Nonetheless, it is important to recognize the contributions made to date by a willingness to cope rather than to seek ideal solutions. It is useful to identify further opportunities that may be achievable by these imperfect ways of making policy.

Ambiguity is only one of the tools available to policymakers, and one of those employed in managing the conflicts between Israelis and the Palestinians. It falls within the category of inducements, or carrots. There are also sanctions, or sticks, in the Israeli policymaker's tool kit. These include economic actions, like the closing of Israeli opportunities to Palestinian workers and businesses, and the use of force against those who threaten force. The Palestinians, for their part, can incite violence if they tire of coping.

This book elaborates the use of ambiguity as a policy tool. I prefer it, and other inducements, over the employment of sanctions, force, and other sticks. Inducements are likely to be more humane, less objectionable, and less costly than the use of sanctions. However, I recognize that carrots might not work if the sticks are not in the background and perhaps occasionally brought to the foreground when their use seems appropriate. Managing the Israeli-Palestinian conflict is not all that different from other political issues. Citizens in well-governed societies are offered the carrots of public services and a decent life in exchange for compliance with tax regulations and other statutes. For those who do not accept this bargain, however, there are the sticks of law enforcement.

The central idea of this book grew out of my earlier writings about Jerusalem, religion, and Israeli policymaking. My first articles on these subjects began to appear in professional journals in the 1980s. The books that I wrote on the way to this one include *Governing Jerusalem* (1996), *Rituals of Conflict* (1996), and *Policy Making in Israel* (1997). Some of the material comes from joint projects with Dr. Gedalia Auerbach of the Hebrew University, Professor Asher Friedberg of the University of Haifa, Dr. Reuven Schwartz of the University of Haifa, and Dr. Yair Zalmonovich of the University of Haifa. I benefited from numerous conversations with other academics and policymakers in Israel and abroad, as well as with my older children Erica and Stefan. They deal with ambiguity and coping in clinical psychology and investments.

Here the focus is the importance of coping by policymakers and other public officials with respect to difficult public problems. Most of the details are Israeli, but the implications are far wider. With problems as difficult as those portrayed here, the search for complete or maximum solutions is neither efficient nor satisfying. Aspirations to solve difficult problems completely produce frustration among policymakers and cynicism among citizens. And when pushed by policymakers who do not recognize the attractions of coping, the pursuit of a full solution may endanger values that democrats rate highly. These include the opportunity to be heard by those who object to the policy being pursued, and the merits of flexibility in dealing with cases that do not permit simple solutions.

The book was already in press when Israelis went to the polls in May, 1999. The results of the election changed the government in considerable detail, but perhaps not the underlying traits of national politics or the style of government. Ehud Barak won the position of prime minister with an impressive 56 percent of the vote, but his political party received only 22 percent of the seats in the Knesset. As in the case of all Israel's previous prime ministers, the government that he assembled blurred his own preferences and the expectations of those who supported him, his party, and the other members of the coalition.

National unity and peace were themes of Barak's campaign. However, it will take a while to see which of the many hopes and fears will find themselves reflected in the policies enacted and implemented. A number of Israelis appeared to be voting not so much in favor of Barak as in opposition to the policies or personality of Benjamin Netanyahu. The support given to the ultra-Orthodox SHAS party, which increased Knesset representation from 10 to 17, may not have indicated an increase in religiosity, *per se*. Some of SHAS's new voters came from former Likud supporters who had abandoned Netanyahu and his party. Others responded to SHAS's campaign of ethnicity directed at Jews of North African and Asian origin. The multiplicity of issues waiting international resolution assured their own uncertainties. Palestinian demands for territorial transfers, economic agreements, and provisions for Jerusalem will compete for attention with Syrian expectations of a total withdrawal from the Golan Heights, both moderate and extreme sentiments heard from various power holders in Lebanon, as well as Israelis' own concerns for security. The new realities seem unlikely to disappoint those expecting the management of expectations and uncertainties by amiguity and other coping mechanisms.

I

Difficult and Interesting Problems

Government and politics are interesting when problems are difficult. The most fascinating problems are likely to be on the agenda for a long time without being solved in any final sense. Attention may come and go. Individual episodes may find their treatment, but the same underlying problems will return.

My study window on the eastern side of Jerusalem looks out on an Arab village 200 meters away and beyond to the Judean Desert and the Jordan Valley. On a clear day I see the Jordanian capital of Amman on the ridge across the valley. One persistent problem in this direction is how Israel will live with its neighbors. Two kilometers in another direction is the troubled street named Bar Ilan. This symbolizes religious-secular disputes about the application of Jewish law in a Jewish state where most of the Jews are secular and some are antireligious.

The Jerusalem Municipality constructed Bar Ilan Street some time ago in order to direct traffic around an ultra-Orthodox neighborhood and avoid a confrontation between religious and secular Jews about driving on the Sabbath. The ultra-Orthodox neighborhood expanded across Bar Ilan Street and the confrontation had to come, sooner or later. Shouts of *Shabbos*, overturned garbage dumpsters, and occasionally the throwing of stones and dirty diapers greeted drivers who used the road between sundown on Friday and sundown on Saturday. Secular and antireligious Jews demonstrated against the threat of religious coercion. The police intervened. The secular minister of transportation who held office under the Labor government of 1992–1996 accepted the recommendation of a transportation planner and ruled that the road was a vital transportation link and must remain open. When a religious minister of transportation came to office with the Likud government after the 1996 election, the same planner decided that the road could be closed during times of prayer. The Supreme Court responded to a citizens' suit and demanded an explanation about the planner's change of mind. The issue went back and forth between the minister, a panel composed of religious and secular citizens who could not agree about a solution, and again the Supreme Court. Currently the road closes during times of prayer on the Sabbath and religious holidays. Insofar as prayers vary with sundown from one season to the next, we must consult the calendar and our watches before setting out to grandma's on the other side of town for our Sabbath meal. Another suit is pending in the Supreme Court to keep the road open all during the Sabbath, and religious activists have demonstrated to close the road during the entire Sabbath.

The United States has no shortage of problems dealing with peace and religion. Potentially hostile borders are not across the street from the study of working political scientists, and Sabbath does not present a problem for secular Americans. However, the country's status as the world's sole great power assures it a role in other people's problems. Israeli-Arab disputes seldom depart from the concerns of American policymakers or newspaper editors. Other problems trouble American policymakers in what used to be Yugoslavia, as well as in Africa, and even closer to home in Latin America. To some nervous Americans, Mexico represents potential hostility, while to others it is the source of yet another difficult problem concerned with illegal migration.

Religion is well placed on the American political agenda. Although the Constitution enshrines a separation of church and state, the United States is a leader among Western democracies in the religiosity of its population. And, as in Israel, religiosity provokes antireligiosity. Some items on the religious vs. antireligious agenda of the United States are not about religion, per se, but they draw their energy from religious doctrine. Earlier in the twentieth century the prohibition of alcohol was a struggle involving religious communities, with a number of Protestant denominations arrayed against the rest of the country. Whereas Catholics tended to be against prohibition, they are now among the religious activists leading the struggle against abortion. Other campaigns that have roots in religious doctrines concern prostitution, pornography, homosexuality, and the teaching of creationism vs. evolution, as well as prayer in schools and the display of religious symbols like Christmas trees and Hanukkah menorah on public sites. Legal experts use terms like "vague and confusing," and "the subject of endless debate" to describe U.S. federal court decisions about what is permitted and forbidden with respect to religious observances on public property or by public bodies.[1]

Crime and drugs, as well as health care and environmental protection, are prominent issues in the United States and many other countries. Like the quest for peace and accommodation on matters of religion, they seem to defy any search for a fulsome treatment.

Political scientists as well as ordinary citizens who are interested in politics gravitate to the more difficult issues. They ignore the great bulk of what government does as predictable humdrum. Most pieces of mail pass through the system and get to their destination in reasonable time. Most traffic flows on the proper side of the road close to the posted speed. Most school teachers keep reasonable order and instruct their students in something useful. Most citizens pay amounts close to the taxes required by law on or before the dates they are due.

Political scientists and journalists who follow public policy generally write about the things that do not work well. They describe problems, analyze proposals, and explain the conditions that keep the problems from being solved. Often the explanation of a problem's insolubility is conflicting interests. Some individuals demand something new but others are cautious about committing resources. Or the problem may be one of competing theories and limited information. The recurrent issues of crime, health care, and poverty have long histories of creative proposals, elaborate programming, and frustration in failing to solve one or another underlying cause of crime. Some programs face hostility in the legislative or executive branches, or run afoul of the convoluted procedures of administrative units that are more inclined to score points in their continuing struggles against one another than to cooperate in serving the public.

Difficult problems reveal the tensions in society. The way the public and policymakers react to them is likely to show politics at its worst or best. Avoidance, groupthink, a retreat to routines, demagoguery, entrepreneurialism, and creativity appear along with crisis and excitement. The result may be a break point or an episode in which the society departs from the past and begins to remake the future. Or it may choose more of the same, and thereby avoid an opportunity. A disaster can occur, in extreme cases even a revolution and social chaos, which produces further tests of the population and its leadership.

The purpose of this book is to portray the ways that policymakers deal with problems that defy solution. Difficult problems were among the attractions that brought me to Israel part way through my career as a university teacher of political science. More than twenty years of residence in Israel has heightened my awareness of how policymakers deal with them. This book is mostly about coping with difficult problems that I experience on a daily basis. However, its message is applicable in other settings. Policymakers in democratic regimes are likely to respond to their most difficult issues by coping, or problem management, rather than problem solution.

While my experiences as an Israeli have shaped the perspectives included here, I have tried to be fair in my assessments of Israeli actions and my portrayal of its adversaries. Currently the most exciting item in the Middle East is the possible creation of a new state of Palestine and the reactions in Israel and among the Palestinians to the prospects and the fears. Israel and the Palestinians claim the same land. Within each national grouping are numerous perspectives and political movements. Each has invested years in building arguments and recruiting supporters. Leaders and followers insist that justice is on their side.

Like the dismemberment of the Soviet Union, which helped to bring about this change, events here require rethinking ritualized expectations and behaviors. More and more Israelis are willing to see the complexity among Palestinians. Not all are terrorists wanting to continue what the Nazis began. Many speak to us in Hebrew about their desire to run their own affairs and to exist in peace. Yet some continue to demand all of Palestine, which to them includes all of Israel. And officials of the Palestine Authority have tolerated or even encouraged violence. Part way through the peace process, the annual incidence of Israeli civilians killed in acts of terror had increased since Israel and the Palestine Authority signed an accord in 1993. Meanwhile, Israelis have lost the image of being peace-loving pioneers. Some have operated in the style of terrorists in killing civilians. The differences between Israelis and Arabs are in shades of gray rather than mythic black and white.

The unresolved questions are:

- How much additional land should Israel transfer to Palestinian control in these conditions?
- Should Israel allow the Palestinian Authority to declare itself a state with full rights to choose its armaments and alliances? Or something short of that?

Only slightly less prominent than Israel's problems with Arabs are the conflicts between Israeli Jews. Religious and secular antagonists call on well-learned arguments of ancient lineage. Current disputes resemble those that separated Judaic zealots from those who emulated the culture of the Greeks and Romans in the period from about 167 B.C.E to 135 C.E.

In countries where the most pressing issues are illicit drugs or sex, environmental protection, poverty, health reform, and crime, the problems are no less difficult. Money, status, physical pleasure, and ideology get in the way of accepting compromises that outsiders see as reasonable. While some authorities offer addicts access to needles and drugs in order to combat crime and AIDS, others view these measures as intolerable.

COPING

Coping is a useful term to describe how policymakers deal with serious problems. Synonyms of *coping* show that is does not seek to solve problems once and for all time: *contend, deal with, endure, fight successfully or on equal terms, handle, hold one's own, manage, struggle, subsist, survive, negotiate, bargain, barter, weather, adapt,* and *satisfice*.[2] These imply decisions that are "good enough," even if they are not what any of the participants really want.

Political scientists have tended to use *coping* casually to describe policymaking in difficult settings, or to prescribe how policymakers should deal with vexing problems. A number of studies include coping in their titles or subtitles, but do not provide any systematic discussion of the concept. In most of these cases, the prominent use of the word seems designed to emphasize the difficulties encountered.[3] Daniel Patrick Moynihan used coping to convey good judgment, or a capacity to anticipate developments that require action.[4]

The concept of coping is more fully developed by psychologists, who use it to describe how individuals deal with stress.[5] More than political scientists, psychologists have been systematic in clarifying a variety of stresses and coping behaviors, as well as the role of a person's resources in helping to cope with stress. Formulations for what some term *active* and *passive* coping are similar to what others call *hardiness* and *helplessness*. Active coping responds to stress with challenge, commitment, creative information seeking, the definition and ranking of goals, organization, and discipline. It includes efforts to salvage something from a difficult situation; to keep a process going in the expectation of greater opportunities or holding off greater losses; surveying options and recruiting support; changing expectations in the face of conditions that are not likely to change in the short range; and ranking priorities in order to achieve the more important at the expense of the less important. Passive coping responds to stress with a lack of control, hopelessness, confusion, rigidity, distortion, disorganization, randomness, disorder, distress, depression, anxiety, withdrawal, flight, or submission. It exhibits pointless emoting that involves loss of control and direction for oneself and potential allies; quixotic choice of options in an effort to *do something* without taking account of likely costs and benefits; and frittering away resources in efforts that do not produce significant accomplishments. Psychologists have made impressive progress in classifying coping behaviors and analyzing data about coping with different kinds of stress. However, there remains considerable dispute as to the capacity of particular coping behaviors to assure a relief of various kinds of stress.[6]

Prominent among the stresses of politics are contradictory demands, as when one group demands increased spending for services while another group complains about taxes or government debt and urges cutbacks. There are seldom enough resources to pay for everything that people want. Among groups willing to innovate, there are further complications among those wishing to put resources into different programs or to pursue specific programs in different ways. There is also likely to be competition between those who want the same prized appointment or contract.

Uncertainty is the bane of public life. Policymakers are not sure that a proposal will accomplish what its advocates promise. They do not know how rival countries, political parties, or individual politicians will respond to an initiative. Well-laid plans go astray if there is an unexpected increase in the cost-of-living index, the exchange rate of the national currency, violence in a neighboring country, or the death of a political ally who was expected to provide important support.

As a strategy for dealing with problems, coping is associated with a variety of tactics. To put it more simply, there are several ways to cope. Among the tactics described in this book are accommodation, improvisation, avoidance, indirection, and ambiguity. There are no crisp definitions of these terms, or clear boundaries between behaviors associated with each. This discussion reflects how the words are used in various writings about policymakers who deal with conflicts. We shall give the greatest prominence to ambiguity, which appears to be the most inclusive of the tactics and the most prominent in politics and policymaking.

Accommodation

Accommodation suggests compromise but can be more subtle. Accommodation in policymaking is not simply a division of the cake in equal shares. Accommodation seeks to keep the peace by anticipating demands, or reckoning with what it may take to keep a potentially active group at least minimally satisfied. It may give something even to those who are not currently making demands. It may entail accommodating oneself to an adversary's perspectives. This enables the granting of political access, policy benefits, or personal opportunities even without them being requested in an explicit fashion. Accommodation shows itself in Jerusalem, where the Arab minority has pointedly abstained from political activity in the Israeli municipality since 1967. Israeli authorities provided concessions that had not been formally requested by official Arab representatives in any established forum of government. They allowed Muslim religious leaders to remain in *de facto* control of holy sites also desired by Jews. They permitted Arab business and professional personnel to stay within existing Arab associations and the East Jerusalem Chamber of Commerce, rather than requiring them to obtain Israeli licenses or to join Israeli associations that govern their members' practices. Israeli officials allowed Jordanian dinars to circulate in East Jerusalem, despite regulations that prohibited Israeli residents from dealing in foreign currency.[7]

There is no assurance that accommodation will obtain the response that is intended. A beleaguered policymaker may have to calculate how much of an accommodation will buy quiet from an adversary and yet not cause the policymaker's own restive allies to rebel against what they perceive as an excess of generosity. Israelis quarrel about the gestures made to Palestinians, with some hardliners taking the position that only force will produce peace. Critics of the efforts by Western governments to accommodate the different sides in parts of former Yugoslavia see only failure and a weakening of prestige for those who make the effort. American officials chastised the Germans for their efforts to accommodate with trade and investment what the Americans saw as the intractable government of Iran. Commentators quarrel as to whether American accommodations of Chinese authorities have done anything to bring about an improvement in human rights.

Improvisation

Dictionaries define improvisation in terms of public speaking, music, and the theater: composition, performance, or speaking on the spur of the moment, extemporaneously, without detailed preparation.[8] The meaning in policymaking and administration is similar. Improvisation is a way of responding to unexpected opportunities and dangers. Hebrew helps to clarify the concept. It uses similar terms for "improvisation" and "immediate." The implication is that improvisation carries an immediate answer for a need in a fluid and uncertain environment.[9]

Closely related to improvisation are *trying something new* and *entrepreneurialism.* Some writers use the terms interchangeably, but these other behaviors may come as a result of careful planning. Improvisation is more free-floating creativity, conceived and tried under pressures that demand an immediate response.

Improvisation is one of those coping mechanisms that we use frequently, in numerous settings. We improvise in teaching, negotiations, and in everyday conversation. Surprise or unexpected developments can provoke the improvisation. We may not realize that we are departing from normal patterns of speech. Improvisation becomes noticeable when the encounter is difficult and our uncertainty causes discomfort.

As in a performance or speech, improvisation in policymaking and administration can be brilliant or clumsy. Improvisation can be just what an organization needs in a difficult situation or a sudden opportunity, or a step toward disaster. Amateurs who go on the stage or newcomers in policymaking risk a great deal when they improvise. Experience provides a wealth of options that may be called upon quickly to help determine what is wrong in the present situation and suggest how to respond.

Avoidance

Avoidance is another way of coping. It is a widely used, if not always acknowledged, shortcut through an analysis of policy options. Why invest in the consideration of options likely to provoke intense opposition, to be significantly more expensive than alternatives, or that are known to have failed in similar circumstances? Committees may deliberate such options briefly and go on to others. The problems associated with these options may be so obvious as to allow them to be passed over without mention.

Avoidance may involve a slipping over issues that would be cumbersome if dealt with immediately. When challenged, policymakers may promise a response at a more opportune time. They can indicate that they have defined general principles and cannot detail all contingencies. Yet the details still in dispute may represent the most serious of conflicts.

On some occasions avoidance is a flight from responsibility. Yet the same instance may actually be a way to take losses in the short run in order to reap greater benefits later. The Palestinians' boycott of Israeli political opportunities in Jerusalem since 1967 has cost them opportunities to elect perhaps 25 percent of the city council and gain benefits in the ongoing allocation of public resources. In the view of Palestinians who demand a boycott, however, it is a way to assure communal unity in the expectation of the greater benefits represented by national independence and a Palestinian Jerusalem. Until now the losses are more apparent than the promise of gain, but history continues.

Policymakers who find themselves hemmed in by contrary demands may avoid the truth. They may lie as to their intentions. Some appear to agree with the last person who speaks with them. Fudging, speaking out of both sides of their mouth, not being pinned down are common ways of describing dissimulation and duplicity. Dictionaries describe these actions as concealment of what really is, feigning, hypocrisy, acting in two ways at different times, deceitfulness, and double-dealing.

Tax law differs in its treatment of *avoidance* and *evasion*. Avoidance is taking advantage of legal opportunities to minimize one's tax obligations, whereas evasion involves lying, fraud, or some other form of deceit. The same distinction is useful in a discussion of coping by policymakers. Those who avoid the undesirable may be thought of as less slippery than those who evade. The avoider does not tell the whole story, while the evader says something that is not true. However, "thou shall not lie" is not an absolute. Physicians may feel justified in misleading patients about a life-threatening illness, and a national leader may stretch the truth or even invent some facts to maintain public confidence. While tax evasion is a crime, political evasion may be an excusable manifestation of avoidance.

Indirection

Another way to cope is to make the appearance of pursuing one goal while the real aim is something else. Indirection occurs in budgeting where a demand for reduced spending is met by cutting outlays for a favored program. The purpose is to cause politicians to object to those particular cuts, with the hope that the entire idea of budget reduction will be lost in the noise.[10] Bureaucratic infighters learn how to oppose a program without clarifying their reasons, or even to oppose while seeming to support: "That's a great idea! It could be even better if we specify more completely what is intended." What comes next is a move to appoint a committee. Its report, by intention, may never be finalized. Also, the indirect explanation of "limited resources" can cover what is really personal animosity between the individual expressing the opinion and the one who proposed an activity.

In the case of Israeli-Palestinian maneuvering in Jerusalem, repeated Israeli threats to close all Palestinian institutions in the city may be a signal to the Palestinians that they should cease particularly offensive actions, such as the seizing of Palestinians opposed to the leadership of the Palestine Liberation Organization (PLO) by security personnel operating undercover in the city, or killing Palestinians who sell land to Jews.

Ambiguity

Ambiguity is a lubricant of politics that appears in many settings.[11] It serves politicians who make numerous promises that are far-reaching in their implications, without specifying just what will be delivered. The deception can be intentional or innocent: associated with a politician who truly is Machiavellian, or an action by a politician who does not realize the implications of all the promises made for the sum of resources that will be available. Voters choose on the basis of generalized affection for a campaign. The successful politician can select among the commitments whose implementation can be reconciled with circumstances. It is a well-practiced craft that reinforces a chronic cynicism about politicians but generally does not threaten a regime.

The appeal of ambiguity for a policymaker is the opportunity to skip over especially contentious issues in the hopes that an "understanding" will facilitate accommodations. Adversaries can reach agreement on the main outline of a program without bogging down in all the messy details. An editorial in the *New York Times* with respect to an agreement between state attorneys general and tobacco companies was headlined, "Accord's Impact: Hazy." The meaning was that the agreement did not assure all that antitobacco activists desired.[12] Subsequent comments indicated that the widely heralded agreement would be an event in an ongoing process rather than a solution for the conflicts between tobacco companies, public health authorities, state governments, and smokers.

Legislators enact laws that describe general lines of action. They do not spell out all the implications, but leave actual rulemaking and implementation to administrative bodies. Typical is the congressional declaration of national environmental policy.

The Congress, recognizing the profound impact of man's activity on the interrelations of all components of the natural environment, particularly the profound influences of population growth, high-density urbanization, industrial expansion, resource exploitation, and new and expanding technological advances and recognizing further the critical importance of restoring and maintaining environmental quality to the overall welfare and development of man, declares that it is the continuing policy of the Federal Government, in cooperation with State and local governments, and other concerned public and private organizations, to use all practicable means and measures, including financial and technical assistance, in a manner calculated to foster and promote the general welfare, to create and maintain conditions under which man and nature can exist in productive harmony, and fulfill the social, economic, and other requirements of present and future generations of Americans.[13]

There is much additional legislation to specify various parts of the congressional intent. However, there are also general grants of discretion to key administrators. For example, one section of U.S. environmental law, dealing with illegally obtained migratory birds, indicates that they "shall be forfeited to the United States and disposed of by the Secretary of the Interior in such a manner as he deems appropriate."[14]

Members of the legislature should know that they will not see the implementation of all that might fit within the frameworks they endorse. They can return to the subject at a later time if they are not satisfied with what administrators actually deliver, or they can rest with the accomplishments achieved.

Policymakers' "mandates" are never precise. The fog of ambiguity may cover a bit of the emperor's nakedness. Vagueness, murky language, and a loosely defined "consensus" facilitates agreement. If one or another constituency eventually loses something in the implementation, the loss may be acceptable in light of other gains achieved. Even where a written agreement appears to be comprehensive, fuzziness about which provisions will actually be enforced allows flexibility to deal with evolving reality, limited resources, and unexpected crises.[15] The test of ambiguity is its workability. If a program survives the charges that it is not exactly what all of its architects intended, it is likely to be a case of reasonable deviations from expectations.

Related to the issue of ambiguity are the unclear boundaries between formal policy and informal rules of the game. These blurred demarcations offer opportunities for individuals to stretch their rights, but without knowing for certain when authorities will intervene and enforce the rules as written. How much faster than the posted speed limit can we drive without being charged with a violation? What claims can we make on a tax return without triggering an audit? Such cases present temptations and potential embarrassment that add a bit of spice to conventional citizenship. Flexibility is an attraction, but ambiguous limits to acceptable behavior invite irresponsible exploitation of flexibility. Especially problematic are situations where there has been a history of violence. If good fences make good neighbors, a situation of undefined boundaries between hostile communities raises the possibility of bloodshed. Deals involving politicians, business firms, and campaign contributions continue despite a host of rules and limitations designed to curb corruption. Political parties need money in order to campaign, investors want to move projects along. Absolute justice is elusive. What should we call corruption, and what should be applauded as shortcuts through official procedures in the service of the public?[16]

Individuals who serve the public deal with ambiguity on a daily basis. Should the police officer write a ticket or arrest a citizen when the violation is not all that clear or not serious? If the decision is to arrest, how much force should be employed? How should one respond to hints from a supervisor? Cases of sexual harassment depend on contrary claims about what was perceived and what was intended by ambiguous comments. Ultimately an administrative superior or a court may have to decide about comments or behaviors that could be interpreted in different ways.[17]

The structure of government is ambiguous. What is within the responsibility of elected officials or the major departments of government? Questions like this lose their meaning in a situation when public authorities include untold numbers of organizations somewhere on the margins of government, with no clear lines of responsibility or means for holding them accountable. The General Accounting Office of the United States reports that there are more than one million organizations with tax-exempt status, presumably because they conduct one or another public service. (The tiny country of Israel has more than 20,000 nonprofit organizations.) Prominent among these are charitable organizations, but these receive only a portion of their revenues from donations. Many of them also provide services to clients of government agencies, under contract with the agencies.[18] There are also profit-making corporations doing work that once had been done by government. Some 5 percent of the inmates in American prisons are confined in facilities managed by private corporations.[19] What once was thought to be the government's monopoly of legitimate force is now shared with prison corporations and guard companies that provide security for government installations, businesses, institutions, and private homes. The problem comes when complaints arise, and government officials do not feel themselves accountable for the actions of a body that has become quasi-governmental.[20]

It is not only the quasi-governmental that presents problems of accountability. Divisions of responsibility between different departments that each touch on a common program, or shared responsibility between national, regional, and local offices are also problematic. When more than one body has formal responsibility, each may try to shift the dirty work to someone else. Shared work may be nobody's work. Avoidance of the unpleasant, as well as simple overload and the temptation to focus on what is entirely one's own tasks, can lead programs that are jointly administered to be poorly administered.

There is much ambiguity in the realm of international diplomacy. Striking the right balance between intentions and vagueness is an art form that facilitates peaceful relations between nations. The diplomats who drafted U.N. Security Council Resolution 242, approved in November 1967, sought to satisfy both pro-Israeli and anti-Israeli perspectives as to the demands being made. The official versions in different languages varied as to whether they affirmed the principle that Israeli armed forces should withdraw "from territories occupied in the recent conflict" or "from *the* territories occupied in the recent conflict." The first version quoted here suggests that partial withdrawal would comply with the U.N. resolution, while the second version implies that the U.N. would expect total withdrawal. After the 1998 Israeli-Palestinian conference shepherded by President Clinton and other U.S. officials at Wye Plantation, Israeli government ministers received a Hebrew-language summary of the agreements that was closer to Israeli preferences than the official English version. Palestinian negotiators had agreed to the conference conclusions without seeing a map of the territories the Israelis would be handing over to them. Perhaps the appearance of agreement was more important than the details.

A veiled threat by one country against another may produce compliance with the wishes of the threatening country, without being so specific as to provoke undue militancy from the threatened country. The United States has sought to navigate the ambiguities involved in a "two Chinas" policy. This involves maintaining diplomatic relations with a mainland government that insists that it is the only China that the United States may deal with, while maintaining important relationships between the economies of the United States and Taiwan and more or less "guaranteeing," security to a Taiwan government concerned about an attack from the mainland.

Yet another example of managed ambiguity is the effort of U.S. foreign policymakers to condemn China's record on human rights, but not to condemn it so greatly as to insult Chinese authorities and thereby endanger U.S.-Chinese economic relationships.

Disinformation has its uses in international relations and domestic politics. It is meant to confuse or mislead. Disinformation can be used for national or personal purposes: to deceive an antagonist about a government's intention, to deceive the public about a politician's actions, or to excuse a subordinate's behavior in a report to a superior. Military campaigns involve feints. "Trial balloons" are hints about prospective activities meant to elicit the response to an activity without clearly indicating that the activity will actually occur. Individuals "test the waters" to judge their support among the voters without formally announcing their candidacy for office. Officials plant stories in the media about impending decisions without risking their reputations before they see how the idea will sell.

Debates about the merits and problems of "limited war" have some relevance for the themes of this book. At issue are national policies that employ military actions for something less than total or unambiguous victory. The topic is clouded by the experience of World War II, which was unusual in the Allies' insistence on fighting until Germany and Japan would surrender unconditionally. The total victory in that war, and the victors' capacity to remake the governments and the societies of the defeated countries, strengthens those who see military action as useful only in the pursuit of far-reaching goals.

Why pursue military action, with its deaths and destruction, without intending to solve a problem once and for all time? Because it may only be possible to achieve limited aims in a situation without the horrendous human and financial costs of total war. When President George Bush decided in 1991 that a limited victory against Iraq was sufficient, he was well within the conception of warfare that has prevailed throughout history. He was adding the pressure of significant but not total destruction in order to achieve a set of demands that he had not been able to win by political persuasion alone. As the German theoretician Carl Von Clausewitz expressed early in the nineteenth century, war is a political instrument, a continuation of political commerce, a carrying out of the same by other means.[21]

Iraq again reached the headlines in late 1997 when it blocked ongoing United Nations inspections. The United States and Great Britain threatened force, began to assemble their forces, but lacked the support they garnered from other nations when Iraq invaded Kuwait in 1990. The arrangement achieved by U.N. Secretary General Kofi Annan in February 1998 was imperfect in being less than a crystal clear defeat of the enemy. The hope was that it was a cheap success, won by the American and British willingness to assemble force. It was less expensive, in material and human terms, than the actual use of force.

Israel also contributed to the exercise. The government saw to the equipping of its citizens with kits against the threat of Iraqi poison gas and acquired massive supplies of antibiotics against a biological attack. It also warned that an unconventional attack would be met in kind, or perhaps with something more awesome. Just as the United States and Britain had columnists who wanted a more clear victory, some Israeli commentators worried about the "waste" of resources used for defensive measures that were not used. There was no waste, however, if the measures convinced the Iraqis that it would not be worth their effort to send unconventional weapons against a population that was prepared. Quite the contrary. It may have proven to be an inexpensive way to avoid the horrors of poison gas or a plague.

There are no assurances in the agreement won by the U.N. Secretary General. American and British governments indicated that they would keep their forces in the Gulf until it was clear that Iraq would abide by the agreement to let U.N. inspectors into suspected sites of weapon manufacture or storage. It would be in the nature of interactions on the boundaries between politics and violence that there would be another testing by Iraq of the limits to its antagonists' resolve.

Politicians have a great deal of difficulty in accepting, or perhaps even in understanding the quintessentially political idea of limited war. They fear going to the public to explain why some of their sons have to die as soldiers in order to accomplish less than clear victories that will put an end to hostilities. Even Israeli officials, who are among the most experienced of limited warriors, shy away from advocating and explaining the use of deadly force, likely to result in the deaths of Israeli soldiers, for anything less than a lasting victory. The country's history shows time after time when the government has sent its soldiers into campaigns of limited retaliation and has pulled back from territorial gains in response to political pressures. In practice, calculation overcomes emotion. Policymakers do not really intend to solve the country's problems once and for all with massive military activity. They attend the funerals of soldiers killed in action, express sympathy for the bereaved, and commit themselves to everlasting peace. Yet their actions indicate an awareness that peace will be limited, and further actions will be necessary when the deterring effect of the recent attack has worn off.

Ambiguity is important in the tactics of limited warriors. Policymakers hope to save human and material resources by threatening to do more than they are likely to do. Political gains may come from threats alone. However, there is the problem of the boy who cried wolf once too often. When an adversary calls a bluff, the country who bluffed may have to employ more force than its officials had intended.

The *New York Times* reported a case of military actions in Bosnia that seemed deliberately confusing:

NATO troops in Bosnia, after saying the rules did not allow it, have quietly begun to help refugees return to the homes from which they were driven in the brutal "ethnic cleansing" campaigns of the war. . . . NATO maintained that protecting returned refugees was not part of its mandate. Now, however, with American troops doing that very thing, senior NATO officers say the Americans are not exceeding the mandate. There appears to be little appetite to try the refugee protection program on a larger scale. But international refugee officials say its apparent success shows that with similar protection, refugees could go home to many other parts of Bosnia. "Someone is going to call this 'mission creep,' but it's the best news I've had in months," said a United Nations refugee official.[22]

Ambiguity prevails when the formal rules do not matter. In December 1997, President Bill Clinton signed a document authorizing the PLO to reopen an office in Washington that officially had to close some months earlier in response to congressional legislation. However, the office had remained open. Both the legislation requiring it to close and the president's authorization for opening it were only formalities.[23]

History is ambiguous. Who did what to whom? Does a previous injustice excuse what looks like a present injustice?[24] It was our land before it was your land! Your ancestors exploited our ancestors! What elements of national myths are true? Napoleon commented that history is fable agreed upon.[25] If those who forget history are destined to repeat it, how do we interpret history in order to learn its lessons but not be deceived by partial knowledge?[26] Part of the ambiguity in history is the feeling that things are changing and uncertainty as to whether changes will continue, their ultimate extent, and their implications.

Our world is ambiguous, and politics is only one of the realms in which it is prominent. Natural as well as social scientists have problems interpreting the findings of their research. In most cases, differences between samples are not absolutely clear, and it is necessary to use judgment as to whether to accept or reject a hypothesis. Experts argue among themselves whether classic concepts like social class have changed their meaning or importance.[27] Researchers worry if the questions asked in interviews are clear to the respondents. If not, their findings may be only a jumble traced to ambiguities, and say nothing that is reliable about the attitudes or behaviors being investigated.[28] And while scientists employ their own terminology in order to be more precise in describing their work, the arcane nature of what they write may actually increase rather than diminish ambiguity. The following sentences, taken from an academic study that assumes a posture of objectivity about religious doctrines, stray rather far from simple English, and hardly seem to clarify the subject being investigated. "Religious ambiguity does not require the assertion of the views which created such ambiguity. It only requires the admission that each view can be held without violating doxastic obligation."[29]

We shall see in Chapter 3 that ambiguities in both religion and politics confound the tasks of determining what is happening where they overlap, as in public controversy about the state's use of religious doctrine in writing its laws. Ambiguities seem to produce stereotypes, perhaps because people crave certainty. Secular and religious Israelis each feel that the other is growing in its influence, while both may be frustrated by their inability to determine public policy.

Academia has its own ambiguities. People who work with money have well-established indices of inflation. Professors who serve on committees that select graduate students suspect that undergraduate grades are also inflating, but there are no measures equivalent to the consumer price index. Average grades are increasing, but this may be the result of students who are better prepared. While the consumer price index measures price changes for an equivalent set of goods and services, there is no index showing the grades for equivalent levels of student performance. An additional feature of academic life is the variety of institutions providing higher education, as well as an increasing number of disciplines, plus interdisciplinary programs and developments within the established departments. One's feeling is that an education earned at an Ivy League university is more creditable than one from a state college or an obscure private institution, but how great are the differences? And how do each compare with the training received from the national university in a Third World country?

Investors should also be familiar with ambiguity. Uncertainty and risk characterize their environment. What stocks will increase in value, while others decline or remain stable? Markets offer a blurring array of possibilities in stocks, bonds, shares in property ventures, and enough mutual funds to fill a complete page in a daily newspaper. Brokers and other advisors suggest that they look at recent performance, interest rates, price-earnings ratios, or numerous other indicators to find opportunities that are undervalued and thus represent good bargains. The label of *guru* that is attached to personalities who claim success in picking investments hints at the amorphous nature of the investment process.[30] Scholars have worked over the years to conceive of devices to minimize risk, but even the most calculated of strategies can run afoul of the many factors that can influence markets.[31] A distant war affects the price of oil or coffee beans, a comment by a leading banker that the stock market is overpriced causes panic among investors, as does a crises in overseas banks or stock markets linked together by globalization.

Subtlety is a close relative of ambiguity that is valued in art, fashion, music, and literature. Metaphor, symbolism, irony, contradiction, paradox, and allegory are ways of blurring and complicating the images that writers present to their audience. A prominent theme in the academic school of postmodernism emphasizes the different levels of meaning and interpretations that imbue expression and behavior. Practitioners of postmodernism are likely to see ambiguity where others see clarity. They also claim a capacity for explicating the unclear in ways that may be creative but are seldom lacking in ambiguity.

Ambiguity is important in the management of private as well as public activities. In an era of corporate mergers, takeovers, and downsizing, ambiguity helps in the selling of an idea to the owners, managers, and workers involved. It is impossible to spell out everything. The details of the near future are too many, and some of them are unknown at the point when a deal is struck. In such a context of uncertainty, a positive spin on the details may minimize opposition from those who fear that they might suffer personally from a change in corporate structure. Privatization is a phenomenon on the boundaries of public and private sectors that combines elements of doctrine and popular slogan. Research into privatization in numerous countries reveals a host of meanings associated with the term. They include selling all or part of government-owned enterprises to private owners, making efforts to increase the efficiency of government activities without transferring them to the private sector, and reducing government subsidies for activities conducted by private enterprises. Some privatization has been thinly disguised exploitation of a fashionable slogan in order to pass resources to political elites, as when a government provides loans to those who will buy the enterprises and then fails to insist that the loans be repaid.[32]

A consideration of South Africa's recent history alongside of Israel suggests that coping and ambiguity are likely to accompany points of great stress. The stresses in South Africa include a huge underclass, with ethnic tensions between black communities, and a great deal of crime that features a rate of murder eight times that of the United States.[33] (The rate of murder in the United States makes it a leader in violent crime among Western countries; it is five times the rate of murder in Israel relative to population.[34]) South African stresses also include an emigration of numerous well-to-do and professionally qualified whites, as well as a delegitimization of state institutions in the eyes of blacks due to the history of apartheid and authoritarianism, and delegitimization in the eyes of whites due to what is perceived as the elevation of unschooled and inexperienced blacks to key positions. Leading black politicians have coped with their problems by promising education, housing, and jobs. Ambiguity appears in the gaps between the costs of the promises and the capacity of the economy to provide resources. The ambiguity adds to stress among whites who fear an increase in redistributive policies for poor blacks at white expense. The same ambiguity may add to stress among poor blacks who see a great shortfall between the promises of black politicians and the benefits actually delivered by their new government.

Some readers may wonder about what may appear to be empathy shown here for the whites of South Africa or for the Jews of Israel. Should not the world be satisfied with the end of apartheid and the victory of majority rule in South Africa, and support the granting of national autonomy to Palestinians? The aspirations of South African blacks and Palestinians have wide support. Like other political goals, however, they represent a threat to some even while they offer promise to their supporters. The toleration of ambiguity and other techniques of coping offer ways to take account of what may seem to be irreconcilable aspirations. The Afrikaners of today might be more secure if those of a previous generation had been more accommodating of black demands. The Israeli Jews and Palestinians of the next generation might be more secure if those of this generation pursue a strategy of coping rather than one of domination.

Problematic Definitions

While it is conventional to define key concepts, the nature of *ambiguity* renders this step less than satisfying. Ambiguity is itself ambiguous! Dictionaries describe ambiguity as doubtful, questionable, indistinct, obscure, not clearly defined, admitting more than one interpretation or explanation, double meaning, of several possible meanings, and equivocal.[35]

Policy scholars quarrel about the differences between improvisation, accommodating, avoidance, indirection, ambiguity, and coping. Elements of each overlap with the other, and there are no unambiguous definitions of the terms that are widely accepted. Without making too much of the distinctions, it may help to distinguish accommodation as seeking to provide a minimum of responsiveness in order to keep the peace between potentially contentious groups. Improvisation is distinguished by being extemporaneous. It is a response to a unique situation. Avoidance is concerned with deferring decisions of potential importance. Indirection substitutes one activity for another. The result of all these actions may be ambiguity as to the real intentions or subsequent actions of policymakers.

Coping and ambiguity are the most inclusive of these concepts. They overlay the terrain covered by accommodation, improvisation, avoidance, and indirection. Ambiguity as well as accommodation, improvisation, avoidance, and indirection are modes of coping. Ambiguity seeks to paper over disagreement by blurring differences. Ambiguity, avoidance, and indirection intrude on one another when policymakers render their actions ambiguous by not specifying how they intend to treat an issue. Ambiguity overlaps with improvisation when the response to the crisis of the moment is not entirely clear. Politicians often try to satisfy with words that sound good but promise little. Doing it on the spur of the moment is an art form that is useful to an aspiring leader. Ambiguity and accommodation overlap when actors do not specify the limits of accommodation. They do not specify how much an individual will receive. "We'll take care of you" and "It'll be all right" are useful expressions. They may not threaten dominant groups who might fear giving up some of their power to the weak. And they do not promise anything concrete to the weak. If participants accept these vague promises (knowing, perhaps, that they offer no guarantees) they allow passage over a difficult moment in politics.

POLITICS

By saying that ambiguity is an umbrella concept likely to be associated with accommodation, improvisation, avoidance, and indirection, we are saying that ambiguity is the essence of politics. Various conceptions of politics concern power, influence, and the division of scarce resources between individuals and groups that make demands that are not easily reconcilable. *Politics: Who Gets What, When, How?* is a classic expression still useful more than six decades after Harold Lasswell published a book with that title.[36]

Ambiguity stands at the center of politics when, as is usually the case, demands are irreconcilable. Different individuals and parties compete for the same offices. Some interest groups demand more resources than the government can extract from the economy or borrow against the future. Others demand reductions in taxes, and thereby complicate even further those who would respond to claimants for more services. The violation of campaign promises comes in for scathing cynicism but summarizes much about politics.

- Politics is the happy science.[37]
- Promise more than you can deliver now.
- You may be able to honor the promises later, or someone else may honor them.
- Politics is about attracting supporters.
- Keep the wolves satisfied and the sheep happy.[38]
- Never say no.

Each of these expressions says something about the role of ambiguity in politics. If you comprehend them and do not perceive a violation of good sense, you have an understanding for what politics can accomplish.

GOVERNANCE

Coping is a political tool as well as a general skill or strategy that includes within it ambiguity, accommodation, improvisation, avoidance, and indirection. There are several points of commonality between coping in policymaking and ambiguity in politics. One such point occurs in the overlap between policymaking and politics. Policymaking is heavily political. Perhaps all public policymaking is political, insofar as it deals with demands on the institutions of government. Yet not all politics involves policymaking. Political activists spend much of their time with issues of public relations, public opinion, elections, and the advancement of individuals and organizations. Only some of politics deals with the advancement of ideas for governmental activity, that is, public policy.

If one statement can sum up the perspective that pervades this book, it is that coping is the essence of governance, and that ambiguity is the essence of politics. Coping appears to be the essence of governance insofar as governance deals with pressures, conflicting demands, and problems whose solutions are elusive. Simple problems, or the use of accepted criteria in responding to clients who request services, are the stuff of administrative routine. Administrative routine may account for most activity of government workers, but it is below the threshold of the more serious issues that merit the term *governance.*

RATIONAL DECISION MAKING

The claim that coping is the essence of governance stands against the aspirations of many reformers to "do things right." It is common for advisers to urge policymakers to be objective and rational. By this they usually mean that officials ought to take everything into account in making their decisions, and should decide ultimately to achieve the greatest good for the greatest number, or the most output for the least cost.

The steps of objective, rational decision making are said to include the following:

- Define the problem that is to be the object of policymaking.
- Recognize the full collection of demands that are relevant to the decisions that are to be made.
- List all policy alternatives.
- Define the resources necessary to achieve each alternative.
- Calculate the benefits and costs associated with each alternative.
- Make the decision on the basis of all relevant information, in a way to achieve the most benefits at the least cost.

For some time now, political scientists have asserted that it is impossible to achieve this idealized set of aspirations.[39] Economists, as well, find that lots of people do not behave in ways predicted by theories based on rational consumers or investors.[40]

One set of constraints is technical. The nature of a problem is seldom obvious. Analysts are likely to disagree about what lies behind the variety of symptoms indicating that something is wrong. Limits of time and information keep policymakers from recognizing all of the demands that are relevant to an issue. It is seldom possible to list all the alternative policies in a way that reflects the many combinations in all of their nuances.

Different pluses and minuses make it impossible to define an intelligible balance of benefits and costs for all alternatives. The values used in judging the good and bad associated with each alternative do not reduce themselves to units of currency or any other common standard that can be arranged to measure benefits against costs. One alternative may lead in popular support. Others may lead in the economic value of the results that are expected. Another may promise to be implemented for the least cost in terms of budgetary outlays. However, the option with the lowest budget cost may threaten high economic or social costs by virtue of the losses it is likely to impose on one or another group in the population. Insofar as the benefits of each differ, none may be clearly more efficient than others.

THE SUPREMACY OF POLITICS IN GOVERNANCE

These technical constraints that prevent objective, rational decision making create a setting in which politics thrives. Politics is a way of reaching decisions according to persuasion and preferences, as opposed to a system that assumes clear answers that can be derived objectively. If persuasion does not lead to consensus, politics provides the option of voting and awarding victory according to some prearranged criteria (e.g., rule by simple majority, by two-thirds or some other extraordinary majority). In its simplest fashion, voting involves a clear choice between alternatives. Where there are more than two parties, candidates, or proposals, however, ambiguity has its role. Some activists figure that it is wise to support a second-ranked option in order to frustrate the prospects of a lower-ranked option. Supporters of "fuzzy logic" embrace the reality of ambiguity and advocate intermediate options even in a decision about programs that seems to involve only two choices. Members of a forum called on to vote could choose from points along a line between options number 1 and number 2.[41]

In saying that politics supersedes rational decision making, there is no intention to suggest that politics is *irrational*. For a modern Western democrat, politics is a form of rationality more suitable than the "objective rationality" defined above. Politics allows the choice between difficult and contentious alternatives. To be sure, not all decisions by persuasion and voting are wise or even reasonable. Errors of omission or commission by political activists are fair game for criticism. They are among the factors that cause serious problems.

Politics takes numerous forms. *Populism* may be the most widely recognized politics. Populists seek the course of action that will get them the most votes at the next election. *Partisanship* is a form of politics that emphasizes the benefit of one's political party or faction within a party. *Patronage* and partisanship often go together. Patronage involves the distribution of favors in a way to benefit supporters.[42] The term *bureaucratic politics* indicates that politics does not only occur among elected officials. Politics also appears in the activities of administrators who jockey for position in order to advance what they consider to be their vital interests.

Politics can be found at all stages of the policy process. Elected officials; the professional employees of government, parties, and interest groups; plus citizen activists compete over the definition of social and economic problems. The group that manages to define the problem will have an advantage in the later stages of selecting policy goals, defining the budget and personnel allocations, and writing the instructions that guide program administrators.[43] Even after a program is underway, political disputes may continue. Opponents might seek to frustrate a program by means of court appeals, by reducing its budget, or persuading administrators to write the detailed rules and apply them in favorable ways. Opponents might also campaign to turn the public against the policy.[44] There is always another year's budget that may alter the implementation of existing policies, as well as another meeting of key officials or the legislature to change decisions already taken.

Politics also occurs when there is a considerable record of program activity, and it is time to evaluate it. This is not an occasion for rational objectivity, but another opportunity for the supporters and opponents of the ruling party, administrative units, program clients, and others to express their praise or criticism.[45] There is likely to be a wide range of indicators to help one or another interest to claim that the program has succeeded or failed.

COPING IS HUMANE AS WELL AS INEVITABLE

It is not the purpose of this book merely to argue that coping and ambiguity, plus the other devices mentioned here, are widespread in politics and policymaking. That is readily apparent and should not be viewed as novel. It is our concern to demonstrate that there is a humane quality as well as a utility to coping and its devices. More than being the best that can be achieved, coping seems valuable in its own right. The tactics of accommodation, indirection, improvisation, avoidance, and ambiguity are ways of keeping together a polity easily split by contending demands and loyalties. They also work to keep competing groups in the realm of antagonists who can negotiate with one another, rather than turning them into enemies who must battle one another.

Governance by coping is untidy and frustrating, but inevitable in settings that truly are democratic. It is inherent in the ambiguity of politics that there are no clear boundaries between what should be permitted and forbidden, or between national purpose, legitimate self-interest, and corruption. The messiness of coping is more likely to be humane than the perfection, discipline, and completeness that, if it were possible, would meet the aspirations of those who demand decision making that is more fully rational.

Israel is not the only polity that illustrates these points. However, it provides sharply drawn examples in domestic and international relations. Some of its problems are difficult but within a normal range, while others portend danger for national survival.

The words *final solution* conjure up the ugly regime of the Nazis. They sought to rid the world of Jews, and killed some 40 percent of those living in 1940. This is one reason that Israeli politicians are disinclined to use the term final solution. Yet another reason might be their awareness that they are unlikely to resolve once and for all time the demands made by different groups of citizens.

My father-in-law, Erich Horn, came to Palestine from Düsseldorf in 1934. We have spent many hours arguing about how governments should operate. His background is typical of many German Jews of the 1930s: His family resided in his home city for several hundred years, with his father and other close relatives having served in the German army during World War I. His mother did not leave Germany and was killed in a death camp. Erich's brother thought that he would be safe in Holland, but he was also transported to the east and then killed. Although his family experience cast a strong shadow on his life, Erich remained proud of his German heritage. He spent summers in Düsseldorf until his late eighties. He timed his visits for the annual reunions of his high school, and ultimately became the sole survivor of his class. Erich rose to a senior position in the Israeli bureaucracy, but groused about the style of government: Individuals were strongly tied to party and personal loyalties; they concerned themselves with the pressures of the moment and not with the principles that should have determined their decisions; lower ranking clerks were not sufficiently disciplined; there was waste and corruption. There is considerable truth in Erich's recollections about Israel in the 1950s and 1960s. The country was more primitive then, economically and governmentally. Applicants who sought government jobs were likely to benefit on account of party activity or other favoritism. Some leaders of the dominant Labor Party emulated Eastern Europeans in the fervor with which they suspected disloyalty of those who did not share their enthusiasms. Yet with all that can be said by way of criticism directed at the crude machine-like politics of early Israel, there remains something troubling in Erich's concerns for principles, rational calculation, and discipline.

Principles sound idealistic, but are more Prussian than humane. They expect more of policymakers than they are likely to deliver. They do not take into account the contrasting demands individuals make in a democracy, where people look after their own needs and not the lofty ideals of the nation. They do not admit to the pressures, accommodations, and other subtleties that are part of democratic politics. All too often it seems that a "principle" is gloss for what someone wants to implement. When linked to the program of a political party or regime, principles may get in the way of those who point to other considerations, as well as the nuances that complicate policymaking and program implementation. The principle of "national interest," in particular, is likely to be an arrogant way of saying that what I want is for the good of you all, even if it overlooks what are the contrasting but equally legitimate interests of distinct regions, localities, or social groups.

When he was a ranking member of the opposition in the Knesset (parliament), Yitzhak Rabin used the phrase "Bang and we're finished" as a derisive criticism against the grandiose plan of the Likud government to end the threat of terrorism via the war in Lebanon. The war, labeled Operation Peace in the Galilee, began in June 1982. It involved a deep penetration to Beirut by Israeli Defense Forces as well as extensive engagements with Syrian forces located in Lebanon. According to plans said to come from the minister of defense and former general Ariel Sharon, Israeli forces would team up with Christian militias and drive both Palestinians and Syrians from Lebanon. It was expected that the humiliation of the PLO would end the support for that organization in the West Bank and Gaza. Palestinians were expected to return to Jordan, unseat the Hashemite monarchy, and turn that country (whose population is perhaps two-thirds Palestinian) into the Palestinian State and end pressures on Israel.

The point of Rabin and his Labor Party colleagues was that the threat of terrorism could only be resolved with the patient application of limited defense measures, plus political accommodations that would undercut the popular support for terror. More than sixteen years after the beginning of Operation Peace in the Galilee, Israeli troops remain in southern Lebanon. Lebanese Shi'ites have replaced Palestinians as the threat to Israel's northern border and the nemesis of the Israeli military. Lebanese Christians reneged on whatever commitments they had made to cooperate with Israeli forces. The Hashemite monarchy remains in power, and appears to be the most friendly of Arab regimes toward Israel. Subsequent Labor and Likud governments have made extensive accommodations with the PLO. The Palestinian Authority may be on its way to becoming a state, but Israelis quarrel as to whether the accommodations have reduced the threat of terror.

Subsequent chapters of this book develop the argument begun here. Chapter 2 explains the choice of Israel as the principal site for examining behaviors that are widely apparent in democratic societies. It also surveys Israeli problems, as well as traits of the country's government and politics that seem to put a premium on skills of coping and ambiguity. Chapter 3 extends the argument about ambiguity in politics to ambiguity in religion. Religion is important in the politics of Israel and numerous other Western-style democracies. Moreover, religion and politics have a number of commonalties, including a central role in both for ambiguity. Chapter 4 portrays a typology of ambiguity, showing it at every stage and level of policymaking and program implementation. Chapter 5 illustrates the utility of ambiguity in a situation of extreme complexity and sensitivities. It explains the potential to be derived from a lack of clarity surrounding the name *Jerusalem* in negotiations about the city's future. Chapter 6 shows the problems of judging activities that include many ambiguous elements. It does this while offering a summary assessment of Israel's performance as a country during its half-century of independence. Chapter 7 describes the ambiguities that are prominent in the peace process. Chapter 8 finds ambiguities in claims of precision and exactitude in social science. Chapter 9 looks at the disadvantages associated with coping and ambiguity and suggests ways of dealing with them. It also explains the limits involved in coping with the downside of coping.

2

Why Israel?

Why choose Israel to illustrate the workings of ambiguity and coping? The country is the size of a tiny American state. It has only about six million residents and is tucked away in a corner of the world far from the academic markets of North America and Western Europe. Its population and political traditions are not typical of the people likely to read this book.

The attractions of Israel for our purposes outweigh all these limitations. Its surfeit of problems and its style of policymaking provoked the analyses that led me to this book. And while Israel is small and different from the countries better known to North American and Western European academics, it is often in the headlines of their newspapers. By some claims, Jerusalem is the home away from home of more foreign correspondents than any other city except Washington, D.C. The interest of the world may stem less from the concerns of political science than from Israel's ancient heritage as the Holy Land. Perhaps 50 percent of the world's people, concentrated in areas of economic and political importance, view Jerusalem as part of their spiritual heritage.[1]

Israel's character and its problems differ in detail from those of other countries, but it shows in sharp outline a condition that is more general: Politicians and policymakers cope with severe problems by employing ambiguity and the other tactics described in Chapter 1. Twenty-three years studying Israeli politics and service with a number of governmental bodies has sensitized me to advantages as well as the problems associated with coping and ambiguity.

NATIONAL SECURITY

Israeli policymakers encounter a high incidence of vexatious problems concerned with national security as well as religion. In the half-century of the country's modern existence, there have been frequent wars and countless attacks by terrorists. There are unsettled boundaries, economic burdens, heavy immigration, the scars of the Holocaust and other persecutions, plus quarrels among Jews about Judaism.

Some 14,000 Israelis have died as a result of military engagements since 1948, not counting civilians killed in terrorist raids.[2] Compared to national populations, this is ten times the rate of American deaths in the Korean and Vietnam wars together.[3] American deaths in World War II amounted to 0.2 percent of the American national population while the Nazis and their allies were killing 40 percent of all the Jews in the world.

Israelis are weary of continued bloodshed. However, their persistence in defending themselves, but not seeking too great a victory, is a prominent illustration for the theme of this book. The protracted but limited war that Israel has waged for all of its existence testifies to the capacity of policymakers and the population to make do with less than a thoroughgoing effort to end their problem of national security. A situation of no war, no peace has continued now for over twelve years since the pullback to a security zone in the south of Lebanon. Frequent casualties result from clashes between Israeli units of a dozen or so soldiers and a like number of Lebanese. The *intafada,* or Palestinian uprising, began in December 1987. It petered out with the onset of serious talks between the PLO and Israel after the Madrid Conference of 1991, but incidents of Palestinian-Israeli violence have occurred since then.

Israelis continue to report for reserve duty, with many of them expecting dangerous patrols, and they send their eighteen-year-old sons into an army that will expose them to danger for three years as draftees and perhaps another twenty years of reserve duty. (Israeli daughters also serve; typically for two years, but seldom are in danger.) Nothing like a clear peace seems to be in sight, either as a result of a "war to end war" or far-reaching diplomacy. The war option has been tried, and diplomacy seems unlikely to satisfy all Arabs who can acquire some explosives, a rifle, or a knife.

Many attempted assaults never make the press, or warrant only a routine report about a bomb that was disabled or a stabbing that left a civilian injured or dead. Family losses add poignancy to discussions of what Israelis are willing to risk by way of physical security for treaties with enemies who only a short while ago called for the country's destruction.

IMMIGRATION

Immigration was especially burdensome during the years 1948 to 1951, and returned to the agenda with the collapse of the Soviet Union. In the early period, the population more than doubled while the economy was small and poor and was recovering from the 1948 war that was more costly in casualties than any since then. Almost all of the migrants in the early period came as refugees from Europe or Arab lands and depended on the Israeli state and other public institutions for aid in housing, job creation, and social services. The immigrants and their children have bitter memories of tent cities in the damp winter, meager rations, manual labor, and authorities who were insensitive to personal needs. The current wave of migrants began in 1988. By 1998 it had exceeded 800,000 and added more than 15 percent to the population. In the wake of the migrants came a sharp increase in the price of housing, construction of new towns, and concerns about crowding, traffic jams, land taken from agriculture, and environmental protection.

The positive sides of immigration are the contributions of additional workers and consumers, who add their skills and purchasing power to the national economy. Some of the recent immigrants have increased Israel's resources in the professions and arts. A spurt in the national rate of unemployment occurred with the onset of this immigration, but then declined as immigrants passed through retraining courses or found work that was close to their occupations in the Soviet Union.

JEWISH MAJORITIES

The Jewish majorities in Israel and Jerusalem (79 percent of the national population and 72 percent of the population in Jerusalem) present their own problems to national authorities. About 10 percent of the Jews in Israel and one-quarter of those in Jerusalem are ultra-Orthodox. There is chronic bickering about religion between Jews who are religious and those who are secular or antireligious. Issues in dispute are Sabbath observance, the availability of nonkosher food, the determination of who is a Jew, who may be married to a Jew, where the body of a non-Jew may be buried, who is a rabbi, the status of non-Orthodox Judaism, and the disturbance of ancient graves for the sake of modern construction. The longevity of these disputes justifies the label of insoluble problems. Specific controversies triggered by religious issues take on the color of political rituals. They generally pass through the stages of initial demands, loud demonstrations, nondeadly violence, and partial and ambiguous resolutions of specific issues without dealing with whatever principle underlies the episodes. The killing of Prime

Minister Yitzhak Rabin by a religious Jew in 1995 raised the specter of religious-secular conflict serious enough to threaten a civil war.

Israel's survival has been a question at several occasions in its half-century of modern history. At first, it was during the War of Independence when deaths of soldiers and civilians amounted to 1 percent of the Jewish population. The second time was when several Arab armies mobilized again in 1967. Israel actually devastated its enemies in six days, but the pre-war concern had led authorities to prepare mass graves for the possibility of civilian casualties. A third time was in the early days of the Yom Kippur War of 1973, when Israel's confidence broke in the face of weapons that took a heavy toll of men, tanks, and planes, and the Egyptians and Syrians moved into the Sinai and the Golan Heights. Israel's existence is still threatened by Arab hostility to its existence, which remains a factor among many Egyptians, Jordanians, and Palestinians despite the formal accords.

The hostility between religious and secular Jews recalls the civil wars of two millennia ago between Judeans who adopted the culture of Greece and Rome, and those who were zealous in their opposition to foreign influences. Flavius Josephus provides a graphic description of the hatred and the bloodletting in his *Jewish War*,[4] and describes how the internal fighting opened the community to conquest and destruction.

Israel's survival in the face of foreign and domestic threats owes something to its leaders' skills in coping and their tolerance for ambiguity. It also reflects the resources of the country. Fifty years into its history as an independent country, Israel has reached a credible level of economic development, and it maintains good relations with the Jewish Diaspora and the government of the United States. The Diaspora has helped with financial support and political influence in the governments of various countries. The largest Diaspora is in the United States, and the U.S. Government has provided financial aid, access to armaments, and political backing to counter what has been the tendency of European governments, along with those of Japan and the Third World, to support Arab demands against Israel.

Israel's willingness to cope appears in how it has dealt with vastly larger enemy forces by moving its own resources from one front to another, by driving its troops to the point of exhaustion, and in later wars by emphasizing technologically advanced weaponry. It has also balanced advantage with restraint. Israel's government heeded the demands of Western powers for cease-fires at points in 1967 and 1973 when the Israelis might have been able to drive deeper into Arab countries. By this mode of coping with international realities, and not seeking to end the Arab threat once and for all, Israel may have denied itself a chance of greater victories. Against this, however, it limited the loss of its own troops and matériel in what probably would have been battles of increased ferocity. And its posture of moderation may have enhanced its access to the technological, political, and financial support of Western nations and given a chance to those who aspired to negotiated settlements.

A similar theme appears in the conflicts of Israel's Jews among themselves. When tempers heat up and demonstrations turn ugly, both religious and secular leaders preach restraint. They recite the lessons described by Josephus and absorbed in Rabbinical teachings. Conquest of one side by the other is threatening to the whole community. So far, there has been no insistence on clearcut victories by religious or secular leaders, and Israelis have stumbled on from one religious crisis to another without solving them. This behavior not only keeps domestic pressures on a low flame, but it has helped in assuring continued support for Israel among Diaspora Jews who themselves show varying degrees of Orthodoxy and religious liberalism.

A CUMBERSOME GIANT

Some of the problems faced by Israeli policymakers reflect a convoluted combination of the formal and informal procedures by which they operate. These, in turn, derive from intertwined conditions that render the state powerful by certain criteria, but also limit its power.

The Israeli state qualifies for the designation of giant by virtue of its domination of the national economy as well as the extent of its military resources and the impact of taxes and military obligations on Israeli citizens. It is cumbersome by virtue of the inelegance by which its officials manage their power. The results are not all bad. Inelegance adds to the humanity of the Israeli state even while it produces shortfalls from the disciplined implementation of declared policies. Individual citizens or municipal authorities who demonstrate extraordinary need may get more from the central government than the formal rules indicate.

The reasons for the inelegance are instructive in their own right. They suggest that vexatious problems can further the pursuit of moral subtlety. Outspoken advocacy of one's needs along with intense criticism of the state and its programs are part of the political culture. Programs of government aid to one or another special school or social program exist alongside claims that the state gives too much to one group and not enough to others. Claims of suffering count for something in Israeli policymaking, and the clout of a party's votes in the governmental coalition may count for more. There is no obvious calculus to determine who gets what. The situation frustrates any simple judgment of this cumbersome giant.

The Israeli state has been strong from its beginning. Like almost all the other new states created with the weakening of European colonialism after World War II, Israel began with commitments to socialism. And like other new states, the lack of resources in the private sector dictated centralized public institutions to marshal resources and build infrastructure. Israel had the additional motivations of Zionist theory: a strong state to protect the people who had suffered from two millennia of statelessness, plus a degree of socialism to protect the weak. Almost all of the founding generation came from central and eastern Europe, and that region's strong states also provided models that guided them in Israel. A major war and mass immigration added to the powers of the state, as well as a Diaspora that was willing to loan and donate money to the state and national institutions closely integrated with it.

The combination of socialism and a chronic problem of security provide government ministries with a major role in economic management. Israel's annual financial outlays for security are five to ten times greater as a percentage of gross national product (GNP) than those of other democracies. In some years the expenditures of government and quasi-governmental bodies have exceeded the GNP.[5] Overseas purchases of military equipment contribute to a high international debt and chronic imbalance in the size of imports with respect to exports. Israel's inflation reflects the pressures on its economy. Price increases were above 100 percent annually from 1979 through the middle of 1985, and since 1992 have been considered modest in the range of 7 to 15 percent. Inflation in other Western democracies is generally below 4 percent annually.

Data from the World Bank provide one insight into the continuing strength and relative success of the Israeli state. Table 2.1 shows that in 1993 Israel led a group of Western democracies in the percentage of GNP represented by central government activities. Table 2.2 shows that Israel stands apart from other states that some years ago aspired to centrally controlled socialist economies for its record of economic growth. In contrast to Israel is a pattern of economic *decline* widespread among former members of the Eastern bloc and a number of states that seem stuck in a Third World syndrome of poverty, corruption, and political instability.

Yet another measure of Israel's strength appears in the demands placed by the state on its citizens. High taxes reflect the involvement of the state in the economy, and citizens' dependence on the state and closely related institutions for almost all of their education, health care, and public transportation. In 1998, even after several years of campaigning for government downsizing and privatization, marginal income tax rates of 50 percent began on monthly gross incomes equivalent to $4,900. A value-added tax of

Table 2.1
General Government Consumption as a Percentage of GNP, 1993

Israel	26.0%	Australia	17.0%
Denmark	25.8%	United States	16.8%
Sweden	24.1%	Ireland	16.6%
Canada	20.6%	Portugal	16.5%
Norway	20.4%	Spain	15.6%
Finland	20.1%	Italy	15.5%
United Kingdom	19.8%	New Zealand	15.4%
Germany	19.8%	Belgium	14.8%
Iceland	19.0%	Netherlands	14.1%
Austria	18.9%	Switzerland	13.1%
France	18.7%	Luxembourg	10.8%
Greece	18.0%	Japan	10.3%

Source: World Data 1995: World Bank Indicators on CD-ROM (Washington, D.C.: The International Bank for Reconstruction and Development/The World Bank, 1995)

17 percent affected virtually all purchases of goods and services. Special taxes of more than 100 percent added to the costs of automobiles and electric appliances. Military service required two years for most young women, three years for men, and continued reserve duty that may exceed thirty days a year for men until their forties or fifties. As opposed to the weekend soldiering familiar to reservists in Western countries, Israeli reservists now in their forties have experienced one or two wars, plus patrolling in the West Bank, the Gaza Strip, or southern Lebanon in conditions of frequent violence.

LIMITS TO ISRAEL'S POWER

The designation of Israel as a giant is likely to evoke skepticism or outright ridicule among those who know it well. The connotation of significant size is one problem. In *God Knows*, a novel about the biblical David, Joseph Heller has his hero boast, "I had taken a kingdom the size of Vermont and created an empire as large as the state of Maine!"[6] Modern Israel is even more modest. Not counting the territories still occupied as a result of the 1967 war, it is a bit larger than New Jersey, a bit smaller than Massachusetts, and less than a quarter the size of Maine.

Table 2.2
GNP per Capita, 1993 (U.S. $ Equivalents), and Change in GNP per Capita, 1990–1993

Armenia	670	-69%	Kiribati	710	1%
Azerbaijan	660	-52%	Kyrgyz Republic	850	-37%
Belarus	2,850	-14%	Latvia	2,310	-49%
Bulgaria	1,170	-46%	Lithuania	1,340	-61%
Czech Republic	2,710	-22%	Moldova	1,160	-50%
Egypt	660	0%	Pakistan	440	10%
Estonia	2,720	-43%	Poland	2,250	26%
Georgia	580	-75%	Romania	1,150	-35%
Ghana	430	8%	Russia	2,330	-44%
Guinea	500	14%	Slovak Republic	1,970	-36%
Hungary	3,520	19%	Tajikistan	410	-53%
India	290	-22%	Tanzania	90	-25%
Israel	13,920	21%	Uganda	190	-44%
Kazakhstan	1,410	-41%	Ukraine	2,210	-20%
Kenya	260	-32%	Uzbekistan	980	-8%

Source: World Data 1995: World Bank Indicators on CD-ROM (Washington, D.C.: The International Bank for Reconstruction and Development/The World Bank, 1995).

More to the point of this chapter than small physical size are the limits that Israelis and their policymakers impose on themselves. Close divisions in the population are legendary. The voters have never granted a majority to a political party in a Knesset election. All governments have been coalitions between the leaders of competitive parties whose records are marked by squabbles and a failure to decide clearly about pressing issues. Even after a decision is announced as official policy, ministers and professional administrators may delay programming or reverse the initial decision altogether. Prime Minister Yitzhak Rabin and his minister of finance argued, acted, and then changed their mind about imposing a tax on stock exchange profits. The recommendations of a distinguished panel with respect to reforms in local governments were accepted in principle but never implemented.

It is easier to measure the geographical size of a state or the weight of its budget in the national economy than to gauge the power of its authorities or the capacity of its public programs to achieve their objectives. On these dimensions there are sharp disputes among argumentative Israelis. To the credit of the state can be laid its success in enacting national health insurance at about the same time when the model democracy and infinitely wealthier United States bogged down on a similar issue. And the incidence of homeless on the streets of Israel seems less than in large cities of North America or western Europe, despite a large recent wave of immigration that continues at a rate of more than 50,000 annually.

Coping and ambiguity rather than forthright problem solving marks Israeli government. The putting together of coalitions and the practice of governing involves promises that are purposely vague, as well as subsequent changes in intention. "I promised to do it, but I did not promise to keep my promise!" is an epigram that Israelis tell about politicians caught between coalition partners with contrasting demands and severely limited resources. As this chapter was drafted, Knesset members and other ranking members of the Likud bloc were accusing Prime Minister Benjamin Netanyahu of breaking several promises to individuals about prestigious appointments as minister or ambassador. A declared policy of compulsory and free education from kindergarten through secondary school has not kept the ministries of finance and education, as well as local authorities, from imposing substantial fees for school-related programs. A law to provide benefits to young Israelis after army service lay dormant for more than a decade without being implemented.

Formal Centralization of Government, but in Practice Something Else

Israel's cumbersome character results partly from a governmental structure that is highly centralized in its formal character but operates in ways that bestow considerable actual power on local authorities and individual office holders. Some of the muddle between formal rules and what occurs in practice reflects the coping of policymakers. National and local authorities bend the rules in order to stretch resources. They may tell less than the complete truth to one another in order to get away with giving less or receiving more than the rules imply. Cynics refer to Israel as a "volunteer state," where officials as well as citizens choose the laws they will obey.

Israel appears to be ruled from the center, with a large role for the professional staffs of national ministries and other government bodies. Centralization is made easy because of small size and the people's identification with the nation. Most Jewish families arrived in the 1930s or later. Compared to countries with long-established settlement patterns, Israelis do not have strong feelings toward a region or locale. National politics operates with proportional representation in a single electoral district. No member of the Knesset is officially a representative of a city or region.[7]

Israel has no written constitution. The majority of the Knesset is virtually unrestrained by anything beyond political will in enacting new laws or in changing the laws that exist.[8]

In practice, the strong centralized regime does not operate quite as the rules suggest. The nature of Israeli politics assures that the official regulations indicating strict centralization are administered in a loose, somewhat chaotic fashion.[9] The inevitability of coalition politics contributes to this. Prime Ministers have been unable to impose their will on minor parties that join the coalition, except with respect to a few key issues like national security and, sometimes, economic stability. Individual ministers have been free to operate as they wish on matters of social policy and the aid that they give to local governments, without having to concern themselves with integrated national policies. A disregard for rules may have something to do with the Jewish experience. Where the learned priority is to cope with an environment that may become very harsh very quickly, the formal rules take second place.

Participants quarrel about how the formal structure works in practice. Some episodes indicate the capacity of central government ministries to rule on the small details of local administration, while others indicate that local officials have considerable discretion in practice. The Interior Ministry must approve the local authority's taxes and expenditures, and determine the general grant to be given each locality. The Finance Ministry must approve the budget of the Interior Ministry (as well as other ministries), and may take an interest in the finances of individual localities. The opportunities of local authorities begin with the inability of the Interior Ministry to learn the intricacies of local government finance and operations. Formal approvals for a municipality's budget proposal may come several months *after* the close of the budget year when all the funds at issue have already been spent.

When the Interior Ministry ordered that local authorities reduce their personnel as part of governmentwide economy measures, a subsequent report of the State Comptroller found that most authorities did not implement the instructions.[10] According to a newspaper report, the Beer Sheva municipality in 1997 appointed a fifth deputy mayor from among the members of the city council in order to facilitate the workings of the political coalition running the city, even though regulations of the Interior Ministry allowed only four appointments as deputy mayor.[11]

Working in favor of clever municipal officials are the separate relations between local authorities and national government ministries. The ministries make expenditures on their own programs in the local communities and provide funds to local authorities for specific programs in ways that are not coordinated by the ministries of finance and interior. Ministry administrators operate under a large number of national government laws, ministry regulations, and precedents that reflect decisions taken over the years for different reasons. In these rules and regulations there are numerous provisions for ministerial discretion. Ministers seek to advance their own reputations by favoring projects in local areas, whether or not they are not supported by the ministries of finance or interior.

Ambiguities between Israel's formal centralization and its culture of informality provide opportunities for finagling. The parliamentary leader of an ultra-Orthodox political party known by its Hebrew acronym as SHAS has been the subject of prolonged criminal proceedings that began with charges that as interior minister he provided special allocations for municipalities to use in supporting programs sponsored by his party. The investigation began in 1990 and reached the stage of an indictment and trial only at the end of 1993. He was found guilty on several charges in March, 1999. As of this writing, however, there is likely to be an appeal to this court decision, and two additional trials on separate charges may follow.

Some of Israel's ambiguity shows up in its financial reports. They are less helpful than they might be in revealing major lines of public policy at national or local levels. The categories used in budgets and financial reports may not be comparable from one year to the next, or from one local authority to another. They do not include the activities of quasi-governmental organizations. The categories of "ordinary budget" and "extraordinary budget" suggest a division between operating and capital (investment) activities. However, some operating expenses may appear in the extraordinary budget.

Quasi-Governmental Organizations: The Ambiguity of the State and Its Accountability

Like parallel organizations elsewhere, Israel's extensive quasi-governmental organizations produce ambiguous lines of control and responsibility. And beyond the kinds of quasi-governmental organizations that are more or less typical of those in Western democracies, Israel's unusual relationships with overseas Jewish communities produce an additional kind of quasi-governmental organization with distinctive political traits. The Diaspora provides the basis for extensive voluntary fund-raising by Israeli agencies and allows outsiders from numerous countries and diverse cultures to claim influence in Israel by virtue of financial contributions. Lines of control and responsibility blur as institutions that receive donations from overseas also receive Israeli government funding. Aggressive administrators claim freedom from an international board of directors on account of Israeli government funding, and freedom from Israeli government oversight on account of voluntary funding from overseas.

Overseas communities have supported activities in the Land of Israel from ancient times. Jews of the Greek, Roman, and Babylonian Diasporas sent annual payments to the Temple that were used partly to support the poor of the city. During the long period of non-Jewish rule, emissaries from Jerusalem's Jewish communities traveled throughout the Diaspora seeking funds. The process became more extensive with the onset of modern Zionist immigration in the 1880s. Now the United Jewish Appeal in the United States and the United Israel Appeal elsewhere are the major fund-raisers, while additional sums are collected by the separate campaigns of Israeli hospitals, universities, religious academies, and other social service agencies. Diaspora Jews who are suspicious of traditional organizations donate to campaigns that advertise themselves as bringing change by their support of programs outside those of the "Israeli establishment." These support programs for women, Jewish-Arab relations, and non-Orthodox religious activities.

Non-Jewish communities also have well-established patterns of international support. Overseas Christians built churches and monasteries, hospices for pilgrims, plus hospitals, orphanages, and schools for coreligionists. Officials of the British mandatory government created a Pro-Jerusalem Society that raised funds in Palestine, Europe, and the United States. It spent them on refurbishing historic buildings, town planning, cultural exhibitions, and publications.[12] Muslim authorities in Baghdad, Cairo, Saudi Arabia, and Jordan, as well as the PLO, have supported schools, mosques, and other institutions.

The historic role of the Labor Federation (Histadrut) also shows itself in quasi-governmental organizations. The Labor Federation sought to create work and social services for three decades prior to Israel's independence. It developed agricultural settlements (kibbutzim and moshavim), a bank and insurance company, pension funds, schools, transportation cooperatives, commercial and industrial enterprises, and what became the country's largest health provider with clinics, hospitals, pharmacies, convalescent facilities, and homes for senior citizens. With the creation of the Israeli state, many of these concerns received some or most of their funding from public sources and so became quasi-governmental. Their fortunes waxed and waned with the power of the Labor Party, which at various times controlled both the national government and the Labor Federation.

Several Israeli municipalities supplement their tax revenues and central government aid with funds collected overseas. Most prominent is the Jerusalem Foundation, created and headed by Teddy Kollek during his twenty-seven years as mayor. More than other institutions, the Jerusalem Foundation confounded the issue of what is governmental and private, and what is controlled by Israel, Jerusalem, or overseas friends of Jerusalem.[13] During Kollek's period as mayor, the Jerusalem Foundation supported over 1,000 projects, from small playgrounds and flower gardens to major facilities for museums, theaters, and cinema. It built or refurbished churches, mosques, and synagogues, subsidizing workshops for young artists and performances for schoolchildren.

Kollek's dual role as mayor of the municipality and chairman of the Jerusalem Foundation provided him with the leverage of private resources over public resources, and the leverage of public resources over private funds. Kollek extracted money from the municipality and the national government to match the nongovernmental funds raised by the foundation. He appealed to donors as a man who could use his status as mayor to push the foundation's projects through to completion and to supplement the private donations with public money. The intimate mixture of public and private roles also gave the mayor unusual advantages when he approached the voters for reelection as a man who added to Jerusalem's amenities. The attractions of these roles seemed to last until the election of 1993, when Kollek's age led even some enthusiastic supporters to withhold their support for yet another term. The Jerusalem Foundation has continued to operate with Ehud Olmert sitting in the mayor's office, but without the close connections to the municipality that it enjoyed during the Kollek period. After Olmert's reelection in 1998, a newspaper reported about the tension between the mayor and the foundation. Foundation personnel claimed that Olmert had sought to hamper the foundation's projects in order to take control of it.[14] A subsequent report in the same newspaper indicated that departments of the municipality stood against the posture of the mayor's office, and continued to benefit from the foundation's generosity.[15]

Accountability presumes knowing what is occurring within one's field of responsibility. In the case of quasi-governmental organizations, however, even the name is problematic.[16] Terms used include voluntary, not-for-profit, quasi-nongovernmental, tax-exempt, as well as Third Sector. The purported meaning of Third Sector is that the bodies are somewhere between the private and public sectors. The medley of terminology parallels the variety of organizational structure, as well as relations with clients, sources of funds, and mechanisms of supervision and control. Expectations are that these bodies provide opportunity for self-help, creativity, effectiveness, and efficiency, as well as passing to some other body responsibilities that might otherwise fall upon already strained officials and financial resources of government.

Organizational differences go beyond labels. No single term does more than approximate a description. Different and similar words are used for overlapping kinds of organizational formats. According to one scholar who examined units that shared the traits of being distanced from government yet having a relation with government:

> . . . confusion over names and characteristics is a not infrequent response of those who first enter this corner of the governmental zoo. "Authority," "corporation," "special district" and "commission" are titles used to identify governmental agencies of unusual shape and temperament; but the zoo keeper seems to have affixed labels almost at random, so that a "public authority" in one cage may be a very close cousin to a "government corporation" pawing the ground in another enclosure, while yet another "corporation" flies from tree to tree, sharing little in common with the first two inhabitants.[17]

The problem of accountability concerns supervision and/or control over this wide array of bodies that somehow, perhaps loosely, remain linked to government. Accountability is itself an amorphous concept. It involves an identification of bodies to be kept within certain bounds, bodies or individuals to whom they answer, as well as a clarification of standards for judging activities, information about the activities of bodies, and sanctions available to discipline bodies found to be deficient. The lack of clarity in terminology with respect to the bodies at issue implies that accountability is likely to be elusive. How can we hold something accountable if we are not clear what the something is?

Several authors identify particular problems of holding accountable organizations that fit within the range of the quasi-governmental.[18] What one author calls the "thickening of government," or the proliferation of service agencies and units to manage them, produces a diffusion of power and responsibility and blurring lines of accountability. Among the problems identified are:[19]

- Explicit distancing from government control and, along with this, a distancing from conventional mechanisms of accountability.

- Difficulties in holding human service providers accountable for the quality of performance outcomes.

- Autonomy of contractors enables politicians to avoid blame when programs sour.

- Some of the providers of funds have an incentive not to look too closely at bodies that receive their largesse. These include those whose leaders profit personally, through their families, or through their political connections with organizations that provide them with favors or "kickbacks" of one form or another.

- Multiple providers of funds or organizations with formal responsibilities for the oversight. When there may be arguments as to which organization should exercise oversight, it may be easiest for no organization to impose oversight.

- Donors tend to support voluntary organizations because of the worthiness of the cause that they serve and because of the voluntary nature of their work. They often see no need for accountability measures and feel uncomfortable about holding committed staff and volunteers to account.

Israel's nonprofit organizations account for a significant and growing portion of economic activity. The value of their services increased by 5.5 percent annually during the 1990–1996 period, and amounted to about 10 percent of gross domestic product in 1996. Many of them qualified for the designation of "quasi-governmental" insofar as grants from the national government and local authorities provided 64 percent of the income to more than 4,400 organizations. Sale of services provided another 25 percent, and contributions 10 percent. Part of the sale of services accounts for additional government support via the purchase of services by governmental bodies.[20] Yet another form of government support comes from tax concessions. Israel's nonprofit organizations pay no income tax and are free from paying value-added tax on noncommercial income. In addition, contributors to organizations recognized as public institutions are entitled to income tax concessions. The designation of "public institution" has been given to organizations operating in the fields of religion, culture, education, science, health, welfare, the prevention of traffic accidents, sport, and the encouragement of Jewish settlements in the territories occupied during the Six-Day War of 1967.

Israel has no shortage of organizations and procedures that are meant to provide for the accountability of quasi-governmental organizations. The Law of Associations requires nonprofit organizations to register with the Ministry of Interior, specify their objectives, submit annual audited financial statements, establish a board of directors and an audit committee, inform the ministry about the membership of those bodies, convene annual meetings, and maintain proper bookkeeping practices. The law grants the Registrar of Associations the power to conduct investigations of an association's management and operations and to recommend to a court that an association in violation be dismantled.

The State Comptroller has found several shortcomings in the implementation of these regulations:[21]

- Many associations submit financial reports beyond the deadline, or do not submit them at all.
- The Registrar has limited means for analyzing the financial reports of the associations.
- There is no systematic updating of information about the associations' boards of directors.
- The Registrar has conducted few investigations of associations, and despite findings that seem to warrant dismantling, the Registrar has never recommended that this step be taken.

With respect to their tax concessions, organizations are required to submit financial reports to the Tax Administration to allow periodic renewal of their status. However, the State Comptroller found numerous cases where organizations have maintained their tax-free status despite not having submitted financial reports for many years.[22] The approval of income tax deductions for donors is good until an organization's status as a body recognized for tax concessions is canceled, but the Tax Administration has no cancellation procedure.

Government ministries have two major points of contact with quasi-governmental organizations: the provision of grants and purchase of services. The Knesset enacted directives in 1992 for the orderly provision of government grants. They require that government ministries set objective criteria for making grants, publish the availability of grant moneys for specific purposes, establish grants committees responsible for equitable distributions, and oversee grantees to ensure that they fulfill grant conditions and use the grant for the intended purpose.

The State Comptroller has audited only a small number of the more than 4,000 organizations that receive governmental grants. Its audits have found cases of governmental bodies using these organizations in order to skirt around regulations that apply to the operations of governmental units, *per se*, as well as cases of party patronage and nepotism in the distribution of jobs and purchase contracts.[23]

For some nonprofit organizations of high prestige, there may be an assumption that formal accountability is unnecessary. This attitude may affect not only donors from the private sector but from the Israeli government as well. The Society for the Protection of Nature has done a good job of selling itself to the Israeli public and the government. An annual grant from the Ministry of Education, primarily for nature education directed at school groups, amounts to about 25 percent of the society's budget. The State Comptroller reported that the ministry exercised little oversight over the use of its funds, and expressed doubt that the society was using government funds economically and efficiently. In response, ministry officials explained that the society was a well-respected organization with support from powerful figures.[24]

Several of Israel's traits may exacerbate the problems of accountability among quasi-governmental or nonprofit organizations. These include perennial coalition politics and the capacity of these organizations to facilitate the distribution of party patronage outside the network of controls designed for governmental bodies, plus the appeal of Israel for donors who live in the Diaspora. However, literature from countries as different as the United States and the Third World point to similar conditions. A report of the U.S. General Accounting Office indicates the huge number of not-for-profit organizations in the United States (more than one million divided into some twenty-five categories), and the incapacity of accountability mechanisms to deal systematically with even the relatively simple issue of whether they merit tax-exempt status.[25]

Parallel to Israeli organizations that receive much of their funding from overseas are activities throughout the Third World that rely on a combination of United Nations, donor government, and voluntary contributions raised in wealthy countries. While there may be formal mechanisms of control, in practice there are tendencies to rely on some other body to do the oversight or to not intervene in the oversight of a program that is partly the responsibility of another country or a multinational organization. As in the case of Diaspora individuals that provide donations for Israel, governments that donate to Third World projects may be more interested in receiving credit for making a donation of aid and the humanitarian sentiments associated with it, than with seeing to the oversight of what happens to their funds.[26]

It is possible to exaggerate the desirability of accountability. We should not aspire to complete and systematic accountability that would entail one clerk always looking over the shoulder of every other clerk. Quasi-governmental organizations, in particular, are justified partly on the basis of their flexibility and their responsiveness to client needs. This flexibility entails a looser net of accountability than suitable to governmental bodies.

The Ambiguous Boundaries of Israel: With or Without the Jews of the Diaspora?

Ambiguous boundaries between Israel and the Diaspora affect not only problems of accountability with respect to organizations that rely partly on overseas donations. Much more prominent are a series of conflicts involving Orthodox and progressive Jewries, whose bases of political support are in Israel and the Diaspora, respectively. Their specific disputes involve the recognition of non-Orthodox rabbis to perform conversions to Judaism, marriage and divorce, the representation of non-Orthodox Jews on the religious councils affiliated with Israel's local authorities, the rituals to be permitted at the Western Wall, and the status of women. Behind the details of these disputes is a larger question involving the nature of Israel: Is it merely a state meant to serve its citizens, or somehow a state for the Jewish people worldwide?

There are several layers of ambiguities and other confusions involved in these disputes. They overlap with the tensions within Israel between religious and secular Jews. Yet the confluence of sides is not identical. Non-Orthodox religious Jews do not mesh with many of Israel's secular Jews. Not only are the non-Orthodox religious Jews mostly North American transplants (or entirely North American who come to Israel in order to protest and then return home), but they are religious while being outside the framework of Orthodoxy. Secular Israeli Jews who protest the power of the Orthodox establishment tend to be nonreligious or antireligious. Many of them see no attraction in the rituals or the rabbis of Conservative or Reform Judaism. For many of Israel's secular Jews, it is sufficient to exploit existing ways around the restrictions set up by the Orthodox. Few of them seem interested in adding yet another set of religious options to the Israeli scene.

The weakness of non-Orthodox religious Jews begins with their limited numbers in Israel. Surveys of Jewish religiosity in Israel carried out by Israeli social scientists tend not even to ask about Reform and Conservative affiliation. The categories that are well known, and questioned by survey research, are Orthodox, ultra-Orthodox, traditional, and secular. Israelis who consider themselves traditional are mostly Sephardi who see themselves as adhering to many but not all of the commandments.[27] One survey of Israeli Jews found 10 percent of the population within each of the ultra-Orthodox and Orthodox categories, 29 percent traditional, and 51 percent secular.[28] Thus, a large majority of Israelis are non-Orthodox. The size of the secular camp varies with the issue at hand and the position of traditional Jews. With respect to using automobiles, cook-outs in public parks, and football (i.e., soccer) on the Sabbath, many traditional Jews stand with the secular. With respect to marriage, burial, or kosher food, traditional Jews may be disinterested or go along with the Orthodox.[29]

The interests of secular Israelis have managed to hold their own against the vocal minority (never as many as 20 percent) of Knesset members who have represented Orthodox and ultra-Orthodox political parties. The interests of progressive religious Israelis do about as well as expected in a democracy where they have only a small number of vocal spokespersons in the population and no party to represent them in the national parliament. What power the non-Orthodox religious movements enjoy in Israel derives from their status in the Diaspora, particularly the United States. The financial contributions of American Reform and Conservative Jews have been crucial in setting up their movements' synagogues, schools, and other institutions in Israel. Their influence in the Diaspora guarantees access for prominent Reform and Conservative rabbis to the Israeli prime minister and other ranking politicians. Those Israeli politicians, however, depend more directly on the weight of ultra-Orthodox and Orthodox parties in the Knesset.

Perhaps the strongest deterrent to a development of non-Orthodox religious Judaisms in Israel lies in the nature of those Judaisms. They developed in the Diaspora. There they have provided a degree of religion acceptable to assimilating Jews, as well as a focus of Jewish education, identity, and social life. Israeli Jews have little need for those services. Their Jewish identity is without dispute. Even "secular" education provides a great deal of Bible study and other facets of Jewish history and culture. Almost all of the national holidays are religious in origin and are celebrated widely. The social life and marriage partners of Israeli Jews are almost entirely Jewish. Israelis in need of marriage, divorce, or burial can obtain whatever incidence of religious ceremony they desire from the Orthodox establishment. Those who wish to avoid Orthodox rituals can marry or divorce overseas in ways that the state will recognize.

There is little room for courtesy in the religious disputes of Israel. An ultra-Orthodox member of Knesset was not holding out much promise of cooperation when he said, "Letting a Reform rabbi sit on the Tel Aviv religious council is the equivalent of letting a terrorist into the General Staff headquarters. The Reform are terrorists, not rabbis." When this same MK was present at a meeting with Reform and Conservative representatives, he called them "clowns" and "liars."[30] A group of Reform rabbis made their own contribution to the holiday spirit just before Passover in 1995 by proclaiming that the custom of symbolically selling products that Jews cannot eat on Passover to an Arab, and then buying them back after the holiday is a "bluff, swindle, and hypocrisy" by the Orthodox Rabbinate.[31]

Non-Orthodox Jewish institutions and programs improved their standing during the Rabin-Peres governments of 1992–1996. For part of the government's term, no Orthodox or ultra-Orthodox party was formally part of the ruling coalition. Representatives of the overtly secular Meretz Party served as ministers of education and culture, and a secular member of the Labor Party served for a while as minister of religions. During this period the Ministry of Education and Culture added instruction in Conservative and Reform Judaism to religious programs in Jewish secular schools. The minister of religions opened to public scrutiny the Rabbinate's list of Jews forbidden to marry in Israel. He also demanded that individuals placed on the list on account of one or another provision of religious law be given an opportunity to appeal their designation, and he proposed public funding for them to travel overseas in order to obtain a secular marriage. With the change in government that occurred after the elections of 1996, the Ministry of Education and Culture passed to a member of the Orthodox National Religious Party (NRP), and the Ministry of Religions was to be headed in rotation by a member of the Orthodox NRP and the ultra-Orthodox SHAS. With these changes, the Ministry of Education and Culture renewed its stress on traditional Jewish values in teaching programs on citizenship. Nothing was heard from the Ministry of Religions about public support for Jews traveling abroad for civil marriages.

Left-wing, secular Israeli politicians would appear to be the most receptive to Reform and Conservative demands. However, some of these have made a point of criticizing the spokespersons of liberal Judaism for being out of touch with political realities in Israel. Former interior minister Haim Ramon and former health minister Efraim Sneh (both members of the Labor Party) have wanted help with the peace process from Jews well connected in America. They have come away from meetings with leaders of liberal Judaism saying that those people were interested only in their own religious agenda.[32] According to Ramon, there are only two important communities in Israel, Orthodox and secular, and the others are insignificant. To change that, he said, would require the Reform movement to send several hundred thousand of its members to Israel as immigrants. Reacting to the American flavor of Reform Judaism, Ramon said, "I don't tell you what to do in the U.S.; don't tell me what to do here."[33]

MOVING TOWARDS NORMALITY

Part of the ambiguity that affects Israeli policymaking and administration derives from the ambiguity that pervades the country itself. It is not a normal state. Differences from other countries confuse in the Israeli case what observers expect to see in a country. Prominent in its distinctive characteristics are the hostility that has kept it from being accepted by its neighbors, a lack of clarity in its borders, its relationships with the Jewish Diaspora, as well as the interest and support shown by countries from outside the region.

Israel is now more of a conventional country than any time in its half-century of modern history. But it is still unusual. Its population has increased by some 15 percent as a result of an immigration wave of more than 800,000 since 1989. Israel is also continuing to negotiate the extent of its territory and its future relations with a Palestinian Authority that may be transformed into a Palestinian State. And in conjunction with these negotiations, Israel is moving to normalize economic relations with a number of Arab countries that until recently were formally closed to commerce with Israel.

One of the advantages in Israel's abnormality has been its access to foreign aid. Donations from overseas Jews and other individuals who supported the creation of modern Israel were prominent from the earliest period of Zionist settlement. German reparations for the destruction of the Holocaust became a major factor in the 1950s. U.S. Government aid has been prominent since the Yom Kippur War of 1973. Figure 2.1 shows the importance of overseas transfers as a proportion of Israel's gross domestic product from 1952 to 1997. The decline since 1985 represents one measure of Israel's movement toward economic normality.

The economic impacts of immigration are most prominent in housing and employment. The area of residential building was in the range of 2.9 million square meters per year during the preimmigration period of 1986–1988, and increased to as high as 7.6 million square meters per year from 1989 to 1995.[34] Along with the pressure on housing came an increase in the prices of dwellings, as well as traffic congestion, road building, and arguments about land usage. The immigration began as environmental protection was becoming more prominent as a policy issue in Israel. The demands for increased infrastructure did not pass without complaints about pollution and the transformation of agricultural land to housing and industry. Environmentalists complained about a change in planning regulations that allowed building to go forward at an accelerated pace, with less time allowed for appeals by those opposed to plans.

A spurt in unemployment was perhaps an inevitable immediate result of immigration. Rates increased from the range of 6 to 7 percent in 1986–1988 to 10 to 11 percent in 1991–1992, but then declined to the 6 to 7 percent range by 1994–1995, as shown in Figure 2.2. The decline owes something to investments supported by loan guarantees provided to Israel by the U.S. Government, as well as the skills brought by the immigrants themselves. As in other waves of immigration, Israel has been able to use the human capital prepared in other countries' schools. A later increase that again topped 10 percent unemployment in 1998 may owe something to a decline in foreign investment that came in response to delays in the peace process, plus the animosity of Arabs and others to the post-1996 Israeli government, as well as a continuing process of privatization that has reduced government subsidies to industry and has resulted in the closing of inefficient plants.

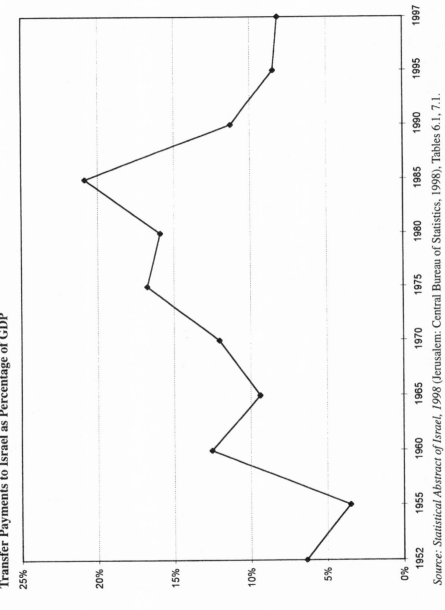

Figure 2.1
Transfer Payments to Israel as Percentage of GDP

Source: Statistical Abstract of Israel, 1998 (Jerusalem: Central Bureau of Statistics, 1998), Tables 6.1, 7.1.

48

Figure 2.2
Percentage Unemployed

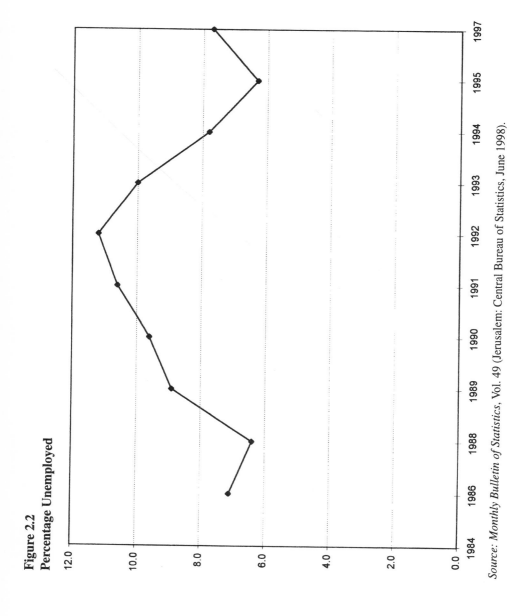

Source: Monthly Bulletin of Statistics, Vol. 49 (Jerusalem: Central Bureau of Statistics, June 1998).

49

Figure 2.3
Defense Percentage of Government Expenditures

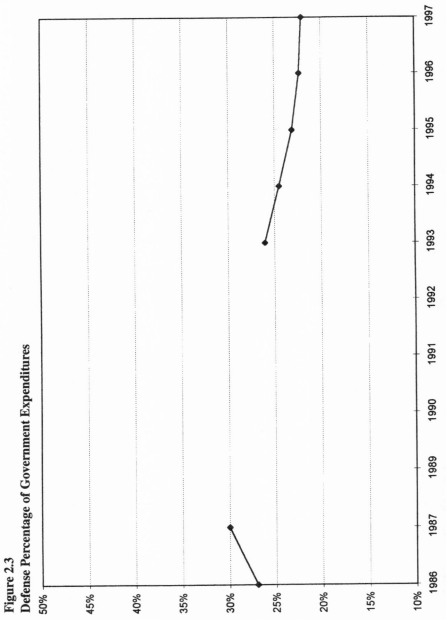

Source: Statistical Abstract of Israel, 1998 (Jerusalem: Central Bureau of Statistics, 1998), Table 20.7.

The implications of the peace process for Israel's abnormalities are multifaceted. And insofar as peace is more an aspiration than a realized accomplishment, projections associated with it are speculative in large measure. Already apparent is a decline in the proportion of resources allocated to defense, as shown in Figure 2.3. The proportions remain high by the standards of Western democracies but are not so drastically far from the mean as previously. As the Arab boycott withers away, more international firms are willing to invest and sell their products in Israel. Somewhat worrisome are the demands for Israel to share the scarce water resources of its semiarid region with Jordan and the Palestinians. Yet the pressures associated with this prospect may moderate as water-rich countries of the region become more willing than in the past to sell some of their surplus to Israel.[35]

Among the numerous indications of Israel's continuing ambiguity is a joke told often about themselves by those who claim to be optimists in their view of the peace process. The peace process continues, along with acts of violence, accusations by various groups of Palestinians, Israelis, and others that Israeli and Palestinian authorities are not doing what they should, and projections are made of apocalyptic catastrophe if the process does not move more quickly. Optimists feel like the person who fell from a high building. The last words heard, as the body plummeted downward, were "So far, so good."

3

Ambiguity in Religion as Well as Politics

Religion and politics seek to accomplish a great deal, and both are ambiguous in doctrine and practice. Israel provides a tantalizing site for the examination of the commonalties, insofar as much of Israeli politics is about religion.

Religion and politics depend on faith and the promise of what is to come. Yet neither has achieved the various forms of paradise that they promise. Sectarians and party activists try to recruit affiliates to their own cluster and to elicit more activity from their members. There are sophisticated theoreticians, crafty leaders, and simple believers in both realms. The behaviors suitable to politics and religion are interchangeable, and the fields overlap. For some, politics is their religion. Pursuing the "art of the possible" is not morally less attractive than many alternatives that are explicitly more spiritual. And religion is the offering of many engaged in politics, ranging from the Christian Right in the United States to the ultra-Orthodox in Israel, along with Protestants and Catholics in Northern Ireland, and Islamic Fundamentalists throughout the Middle East. Religion and politics can provoke intense belief and as a result are said by some to be improper topics of polite conversation.

The focus of this chapter is the ambiguity of religion. Like intellectual leaders in politics, those in religion are not precise in their doctrines. Antagonists who criticize religious and political figures need be no more precise than those they censure for failing to deliver on their commitments. There is more vagueness and contradiction than exactness in classic texts as well as the most recent commentaries, sermons, or campaign rhetoric.

There are proof texts for wide ranges of theologians, preachers, candidates, and officeholders who nonetheless manage to exist within the generous boundaries of religious and political movements. Doctrines that promise much in the future are safe against proof that they are wrong. Themes of organizational theory that focus on the pursuit of institutional self-interest are often more successful in explaining the actions of religious and political figures than the doctrines that they proclaim.

Ambiguity is part of the successes and failures of religion and politics. A lack of clarity in goals aids in recruiting support but also assures frustration in judging accomplishments. The payoffs are never as great as the promises. An Israeli popular song complains that the Messiah has not come and has not even phoned to explain the delay. There are never enough resources to satisfy all those who look to government for salvation.

Religion is prominent in the politics of numerous Western democracies. It should be no surprise that Israel is among these. Not only are its location and its people important in the history of religion, but Israel's proclamation as a Jewish state in 1948 seemed to set it off from other democracies where the movement of the past two centuries has been in the secular direction. Religion and politics proceed at high levels of intensity, and much of the country's politics is about religion. Israeli Jews may agree that theirs is a country for Jews, but they do not agree that religious laws should prevail.

AMBIGUITY IN RELIGION

Religions claim to purvey revealed truth, sometimes of the most absolute variety. Yet the history of their doctrines and commentaries is one of continuous dispute and change. Among the quarrels are whether miracles central to their doctrines really happened or are metaphors for the power and glory of the Almighty. "Stories for children" are the way some commentators describe biblical testimonies of the unbelievable, that is, tales that are meant to convey great ideas to individuals of limited capacity. Others assert that all described in the Bible is true and really happened the way it is portrayed. The parting of the Red Sea and the epiphany on Mount Sinai are important landmarks in Judaism, while the virgin birth and the resurrection are central points in Christianity that are arguably miracles or metaphors.[1] One scholar writes that the ancient audiences who listened to oral renditions of biblical stories were made up of more- and less-sophisticated persons, with the more sophisticated able to tell the difference between the report of a historical record and the use of a literary device.[2] The differentiation exists today. Arguments continue as to what is fact or what is fiction meant to enlighten. The phenomenon has its parallel in political audiences that differ as to how much of a campaign speech they take seriously, or how much of new legislation they expect to be implemented.

Holy texts claim absolutist doctrines and illustrate contradictory themes. Against the power and omniscience of God portrayed in the Hebrew Bible are stories that show God to be unsure of himself and willing to bargain with humans (as with Abraham and Moses in the case of punishments to be meted out to residents of Sodom[3] and wayward Israelites in the desert[4]), concerned with avoiding a head-on confrontation with adversaries who may be too powerful,[5] and who blustered at Job rather than answered his challenges in detail.[6] Each of these problematic passages has been subject to commentary time and again by those who find cause for skepticism, and those who read the same passages in a way to justify the view that the Lord is absolute in his power and justice.

Among the ambiguities in the Hebrew Bible that also relate to ancient politics are passages about kingship. The Book of Deuteronomy calls on the Israelites to appoint as king the man chosen by God.[7] The prophet Samuel was willing to help the Israelites identify a king but warned them about unpleasant consequences.[8] Also, the final passage in the Book of Judges is a classic expression in support of individual freedom: ". . . the children of Israel departed thence at that time, every man to his tribe and to his family, and they went out from thence every man to his inheritance. In those days there was no king in Israel: every man did that which was right in his own eyes."[9] No king of Judah or Israel escapes the wrath of biblical critics. It was Samuel against Saul, Nathan against David, Elijah and Micaiah against Ahab, Elisha against Jehoram, and Jeremiah against Jehoiakim and Zedekiah.

A simple reading of Ecclesiastes finds expressions of emptiness, futility, and meaninglessness that challenge precepts of absolutism that appear elsewhere in the Bible. Death is the end of us all, the wise as well as the foolish.[10] The book professes change as opposed to constancy, and urges judgment about the situation as opposed to a faith in simple rules. "Everything has its season . . . a time to be born and a time to die; a time to plant and a time to uproot; a time to kill and a time to heal . . . a time to love and a time to hate; a time for war and a time for peace."[11] We read in Ecclesiastes that wisdom is to be preferred to foolishness and is better than money or possessions. However, the pursuit of too much wisdom, or too much of anything, is like chasing the wind. One should not be overly righteous or overly wise. Why make a fool of oneself? It is best to enjoy what can be attained and to live the best life possible.[12]

Ecclesiastes has its own ambiguity. It supports pious reverence along with skepticism. Man has a sense of time past and future but no comprehension of God's work from beginning to end.[13] Earth, the heavens, and the

Lord are everlasting.[14] It will be well with those who fear God and obey his commands.[15] God knows all our secrets and brings everything we do to judgment.[16] The final passages are not helpful to the reader who wishes to clarify what seems confusing. They say that the speaker turned over many maxims in order to teach, that he chose his words carefully in order to give pleasure, even while he taught the truth. The third verse from the end is the often-quoted remark against too much study, which urges skepticism to someone who would understand the material at hand: ". . . of making books there is no end; and much study is a weariness of the flesh."[17] The last two verses urge the reader to fear God and obey his commands.

Commentators quarrel as to whether the God-fearing passages in Ecclesiastes reflect the sentiments of the original author, or if they were added later in order to make the book acceptable to those who debated about the inclusion of the book in what became the Hebrew Bible.[18] Those who supported the inclusion of Ecclesiastes in the Bible argued that insofar as it was written by Solomon, ordinary mortals could not presume to understand its wisdom. Against this view, skeptics note the presence of Persian words in the text that date it at least several hundred years after Solomon's death. According to one scholar, the claim that Solomon wrote the book "is like saying . . . that a book about Marxism in modern English idiom and spelling was written by Henry VIII."[19]

The ten commandments are at the heart of Biblical law, but they are not without their ambiguities. The original Hebrew of the sixth commandment is לא תרצח (lo tirtzach).[20] Modern Hebrew speakers are likely to translate it as Do not murder. Thus it appears in the 1955 translation of the Jewish Theological Seminary of America, as well as the New English Bible. The meaning, perhaps, is premeditated intentional killing. However, the same passage is translated as Do not kill in the King James Version and the Revised Standard Version. This suggests a more sweeping prohibition that may bar self-defense and support pacifism.

The ambiguity in translation derives from the Bible's mixture of the words now used for kill and murder in ways that defy comprehension. The word רצח (retzach) usually associated with murder appears in other episodes when the intention appears to be kill rather than murder, as in the case of individuals who kill without prior intention and can seek protection from vengeful relatives of the deceased in a city of refuge.[21] The Bible also uses the word usually translated as kill in modern Hebrew (הרג : hereg) when the intention appears to be murder, as in the story of Cain and Abel.[22]

Alongside the knotty problems of translation from material written two millennia ago in a culture much different from our own are the Bible's use of what appears to be metaphor, allegory, and symbolism. They all contribute to ambiguity and provide the basis for widely varied commentaries. According to a Christian theologian: "the structure and style of Scripture . . . [is] so unsystematic and various, and a style so figurative and indirect, that no one would presume at first sight to say what is in it and what is not.[23] What is said about the biblical interpretations of the apostle Paul can apply to many other readings by Jews and Christians. "The . . . exegesis . . . have an air of freedom. We cannot be sure that if Paul had interpreted the same passage twice he would have interpreted it in the same way."[24]

Jewish and Christian commentators often differ in their interpretations of ambiguous passages. One source of Christians' perception of allegory is the view that the Hebrew Bible is the Old Testament that prepares the way for Jesus Christ, and the failure of the Hebrew Bible to acknowledge that status explicitly. A prominent contention is that the suffering servant in the Book of Isaiah predicts the life of Jesus. The text of Chapters 52 and 53 tells of a man to whom the power of the Lord was revealed, who was despised, and who was wounded for human iniquities. (A Christian translation that he was "pierced" fits the story of the crucifixion, but is not supported by the Hebrew words מכה or מחלל (m'chlal or makoh) that appear in the text of Isaiah and may have given rise to the translation.[25]) Traditional Jewish commentators view the suffering servant as a symbol for the Israelite nation, or as Isaiah's view of himself.[26]

Religious Jews have also been creative in finding their own hidden meanings in the holy text. The Song of Songs has been viewed as an expression of God's love for his people, and not an expression of carnal desire as its text suggests. About Philo, an Alexandrian Jew at the beginning of the common era, a modern commentator writes: "So skillful was his manipulation of the allegorical method of interpretation that [he] could surely have extracted a statement of Plato's Theory of Ideas from a railway timetable!"[27] A leading Jewish scholar was referring to the lack of precision in the ancient documents, and the invitation they offer for interpretations of great variety, when he wrote that "the only possible interpretation of Torah and Talmud is mystical interpretation."[28] A commentator on the Book of Job finds that it ". . . was recreated by its interpreters in their own image. . . . [It] is . . . destined to live a life of peaceful coexistence with, and adaptation to, a broad spectrum of philosophies, Jewish, Christian, humanist, secular, existentialist and nihilist, medievalist and modernist."[29]

Judaic revisions of the earlier books appear in the Bible's own Books of Chronicles. The David of Chronicles is more God-fearing and properly Jewish than the David of earlier books. As the story of David's defeat of the Philistines at Baal-perazim is told in II Samuel, it ends with David and his men carrying off the idols left behind by the Philistines.[30] As the story is told in Chronicles, David orders that the idols be burned.[31] Chronicles leaves out the young David's offer to fight against the Israelites alongside the Philistines. Bathsheba does not appear in Chronicles, neither as the cause of adultery and killing nor one who schemes for the selection of Solomon as David's successor. The succession story from David to Solomon in Chronicles is a smooth one, without a plot by Adojinah or mention of a young virgin who must warm an aged David.

The chronicler's repair of David's image was nothing compared to what has been done for him by postbiblical Jewish legends.[32]

Even after David became king he sat at the feet of his teachers, Ira the Jairite and Mephibosheth. To the latter he always submitted his decisions on religious questions, to make sure that they were in accordance with law. Whatever leisure time his royal duties afforded him, he spent in study and prayer. He contented himself with sixty breaths of sleep. At midnight the strings of his harp, which were made of the gut of the ram sacrificed by Abraham on Mount Moriah, began to vibrate. The sound they emitted awakened David, and he would arise at once to devote himself to the study of the Torah. . . .

Scholarship about the New Testament is no more precise than that which focuses on the Hebrew Bible. About one unclear passage, one commentator wrote, "there are probably as many approaches to the . . . problem as there are New Testament scholars."[33] A group of Christian scholars sought to put some order in the speculative and contentious work by voting about numerous episodes concerning Jesus, and expressing their judgment as to the degree of certainty that they really occurred, as opposed to being the inventions of later authors. Among the results of this seeking after scholarly consensus is that details about Jesus' virgin birth and last days, including descriptions of his arrest, trial, and resurrection, are widely seen as mythic inventions composed sometime after his death.[34]

Paul himself would have trouble with such voting: ". . . if there be no resurrection of the dead, then is Christ not risen: And if Christ be not risen, then is our preaching vain, and your faith is also vain."[35] This passage also suggests that Paul was struggling with listeners who were hard-pressed to believe stories of miracles.

Modern scholars conclude that the Gospels of the New Testament were written forty to sixty years after the death of Jesus, and that they reflect problems of Christian communities at those times.[36] They were concerned to justify Jesus' status as messiah despite his execution as a criminal, to blame the Jews for his death, and to remove the onus from the Romans. The

Jews were the religious antagonists of the Christians, and the Romans had power to persecute those who complained about their officials.[37]

A Catholic scholar writes that the New Testament "is polemical and must be used with extreme caution."[38] A Jewish writer calls the Gospels "dramatizations with policy features."[39] A recent book describes the Gospel According to Mark as "not a documentary record of the past but an aesthetic literary creation, like a novel, . . . its subject matter is [not] historical but ideological."[40]

The New Testament includes numerous anti-Jewish passages.

- it refers to Pharisees as vipers[41] and blind guides;[42] and hypocrites who preach one thing and do another;[43]

- Jews are said to have demanded the death of Jesus, while the Roman official Pilate saw him as innocent of a capital charge;[44]

- Jewish priests are described as bribing Roman soldiers to testify that disciples stole the body of Christ from his tomb, in order to create the image that he had not risen from the dead;[45]

- Jews are said to poison the minds of Gentiles against Christians;[46] and

- Gentile authorities are said to act against Christians in order to curry favor with the Jews.[47]

These expressions not only reveal the tensions between the early Christians and the ancient Jews, but contributed to Christian anti-Semitism and must be counted among the elements that laid the ground for medieval persecutions and ultimately the Holocaust.[48] It is seemingly in response to the Holocaust that numerous Christian commentators now cite the New Testament as polemical.[49] The prestige of an independent Israel may also affect what scholars see in the sources from 2,000 years ago.[50]

Criticism of the historicity of the Hebrew Bible or the New Testament need not reflect a rejection of the spiritual messages found in them. Individual Jews and Christians who question the accuracy of many details in Holy Scripture are inspired by principles that they also find. There are standard responses for those who focus on confusing passages in holy texts. Religious commentators see the texts as the works of God or those who are inspired by God. And the Lord's works are unfathomable to mere humans. The incorporeal nature of God, and God's inscrutability are sufficient to guard against all criticism.[51]

Integral to the development of Judaism are the decisions in cases brought before religious courts. By tradition, the rabbis who serve as judges are explicating the Oral Torah in a process that began with Moses. However, more than two millennia of decisions, as well as commentaries on them, provide for numerous ways of viewing current cases and previous decisions—or precedents—that appear to be relevant. Among the accusations said about Judaism is that it is "hair splitting," or that it employs the definition of fine distinctions that allows or prevents one case from being used to set a decision for another. What to anti-Semites may be excessive arguments about insignificant issues, are to religious Jews the way of discerning God's intentions.

The process of legal exegesis introduces ambiguities in some eyes even while it produces clarifications from other perspectives. The following abstract of a rabbinical decision illustrates a pursuit of justice that makes a point of avoiding absolute clarity (in this case, about the time allowed for a publisher's exclusive right).

Praise be to God for the clarity and beauty of the new Talmud published by the illustrious traders Joseph and Jacob Propes Katz. . . . No man shall dare to print the Talmud before the elapse of twenty-five years from the date of its completion by them. It is true that there still remain a few years of the twenty-year ban issued on behalf of the previous publishers. Just as they encroached slightly on their predecessors, so it is permitted to encroach on them and it is not necessary to insist on the full complement of years.[52]

A lack of clarity in religious expression is not only something from the Bible and its commentaries or from legal decisions. A number of distinguished rabbis in modern Israel are inclined to express themselves in parables, which depend for their comprehension on the insight or imagination of their followers. The spiritual leader of the ultra-Orthodox Sephardim said in the midst of one political controversy, "the head of the flock is a blind man who stumbles and falls." This caused something of a problem for the rabbis' followers in the government coalition, but they were quick to assert that the rabbi was not referring to the prime minister.[53]

THE POSITIVE AND NEGATIVE SIDES OF AMBIGUITY

The problems of ambiguity in politics are well known. Participants do not know exactly where they stand. There are no fixed boundaries or guidelines to behavior that can be described as legitimate, reasonable, or acceptable. At the very least, ambiguity produces the stress of not knowing one's own limits or those of one's adversaries.

The situation is similar in religion. In the case of well-established faiths, adherents must study for years to learn the acceptable interpretations of ambiguous or contradictory doctrines. And even then they may be led by error or intention to express something that is unacceptable to someone. Ecclesiastical trials, excommunication, banishment, and worse have been the fate of heretics and apostates.

The other sides of these coins are the opportunities to recruit widely on the basis of doctrines that are attractive without being precise. Salvation and Paradise in religion have their political equivalents in the promises made by advocates of various modes of collectivism and individual freedom. There are political as well as religious mantras designed for ritualized repetition. A little boy at Sunday School once defined "faith" as "believing firmly what you know isn't true."[54] Political commentators perceive widely different themes in the New Deal, Fair Deal, New Freedoms, New Federalism, decolonialization, and peace with honor. They all promised more than they delivered. In their time, however, they served as the ambiguous slogans of winning movements. Prime Minister Benjamin Netanyahu won the 1996 Israeli election with slogans that promised peace with security as well as a united Jerusalem. During the campaign, and even more so later, his opponents asserted that he made peace insecure and assured the division of Jerusalem.

RELIGION AND POLITICS IN THE JEWISH STATE

Israel offers an enticing opportunity to examine the ambiguities of religion and politics. Politics is intense and elicits wide interest and participation.[55] Politicians cope with problems that are too difficult to solve in a forthright manner, and ambiguity often appears as one of their coping mechanisms.

Israel declared itself a *Jewish* state in 1948 when other democracies were well on their way to secularization. However, the picture was blurred from the beginning by numerous ambiguities in Judaic doctrines. A prominent theme in Judaism renders Jews an ethnic group as well as a religious community. Included in the community are those Jews who profess a range of religious views or none at all. Jewish humanists, agnostics, and atheists are no less able to claim a home in Israel than the ultra-Orthodox. Moreover, one can acquire Jewish ethnicity through a religious ceremony of conversion. Jews span all racial categories. There are Jews with Slavic faces and blond hair, as well as dark-skinned Jews from Ethiopia, Yemen, and the Indian subcontinent, plus the motley rest with roots in Europe and the Middle East.

It is common for articulate Israelis from among the ultrareligious and the antireligious to claim that the society is sharply divided along lines of religiosity. According to recent surveys, however, large percentages of Israelis observe at least some practices that can be called religious: a Sabbath meal with members of the family that includes lighting candles, drinking wine, and traditional prayers; a Passover *seder*; fasting on Yom Kippur; and saying that their Jewishness is important to them. Lesser but still substantial numbers claim to eat only kosher food. While the ultrareligious and the antireligious tend to be socially isolated from one another, there is substantial social mixing among the large majority of Israelis who tend to be religious or secular, but not at either extreme.[56]

The ambiguity in the nature of Judaism supports numerous contentious postures among religious and secular Israelis about Judaism and their Jewishness. Is Judaism simply what Jews believe and do, or does it require the acceptance of certain doctrines? If there are mandatory doctrines, what are they? Should the Sabbath meal enjoyed by Israelis who call themselves secular be categorized as simply part of the national culture as opposed to a religious ritual? Does the widespread support of the Israeli military signify only that Israelis like many other nationalities are patriotic? Does it reflect the development of a civil religion, or something closer to a multifaceted and evolving Judaism?[57]

Lacking a unifying central authority since ancient times, Judaism has been free to evolve without fracturing into distinct faiths. Moreover, dispersion has exposed Jews to the influences of many cultures. The gathering in Palestine/Israel during the last century has brought a diversity that continues to evolve.

The American Jewish scholar Jacob Neusner has written about *multiple Judaisms*. He claims to identify eight varieties, but he seems to identify at least ten: that which preceded the Judaism of the dual Torah, which Neusner dates from the fourth century c.e.; the Judaism of the dual Torah; Reform, Orthodox, and Conservative Judaisms; Zionism; Jewish socialism; American Judaism; Israeli Judaism; and a Judaism of "reversion" which advocates a fresh encounter with the Judaism of the dual Torah.[58] (The dual Torah refers to the written Torah, i.e., the first five books of the Bible and the oral Torah. The oral Torah is the accumulation of Rabbinical commentaries on the written Torah and religious law derived from it.) In writing about the Jewish experience in the United States, Neusner adds some ambiguity to his own concepts by asking if it is Jewishness without Judaism. He calls some efforts of American Jews "grotesque," but concludes nonetheless that they represent efforts of Jews to survive that so far have been successful.[59]

Israeli authorities and intellectuals have claimed leadership and protection of the Jewish world. However, Israeli governments have been selective in applying its protection, and Diaspora Jews waffle with respect to their acceptance of Israeli leadership on matters of faith or politics.[60] Non-

Orthodox Jews are dominant in several Diaspora communities, especially the United States, and they express protection of the non-Orthodox religious minority in Israel. Confrontations between Orthodox and ultra-Orthodox Jews on one side and progressive (i.e., Conservative, Reconstructionist, and Reform) Jews on the other side pit Jews with little direct support in the Israeli electorate against Orthodox and ultra-Orthodox parties that are well situated in the Knesset. Israeli prime ministers welcome overseas financial donations to their own campaigns as well as to Israeli institutions, and the political assistance that non-Orthodox Diaspora Jews can wield with their own overseas governments. They are less welcoming of Diaspora involvement in Israeli politics. When Diaspora leaders say what they want the Israeli government to do, the responses are likely to be vague commitments ambiguously implemented.

Religion is prominent among the country's political disputes, and ambiguity summarizes their outcomes better than any other word. Issues often on the agenda of public debate are:

- Which aspects of religious law should be enforced by state authorities, and which bodies should have the final say in determining the nature of religious law and its application to individual cases? This cluster of problems includes activities permitted on the Sabbath and religious holidays; the sale of nonkosher food; rules of modesty and decency; abortions, organ transplants, and other medical practices; the treatment of ancient Jewish graves uncovered in construction projects; who should be considered a Jew; and who should be given the designation and authority of "rabbi" to perform marriages, divorces, and conversions to Judaism.

- What should be the rights and privileges of various categories of Jews? Religious and secular Jews, ultra-Orthodox, and non-Orthodox, as well as Jews from North Africa, Ethiopia, and Asia feel that they have been treated unfairly by other Jews.

- What should be the rights and privileges of non-Jews, including access to public positions and other benefits of public policy?

- How much of that imprecise landscape called the biblical Land of Israel should be insisted on or bargained away for the sake of peace?

- How to manage the holy places of Jerusalem, where Jewish, Muslim, and Christians have internal disputes alongside conflicts with one another. Jews quarrel about the use of Orthodox or non-Orthodox rituals at the Western Wall. Christians do not agree about the rights of Latin, Greek, and Coptic denominations in the Church of the Holy Sepulcher. Muslims with political loyalties to Jordan, Saudi Arabia, and the Palestine Liberation Organization quarrel about the maintenance of Haram Esh Sharif and the appointment of Muslim religious authorities in Jerusalem.

The intensity of tensions between religious and antireligious Israelis appears in expressions by and about Shulamit Aloni. As an outspoken woman and successful politician, she was likely to prompt some kind of response from Orthodox Jews. Her campaigns against the religious establishment assured that the response would be extreme. For several years she was the leader of a small party that campaigned for civil rights, including those of secular Jews against the demands of Orthodox Judaism for monopolies in dealing with marriage, divorce, and burial. She became even more of an issue as Minister of Education and Culture in the Rabin government from 1992. The dossier against Aloni included:

- A photograph taken of her sitting at a table laden with bread and beer in a restaurant in the Arab city of Nazareth during Passover in 1993.

- A proposal that the name of God be removed from the memorial prayer at military ceremonies.

- Opposition to teaching that the world was created in six days.

- Reference to the chief rabbis of Israel as Israel's two popes.

- Saying that it is no longer necessary to keep kosher in Israel since Jews now live in their own sovereign state, and the laws of *kashruth* were meant to distance Jews from non-Jews.

- Referring to a site revered by some religious Jews as the Tomb of the biblical Joseph as the tomb of Sheikh Yusuf. She based her assertion on archaeological evidence that it was the tomb of an Arab sheikh, perhaps no more than 200 years old.[61]

- Saying that the government is excessive in bribing the ultra-Orthodox, or paying them to move step after step towards a religious fundamentalist, "Khomeinistic" state.[62]

Aloni also directed her barbs at the religious Zionists who have settled in parts of the West Bank and Gaza. She called on the government to stop the "vile, contemptible methods of rioting and Jewish intafada" which endanger not only the peace process but Israeli society.[63] On one occasion she said, "Some of the [Jews living in Hebron] are racists who want to expel the Arabs. . . . We remember how in the night they threw out the people who were living there. They urinated on them, destroyed their houses and shot at them." This statement was made after Prime Minister Rabin had given in to religious demands, taken the education portfolio from Aloni, and demoted her to Minister of Culture and Communications. A Knesset member of the National Religious Party (NRP) responded with a call for Aloni's dismissal as culture and communications minister and referred to her as "mentally unstable." He made the point that her remarks about Hebron settlers came only a day after the funeral procession for two victims of Arab terror in Hebron had been stoned by Arabs on its way to the cemetery.[64]

One ultra-Orthodox rabbi prophesied that Aloni would do to Israeli youth what Hitler had done to one million Jewish children fifty years earlier.[65] Another said that he would "declare a celebration and throw a banquet the day that wicked woman Shulamit Aloni dies."[66] Aloni's response was to wish the rabbi, "a very long life, so that he would one day indeed get to throw the banquet he wished for."[67]

Then a number of religious Israelis also condemned the rabbi who said he would celebrate Aloni's death. This made clear once again that the religious bloc has its own inner tensions. A religious Knesset member of the Labor Party asked if the rabbi was empowered to pass a sentence of death on anyone.[68] According to a Knesset member of the Orthodox NRP, "What Rabbi Yosef said was narrow-minded, immoral incitement and is distinctly un-Jewish. He should not be seen as a Torah great, no matter how many pages of the Talmud he knows by heart. His words drip with personal hatred and have nothing to do with an ideological disagreement." In response, the ultra-Orthodox Rabbi Yosef was hardly modest in condemning the NRP: "the NRP's religion can be dumped in the garbage can—it and the NRP both. . . . This party calls itself a bridge?. . . It's a bridge all right—a bridge straight to hell for teaming up with Labor. They are both bound for hell."[69]

The ambiguity in the treatment of religious disputes among Jews is apparent when both religious and antireligious activists claim losses in what seems like an ongoing tug-of-war. Both can also claim gains, but they tend to avoid boasting in order to play the downtrodden at the next encounter. On some occasions, each can claim both victory and defeat, as when authorities enact measures that seem to favor one side but fail to implement them.

Ambiguities are assured insofar as religious vs. secular religious disputes focus on particular cases and avoid any effort to resolve once and for all time the general issues that are at stake. The individual cases find a solution or disappear from the public agenda without resolution, and the same underlying conflict returns again at another time or another site. There is no clear indication whether religious or secular is winning, or what is general policy with respect to Sabbath activities, rules of modesty, or the status of non-Orthodox Judaism.

- In the case of the construction of roads and a new stadium that was opposed by religious activists on account of causing violation of the Sabbath, the outcomes were delay or alteration in the implementation of policy rather than total reversal. One road project was delayed and its roadbed shifted slightly to avoid ancient graves discovered during excavations. The project then went forward despite additional graves located along the line of the new plans. A long-running conflict over a road through a religious neighborhood in Jerusalem currently stands with the closure of the road during certain hours on Sabbath and religious holidays. This resolution is under appeal in the Supreme Court.

- The issue of "indecent" advertising in bus shelters has produced waves of burning shelters, then agreements between the advertising company and religious representatives. The issue has emerged and receded again and again, as when religious activists object to particular posters with women in short sleeves. Religious critics failed in their protests against Yad Vashem's display of photographs showing nude concentration camp inmates. The museum has stood by the position that the pictures are an important part of exhibits that depict the humiliations that were part of Nazi policy toward Jews. Ultra-Orthodox rabbis threatened to open their own Holocaust Memorial if the offending exhibits are not removed, but have not done so.

- Laws prohibiting the sale of nonkosher food are enacted but generally not enforced. A newspaper report from May 1995 indicated a significant increase in the shops selling pork in response to immigration from the former Soviet Union.[70]

- The status quo remains to provide Orthodox rabbis a monopoly of official functions with respect to marriages and divorces performed in Israel. In November 1995 the Supreme Court found a flaw in the procedure that had provided Orthodox rabbis sole rights to conduct conversions to Judaism in Israel. The court did not recognize conversions by non-Orthodox rabbis, but indicated that the Knesset should consider a revision of existing legislation.[71] Three years later the Knesset was still struggling to resolve the issue, under pressure on the governing coalition from ultra-Orthodox parties on the one side and from overseas representatives of non-Orthodox congregations on the other side.

- The contrasts between religious law, the rules followed by state authorities, and actual practices are especially muddied in the fields of marriage and divorce. Israeli couples who cannot be married by the Orthodox rabbinate on account of one or another provision of religious law, or who do not wish to be married in an Orthodox ceremony, can marry overseas; couples wishing to separate can similarly go through legal procedures outside of Israel, sometimes arranged by mail without leaving Israel. The Israeli Interior Ministry and Israeli courts accept foreign documents concerned with marriage and divorce, and register individuals accordingly.

- The most overt secular victories have been the opening of restaurants, discotheques, and cinemas on the Sabbath. The municipal bylaws that had kept them closed were ruled to be flawed in a 1987 court decision, and religious politicians have not succeeded in several efforts to enact a national law to resolve the issue in their favor.

• During an earlier wave of religious-secular dispute in the 1980s, a government decision required that El Al Israel Airlines end its Sabbath flights, but other Israeli airlines expanded theirs. The criteria for allowing abortions in public hospitals were changed to exclude "social distress," but applicants learned to explain their problem as one of "emotional distress." The religious parties did not succeed in changing the Law of Return, which evades an explicit definition of who is a Jew and allows the immigration of non-Jewish relatives of Jews.[72] The issue of Sabbath flights by El Al returned to the agenda in 1997, as part of a campaign to make the airline more attractive to investors in order to privatize it.

The lineage of disputes between Christians about the management of their holy sites testifies to their lack of final resolution. A traveler during the late seventeenth century left the following report of violence in the midst of a religious ritual. "Greeks and Latins . . . in disputing which party should go in to celebrate their Mass . . . have sometimes proceeded to blows and wounds even at the very door of the sepulcher, mingling their own blood with their sacrifices."[73] Arguments between Greek Orthodox and Roman Catholics about the Church of the Holy Sepulcher in the nineteenth century contributed to the cause of the Crimean War, and continue today whenever it is necessary to undertake repairs in the old and crumbling structure.[74]

Israel's practice of ambiguity in religion has not been free of problems as in other issues. The problems warn that ambiguity is no magic tool capable of dealing with all problems in a satisfactory manner. Neither religious nor antireligious activists have been able to dominate, and neither is satisfied. Some Jews suffer because the state does not enforce religious law strictly enough. Others suffer because the state is too Jewish. The intensity of hatred appears on the faces and in the screams of religious and antireligious Israelis when they demonstrate against one another. Still others suffer because they cannot tolerate a situation where there are no clear outcomes to the chronic disputes.

We will return to the question of "who wins?" in conflicts between religious and secular Israelis in Chapter 6. There we will find additional indications that there are no final answers to the question. Ambiguity prevails. It is not ideal, but may keep Israel from even more destructive conflict among the Jews.

RELIGION AND POLITICS IN UTAH

Life in Israel is fascinating for its multitude of difficult problems and the opportunity to observe how officials and citizens cope with the pressures. Yet at close intervals the pressures mount and the excitement reaches the limits of personal tolerance. On one such occasion I was attracted to an invitation to spend a sabbatical year at Brigham Young University in Provo, Utah. The occasion promised not only access to the natural beauties of Utah, but an opportunity to satisfy my curiosity about a distinctive religious community. Several years later, when I needed another rest from Israel and my curiosities about Utah were still unsatisfied, I responded to a similar invitation from the University of Utah in Salt Lake City.[75]

Perhaps the greatest mystery of religious faith is its strength two centuries after the Enlightenment and French Revolution. Although intellectuals in each generation have declared the imminent demise of the Almighty against the challenges of science and individual freedom, substantial numbers of people in most Western democracies express a belief in God.[76] Another mystery is the widespread tension and unresolved disputes in Western democracies among religious communities, as well as between the religious and the secular or antireligious. Religion and antireligion appear to be important enough to assure their places on the public agenda, but not strong enough to dictate public policy on issues of major concern.[77] Also among the mysteries are the varieties of belief and behavior within the same communities. Sacred texts support numerous interpretations. It is as if religious traditions presented interchangeable parts.[78] Assertions of similarities or differences between religious communities are likely to stumble on the lack of uniformity within each and an overlapping of doctrines rather than clear differences.

There appears to be a commonality between these different mysteries. The appeal of religion is strong enough to assure a certain degree of loyalty, but not so strong as to support concerted efforts to render each community clearly distinct from others or to overcome the strength of competing loyalties to secular values. The Mormons of Utah and the religious Jews of Israel illustrate this picture of similarities as well as differences within the same religious tradition, and both participate in unresolved disputes about religion and public policy.

No two religious groups seem more different than the strictly hierarchical Mormons and the assertively pluralistic Jews. Mormons (i.e., members of the Church of Jesus Christ of Latter-day Saints, or LDS) set themselves apart from Jews by their acceptance of Jesus as the messiah. Mormons go beyond other Christians in describing an additional episode of resurrection and other stories that do not appear in the New Testament. One Mormon version of the Book of Genesis, said to be a correct translation by Joseph Smith, begins with a conversation between God and Moses about Jesus. [79] Mormons claim continuing revelations to their ruling prophet, while Jews say that there has been no prophet since Malachi. Moreover, the Hebrew prophets were critics of the elites rather than rulers. Mormons continue to employ church tribunals to banish those who speak or act against official doctrines. Judaism has a long history of accommodating dispute, and Jewish ethnicity provides a collective for those who identify along a wide spectrum from ultra-Orthodoxy to Jewish humanism, including agnostics and atheists.

Yet the behavior of certain ultra-Orthodox Jewish communities in Israel complicates this comparison. They resemble Mormons in declaring bans against those who speak or act improperly. Ultra-Orthodox toughs call themselves committees of modesty and punish the wayward. The Mormon leaders in Utah also resemble leaders of Orthodox Jewry in Israel in their political struggles. The Jews of Israel are 79 percent of the population of a country declared as a "Jewish state." Utah is the center of a religious community with perhaps 11 million members worldwide. While more than 90 percent of the people in some localities of Utah are Mormon, it is estimated that the state as a whole is 67 percent Mormon and the state capital Salt Lake City less than 50 percent Mormon.[80] In both Israel and Utah there is similar conflict involving religion and the state. The diversity of Utah's population along with the encompassing legal and cultural influences of the United States make Utah no more of a theocracy than Israel. A comparison between Israel and Utah shows not so much the power of religion but a standoff between religious, secular, and antireligious activists.

Mormonism began in upstate New York in about 1830 when Joseph Smith reported that he had been visited by angels who led him to a book of golden plates and magic devices that he used to translate them. In this and subsequent revelations he produced the *Book of Mormon* that recounted a migration of Israelites from Jerusalem to the Americas about the year 600 B.C.E. Smith and his followers proclaimed that the new Zion was in America, and that theirs was the one true church. To the basis of Christianity they added rituals for the baptism of family members already dead, and elaborated concepts of other worlds, prelife and afterlife. Mormon conceptions of God, Christ, and other biblical figures differ from those of other Christians.[81]

The Mormons came to Utah from 1847 onward in search of a place where no one was likely to disturb them. They had been driven from several locales further east where mobs had murdered, raped, and plundered, and lynched their founding prophet. They separated themselves not only doctrinally from more conventional Christians but economically and politically. At various times church leaders were seen as threatening their neighbors by a united economic order, block voting, and intentions to create an independent theocracy. They added to their numbers by proselytizing in the United

States and overseas, and by encouraging the converts to concentrate in their American community. Polygamy was the most spectacular and offensive Mormon practice. It provided the material for lascivious publications, local harassment, and national scandal. Utah could not become a state until church leaders renounced polygamy in 1890.

Contemporary Mormons are a long way from the farmers, tradesmen, and artisans who joined Smith in the first generation. Among American religious groups, their years of education and their family incomes surpass Catholics and most Protestant denominations, and fall slightly below Unitarians, Episcopalians, and Jews.[82]

Mormons couple their secular achievements with a commitment to the church which is no less impressive than that of ancestors who sailed the ocean and walked across prairies and mountains. Mormons are expected to tithe and to abstain from coffee and black tea[83] as well as alcohol, tobacco, gambling, and sex outside of marriage, and to abide by the legal requirements of secular authorities. They are encouraged to marry early and reproduce often. Families with six to ten children are not unusual.

One attraction of the Mormon church is its lack of a professional priesthood, but with many functions to be filled. Some years ago it was reported that there were enough offices in the church or its affiliated organizations for 55 percent of the membership over the age of twelve. "The church has provided a job for everyone to do."[84] Many teenagers spend fourteen hours per week in church activities.[85] While religiosity generally declines along with increasing education in the United States, that of Mormons increases with education.[86] Among the reasons offered for this is the opportunity to hold a function and title that bestows prestige. It is the educated Mormons, with higher than average ability to speak in public and to organize others, who are more likely to serve. The lifestyle associated with Mormonism is healthy and produces lower mortality rates than those shown by other Americans.[87]

For a political scientist, the Mormons of Utah offer an attractive subject of research. Not only do they dominate the state numerically, but several other traits should maximize their impact on state politics and public policy. Mormon history features communal separateness, reinforced by persecution, mass migration, and the attempt to establish an independent nation.[88] The LDS Church has a disciplined hierarchy that can communicate effectively with every active family. According to one Utah scholar, "undoubtedly the most significant factor of Utah politics is the Mormon church."[89]

In fact, certain traits of the Mormons and Utah limit the impact of the church on state policy. The scholar who wrote that the church is the most significant factor in Utah politics also documented several failures to determine election outcomes or public policy. He concluded that the church is influential but not dominant.

There is anti-Mormonism in Utah that pits a number of people against the church. Organizations distribute tracts that ridicule the church's doctrine, and describe scandals involving Mormons.[90] The Utah newspaper with the largest circulation, the *Salt Lake Tribune*, as well as the University of Utah, are said by some of the faithful to be anti-Mormon. Occasionally the *Tribune* advocates policy changes (e.g., legalized gambling) in a way that seems calculated as much to annoy the LDS hierarchy as to change the law. Ranking members of some University of Utah departments say they have worked successfully to deny faculty positions to Mormon applicants.

The principle of continuing revelation provides a means for the leadership to change the church's position, as in the well-known reversals on polygamy in 1890 and the access of blacks to the priesthood in 1978. Yet the collegial nature of the church leadership may blunt its political activities. Lower echelons are subject to review and correction by the upper echelons (General Authorities). The most supreme leadership[91] operates collectively, with a great deal of discussion before major decisions are announced.[92] The terms "cautious" and "conservative" are used to describe the church's political style.

Along with what appear to be unifying doctrines and strict discipline, Utah Mormons exhibit some of the pluralism apparent among Israeli Jews. Individuals vary in the extent to which they take part in church activities, adhere to its precepts, or identify with the attitudes that prevail among the members. Roughly one-third of the readers of *Dialogue*, a journal that describes itself as Mormon but nonofficial, responded to a questionnaire in a way to suggest that they do not accept basic doctrines.[93] Some Mormons distinguish between doctrinal requirements of the church, which they must accept under penalty of being denied access to a temple and its sacraments, and the advice of church leaders, which they can ignore without penalty (e.g., to avoid excessive debt or overeating). Individuals also describe matters of political conscience where the Church should not assert itself.

Numerous Mormons voted against the advice of church authorities in referenda dealing with legislative apportionment in 1954 and the "Utah Cable TV Decency Initiative" in 1984. The positions favored by the church lost in both of those referenda. A number of Mormons also voted against their church in a liquor referendum in 1968. The church position won, but not by the overwhelming majority that its leaders wanted. At the next session of the Utah legislature, church spokesmen acquiesced in the passage of a bill that liberalized access to alcohol, seemingly in a spirit of compromise.[94]

Sometimes the leaders are led by their followers. A well-placed professor at Brigham Young University indicated that ranking members of the hierarchy expressed their own opposition to prayers in public schools but refrained from pressing their stand out of concern for the many church members who supported school prayer.

Church doctrine is sufficiently ambiguous to provide the current leadership substantial discretion in defining postures on contemporary issues. This ambiguity also permits church members to differ among themselves and to disagree with church leaders. Some say that the doctrine is clear but that its application to specific issues is open to dispute.

Certain Mormon practices derive from popular interpretations of doctrine, which differ from those proclaimed by church authorities. A number of Mormons insist that they should abstain from all drinks with caffeine even though the doctrine has been interpreted officially as requiring abstinence only from the "hot drinks" of coffee and black tea. During my yearlong visit at the Brigham Young University it was not possible to purchase cola drinks with caffeine on campus, but some active Mormons on the staff brought them from home.

Individual Mormons take pride in identifying themselves as politically different from the mainstream.[95] Non-Mormons who do research on the Mormons or the state of Utah have been approached by Mormons who are sharply critical of the church leadership, both for the substance and the style of its political activities.[96]

Mormon culture is not simplistic in being clearly "left" or "right" across a wide range of attitudes. Attitudinal surveys find that Mormons resemble conservative Protestants in their opposition to the "new morality" of casual sex, pornography, and abortions. Yet they are closer to liberal Protestants and Jews in their attitudes about racial justice and civil liberties.[97]

One scholar describes several sides of a complex, amorphous relationship between church authorities and members of the state's legislative and executive branches. He reports numerous instances of church authorities expressing themselves on large public issues like state policy on liquor, and small issues like the location of individual liquor stores. Yet he argues that it may be difficult to determine if one of the approximately eighty members of the upper echelons is actually speaking for the church or simply expressing his own views.[98]

The church is sufficiently important for the state's officials to court its support. Governors and members of the legislature visit church headquarters and discuss current issues. One of the major state newspapers (*The Deseret News*) as well as major radio and television stations (KSL in Salt Lake City and KBYU in Provo) are church affiliated. More than 80 percent of the legislators in a typical session are likely to be church members, with some of them highly active as ward bishops or stake presidents. It may not be necessary for church authorities to proclaim formally what they want, much less to lobby the members of the legislature.[99] A Salt Lake City newspaper reported that church authorities contacted each of the twenty-eight Mormons in the State Senate during 1989 on a liquor issue. The lone non-Mormon in the Senate was quoted as saying, "Nobody called me. . . . I feel sort of left out."[100]

At times church leaders are embarrassed by members of the legislature who assert that they are speaking for the church in order to advance their own standing.[101] The church frequently reiterates its official policy that members should not claim to be speaking in its name when expressing their own views about candidates or issues. However, this policy is overlooked by some local and intermediate authorities.

Utah stands apart from other states in several traits, some of which may flow from the influence of Mormon doctrine or culture.

- The picture is clearest, and least surprising, on the traits of births, abortions, and college education. Mormon leaders have long emphasized family and education, and have opposed abortion. Utah ranks high on the incidence of births and adults who have at least four years of college. It ranks low on the incidence of abortions.[102]

- Utah has a low incidence of families below the poverty level. This reinforces the Mormons' reputation as middle-class strivers.[103]

- The church's efforts to inculcate good citizenship and to assure a maximum of political leverage via voter participation appears in the state's high ranking on the measure of turnout. Sixty-five percent of Utah's voting age population cast ballots in the 1992 presidential election, while the national average was 55 percent.[104]

- On some traits Utah is a conservative, minimalist state whose citizens rely on themselves or their Church. The state and local government workforce in relation to population is small.[105] Utah voters gave higher percentages to Republican candidates than any other state in the 1980, 1984, 1988, and 1996 presidential elections, as well as a higher percentage to Ross Perot in 1992 than any other state.

- Like the religious establishment of Israel, the LDS Church has a mixed record in trying to legislate issues of doctrine. Liquor and gambling illustrate the points. The church has worked to curtail or limit both activities. Utahns can buy alcohol in state liquor stores and purchase drinks in many restaurants. While drinking is not as convenient in Utah as in some states, it is not more inconvenient than in a number of other states far from the Mormon homeland. On the matter of gambling, the church has been successful in resisting on-track betting and casinos. But there is a limousine service from Salt Lake City to the casinos of State Line, Nevada, and Utahns make day trips to horse racing in Wyoming.

Utah's neighboring state of Nevada also shows Mormon flexibility and pragmatism. Brigham Young established several colonies there, and now the Mormons are the state's second largest religious denomination.[106] They are politically active and have made their peace with legalized sin. While some assert that their coreligionists live pristine lives that are isolated from Nevada's tourist industry, others admit that this is impossible in a state with few economic options. Active church members serve the casinos as dealers, corporate officers, accountants, and attorneys. One Mormon has been chair of the Nevada Gaming Commission.[107]

Mormonism and Judaism

Jews figure prominently in the Mormons' world view. The *Book of Mormon* and other holy writings link the believers with ancient Israel. Joseph Smith studied Hebrew and sent an early convert to the Holy Land. Individual Mormons are given affiliations with the ancient tribes of the Israelites. Some report their tribal identity with an embarrassed grin. Others say that an inspired assignment made by a church authority signifies a biological linkage with the ancient people. Mormon leaders have expressed support for the Israeli government. Church doctrines connect the reestablishment of Israel with the return of Christ. Brigham Young University has an overseas study center in Jerusalem with an impressive building on the Mount of Olives.

There are tensions between the communities. A number of Mormons and the student newspaper of Brigham Young University have expressed support for Palestinian national aspirations. Numerous Israelis oppose Christian missionaries. The government imposed a ban on proselytizing Israelis as a condition for the construction of BYU's Jerusalem Center. Yet these strains have not kept Mormons from continuing as Judeophiles. The public schools of Utah teach about Chanukah and Passover, and seek out Jews to explain the rituals.

There is no exact and objective manner to array the doctrines and practices of Jews and Mormons. Judaism differs from the LDS Church in being overtly pluralistic without an authoritative center. Liberal rabbis and Jewish humanists range far from Orthodox doctrines and practice, and suggest that Judaism is more open to diversity than Mormonism. The Jewish posture that Malachi was the last prophet stands prominently against the Mormon doctrine of latter-day sainthood and a contemporary prophet who is ruler of the LDS Church. The end of prophecy and with it God's communications with his people is cited by rabbis who say that individuals who speak with angels are a medical and not a religious phenomenon. Jewish traditions of acerbic criticism and intellectual creativity appearing in the biblical books of the prophets, Job and Ecclesiastes, contrast with Mormon trials for heresy. The biting humor that Jewish writers have directed at biblical figures, as in Joseph Heller's *God Knows* or Stefan Heym's *The King David Report*,[108] contrast with the piety that marks Mormon fiction about biblical characters.[109] The ancient heritage and the doctrine of the chosen people may free Jews from the Mormons' need for a repeated insistence that theirs is the one true religion.

With all of these differences, individual rabbis and other learned Jews show a number of the behaviors associated with Mormons. The excommunication of Baruch Spinoza by the Amsterdam community in 1656 was not the last action of its kind. Local rabbinical courts in modern Israel declare individuals as dangers to their community on account of aberrant expressions or behaviors, and warn other Jews from having any contact with them. The shrill insistence on absolute truth in interpreting doctrine that occurs among some Mormons also appears in Judaism. In response to a road accident that killed schoolchildren on a class outing, the communal Sephardi rabbi of Rannana, who later became minister of interior, said that the tragedy was due to the practice in their town of opening places of entertainment on the Sabbath. Another rabbi, the spiritual leader of the ultra-Orthodox Sephardi movement, has proclaimed that early death and a designation as non-Jews are appropriate punishments for Jews who violate the Sabbath.[110]

Jews who smile at the Mormons' stories of being helped by angels should not overlook their own coreligionists who ask for favors at the tombs of revered figures or visit rabbis with reputations for working miracles. Individual rabbis of all traditions—from the ultra-Orthodox to the Reform—express their belief that the Lord provided the written and oral Torah to Moses on Mount Sinai. (The oral Torah is the accumulation of Rabbinical commentaries on the written Torah and religious law derived from it.) Alongside the sarcasm of writers like Heller and Heym there are pious Jewish tales that create wholly admirable characters out of the complex figures described in the Hebrew Bible.[111]

Personal encounters in Utah and Israel cautioned me against simplistic comparisons between the religious communities. In Utah I met serious Mormons and other Christians who did not recognize the name of our daughter, Tamar. I learned that problematic biblical episodes were not given prominence in church lessons: that of Judah's daughter-in-law Tamar who seduced him in order to give birth to a child who would continue his family line;[112] another Tamar, the daughter of David, whose rape by her half-brother is an important incident in the king's troubled history; or the whole of the Song of Songs.[113] Surely, I thought, the Jewish practice of reading the entire Hebrew Bible at one or another occasion during the ritual year would free learned Jews from such narrowness.

Later I met an ultra-Orthodox Jew in Israel who seemed well versed in religious doctrines but did not know the Tamar episodes. When I expressed surprise, he said that it was forbidden to read the Bible without the guidance of a rabbi due to the danger of unacceptable interpretations. This same individual took the position that David was a model of piety who did not sin; and that those who say that David sinned express improper interpretations of biblical episodes.

Both communities have movements that employ religious doctrine to justify violence. Elements associated with Israel's religious nationalists have killed individual Arabs and Prime Minister Yitzhak Rabin.[114] Communities of Utah polygamists whose members claim to be the true Mormons have killed errant members of their own groups and resisted law enforcement with violence.[115]

ON THE NATURE OF RELIGION(S)

Similarities in detail among communities as distinct as Judaism and Mormonism illustrate one of the mysteries at the heart of religious practice. Despite the looming difference on the status of Christ, contrasts on the dimension of doctrinal pluralism, and all the lesser points that separate Jews and Mormons, individual Jews as well as Mormons act as pre-Enlightenment zealots. They cite proof texts for their beliefs. They affirm the reality of miracles, call down the punishment of heaven on those who articulate improper doctrines, and in extreme cases seek to do the Lord's work by employing violence.

Both the religious Jews of Israel and the Mormons of Utah make persistent efforts to expand their influence through the power of the state, and both fail to overcome their opponents. In Israel and Utah, religious issues are often on the public agenda. Critics of both polities term them theocracies, but they fall far short of Saudi Arabia, Iran, Pakistan, or Sudan. While religious authorities in Utah and Israel have substantial power over their adherents, those who do not adhere can follow their own consciences on matters of marriage and divorce, abortion, Sabbath observance, liquor, gambling, and other issues that the religious would regulate.

There may be a common explanation of both phenomena considered here: the plurality of practice within the same religious communities and the modesty of political power shown by religious activists in Israel and Utah (and, by extension, other democratic polities). These phenomena suggest that the importance of religion is considerable but limited. Religion is important enough to assure its presence on the agendas of Western democracies, but religious leaders are neither capable of dominating their congregations on matters of doctrine nor capable of dominating their polities on matters of public policy. Religious loyalty has a prominent role in democratic societies. It has proved able to resist two centuries of secularization. Yet while religious leaders in Israel, Utah, and other democratic polities speak out against secular norms, they seem to have accommodated themselves to the strength of values that are not their own. Perhaps they are led by a sense of realism or a recognition of the costs associated with doctrines that proclaim a monopoly of truth. In the terms of this book, religious leaders are coping on two planes: (1) with individuals who are tempted to follow secular as well as religious norms; and (2) with religious doctrines that some see as clear and demanding, but which in reality are ambiguous and flexible.

In situations of competing demands and multiple uncertainties, believers in conventional religious doctrines may have an advantage over activists in democratic polities. Religious Israelis, like their counterparts elsewhere, can fall back on centuries of well-formulated explanations for the delay of salvation and other heavenly promises. Political activists have no such explanation to excuse the failures of competing parties or candidates to deliver on their commitments. Each may claim that it can accomplish more in the interval between the next election and the one after that, but we all know that, at most, only part of what they promise will come to pass.

A Typology of Ambiguity in Policymaking and Administration

Ambiguity appears at all stages of the policymaking process and at all levels of the polity.[1] It occurs in the most prosaic routines of program implementation as well as in the definition of policy goals involving great expense and sensitivity. Low-ranking clerks in the bureaucracy as well as high-ranking ministers employ ambiguity in order to avoid undesirable decisions. In confusing policymaking and implementation, ambiguity touches issues of accountability, justice, and other moral values.

WHO, WHERE, WHEN, HOW, WHY, AND WITH WHAT EFFECTS?

Harold Lasswell's classic conception of politics (*Politics: Who Gets What, When, How?*) serves as our guide for a typology of ambiguity.[2] Subsequent sections of this chapter identify the categories of the typology. The categories are not without their overlaps, and some activities deserve mention in more than one. We must recall that the subject of the typology is ambiguity. It does not lend itself to crisp definition or categorization.

Many of the cases used in creating the typology come from published reports of Israel's State Comptroller, the supreme audit body, responsible to the Knesset. The source carries with it both problems and advantages. Most apparent is the pervasive criticism that marks the activities of the State Comptroller. Like its counterparts in other countries (e.g., the U.S. General Accounting Office and the National Audit Office of the United Kingdom), the State Comptroller's personnel see their task as identifying faults. They seldom praise or seek to justify the shortcomings of audited programs. Israel's State Comptroller, like others of its kind, is also guilty of excessive legality and saccharine morality. It is insensitive to political pressures and the attractions of deals that include some measure of ambiguity. Insofar as the State Comptroller is not tolerant of those who create ambiguity or exploit it, it is appropriate here to indicate the positive as well as the negative implications of the ambiguities to be described.

The advantage of using State Comptroller reports to identify cases of ambiguity is that the State Comptroller is especially active in ferreting out cases of doubtful policy and management. Its law is inclusive in granting it authority to audit governmental and quasi-governmental bodies against the criteria of moral integrity as well as the more conventional standards of legality, economy, efficiency, and effectiveness. Reports of the State Comptroller have criticized issues of poor judgment by the highest ranking of Israel's policymakers, as well as more pedestrian cases of poor administration.[3]

Who Engages in Ambiguous Behavior?

This most elementary of questions can be answered simply: Ambiguity touches virtually everyone who deals with government. We find it in program criteria that are not clear, which lend themselves to differential treatment of high- and low-status social groups and of high- and low-ranking members of the state service. Some ambiguities distribute benefits widely, whereas others cause many to suffer.

Israel's State Comptroller has commented about the discretion that is found in the activity of state employees at the lowest levels, or what Michael Lipsky labeled "street level bureaucrats."[4] One report described how the police misuse their discretionary power to confine individuals suspected of offenses, a great many of whom are never formally charged.[5]

Also touching widespread behavior was a report about fictitious fringe benefits that provide payments to employees throughout the public service. It is difficult to change "salary," *per se*, in Israel, because different categories of public and private-sector workers are linked to one another's salaries, and a change in one will trigger automatic adjustments throughout the economy. The result is a charade in which workers demand special fringe benefits, supposedly tailored to the unusual conditions of their occupation. Some years ago health workers won a special benefit for being on call at all hours of the day and night. The idea spread throughout the economy. Eventually university academics received the fringe benefit, on the basis of a claim that we are subject to calls at home about university business from colleagues and students.

The result of this is that Israeli pay slips are lengthy and detailed, with allowances for transportation, clothing, and vacation, as well as oddities like payment for occupational dangers paid to individuals who work at heights on utility poles or laboratory technicians who handle toxic substances. There are special payments to university academics who have published recently or teach large classes, and who devote full time to their home university. After a while the system becomes unwieldy, and committees of employees, employers, and the Finance Ministry fold all the benefits into salary, except for some very special allowances which then begins the process anew. I have heard of some innocent creatures who take all these allowances seriously and use their clothing allowance only for that purpose. Most of us recognize the fictions and treat the bottom line as take-home pay.

The State Comptroller reported about the fictions involved in a fringe benefit for transportation, presumably paid to workers who used their private cars for public business. It had spread so far as to be available to workers without cars or driving licenses. When a case reached the Israeli Supreme Court, the justices refused to impose sanctions against workers who violated the letter of the rules by claiming a car allowance when they owned no car, insofar as the practice had become an "accepted lie."[6]

Ambiguity also affects the appointment procedures for Israel's public employees. Israel's Civil Service Law requires competitive procedures of appointment and provides for exempting certain positions from the rule. Over the years, the number of positions exempted has grown. The formal reasons given to the committee charged with exempting a position may be a thin veil for the real concern to appoint a person favored by the minister in charge. Once a position is exempted from a requirement to be filled with a competitive procedure, it remains exempted even with turnover in the person filling the position. Reports of the Civil Service Commission have shown that 20 percent to 40 percent of appointments to national government offices are not made according to competitive procedures. Even where appointing officers follow the formal requirements of competitive examinations, the competition may be "sewed up" in advance to favor a particular candidate. Government officials become expert at arranged outcomes. Among the tricks are advertising for combinations of skills likely to be possessed by few if any candidates other than the one favored, and assuring that members of the examining committee will be cooperative. If these tricks do not produce the desired outcome, it may be possible to declare that no one has won the competition. In this condition, the favored candidate can be appointed "temporarily." At the next round of competition, this candidate can add experience to the qualifications offered, and thus have an advantage in competing with other candidates for the position.[7]

Where Does Ambiguity Occur?

The answer to the *where* question is no less extensive than the answer to the *who*. State Comptroller reports identify ambiguity in government ministries, local authorities, government companies, and other quasi-governmental entities like health maintenance organizations and the activities of agricultural cooperatives (i.e., kibbutzim and moshavim).

A number of reports have focused on the linkages between organizations. They suggest that a lack of clear responsibility is endemic to the joints between the different units in government that are expected to cooperate, and that these provide a fertile ground for the exploitation of ambiguity. The State Comptroller often faults central government ministries for failing to invest more effort in the supervision of local authorities and quasi-governmental bodies, and details striking departures from official salary scales and procedures of appointment that occur in those settings.[8] One problem of land usage developed in the gaps between regulations supposedly enforced by the Ministry of Interior and the Lands Authority, and fed on the acquisitive interests of agricultural cooperatives. The cooperatives sold their land rights to developers for housing and commercial construction, which went forward to completion and occupancy without the responsible bodies changing the land-use designations from "agriculture."[9] Some of this occurred during the period of rapid building for the wave of more than 800,000 immigrants who began arriving in Israel with the collapse of the Soviet Union and the opening of migration for Jews from Ethiopia. However, much of the building described by the State Comptroller's report was upscale, for Israelis not directly affected by the migration.

Ambiguity also appears at sensitive issues where bureaucrats deal with the population. Israeli regulations forbid the construction or modification of buildings without the approval of planning authorities. At the beginning of 1992, the Ministry of Interior estimated that there were 1,500 illegal dwellings in the Palestinian neighborhoods of Jerusalem. Obviously some officials had not followed rules designed to prevent illegal building. Ministry officials criticized the municipality for lax supervision of building. A representative of the city rejected the estimates of the Interior Ministry and remarked that on one occasion ministry officials destroyed Palestinian dwellings for being built illegally in Jerusalem, only to discover that some of the dwellings had been outside the city's boundaries.[10] Some months later, Mayor Kollek announced that his conscience would not tolerate his signing demolition orders for Arab housing, despite their being built illegally. He cited one especially painful case, involving a family with fourteen children. In response, the district commissioner of the Interior Ministry accused the mayor of encouraging illegal building, and promised to use his authority to sign demolition orders if the mayor refused.[11]

Jews also build illegally. There hardly seems to be a building that does not have one or another style of aluminum windows used to turn balconies into spare rooms, virtually all of them in violation of planning regulations. They are ugly or charming, depending on one's aesthetic sense and toleration of variety. The Knesset ignored the rules when it added a Star of David to the roof of its building without the approval of the Planning Commission.[12] The former Chief Ashkenazi Rabbi Shlomo Goren did not ask for the approval of the Planning Commission when he erected a modernistic monument to Holocaust victims on the roof of a building overlooking the Western Wall. What to the rabbi was an artistic achievement was to others an abominable desecration of a site that should be left unadorned. Four years after the squabble began, the sculpture was still in place while municipal officials were unable to obtain the rabbi's agreement to erect a stone parapet that would partially obscure the monument, in exchange for retroactive authorization from the Planning Commission. Before he died, the rabbi was quoted as saying that the monument would remain until the Messiah arrived to move it to His newly erected Temple.[13] Meanwhile, the monument would commemorate Israel's problems in implementing decisions of its planning authorities.[14]

Officials of the municipality and the Interior Ministry estimate or guess that between 10,000 and 100,000 Palestinian residents of the occupied territories live illegally in Jerusalem.[15] Being without proper documentation, they would not qualify for the social services available to the Palestinians of East Jerusalem. They would encounter no problem finding work, renting a dwelling in a Palestinian neighborhood, and sending their children to a private school. Their situation resembles that of illegal immigrants in other societies. The economy attracts them, and provides them with work that is low paid and undesirable in the eyes of legal residents. Israeli builders, as well as proprietors of restaurants, auto repair shops, and small industries profit from the low wages they can pay. The employees, in turn, earn more money than they can find in their home villages.

Another variety of illegal resident came to Israel with the collapse of the Soviet empire in eastern Europe and with several extended closures of the West Bank and Gaza in response to suicide bombings by Palestinian terrorists. Romanians and Chinese came to work in the building trades, Thais in agriculture, and Filipinos in household chores. Many come as documented temporary workers, but others come as tourists and overstay their visas. Insofar as the vast majority are single men, they have spurred an expansion of prostitution, often staffed by eastern Europeans who also work illegally in Israel.

According to the Israeli political scientist Ehud Sprinzak, illegalism is a feature of Israel's political culture that shows up in numerous prosaic and profound ways. At one end of the spectrum are the small and larger favors done by bureaucrats for friends and relatives, usually without explicit compensation. A typical small favor is dealing with a file ahead of turn. A larger favor is granting a benefit that according to a strict reading of the criteria would not be granted. At the other, more profound end of the scale Sprinzak describes land-grabbing and violence perpetrated against Arabs by religious nationalist settlers in the occupied territories.[16]

The entire relationship involving Israel, its Arab neighbors, and Arab residents is ambiguous at numerous points. When they work well, the ambiguities in Israel-Arab relationships work to defuse, lessen, or avoid potentially serious problems by not requiring them to be faced in a forthright manner. Several points have been described in previous chapters, or will be described in subsequent chapters. Ambiguity appears in:

- Israel's compromise of its sovereignty and claims of a unified city in Jerusalem;
- Israel's defining the boundaries of Jerusalem to exclude numerous Arab settlements in the surrounding area, a failure of either Israel or the Palestinian Authority to define the Jerusalem metropolitan area, and Israeli laxness with respect to Palestinians who live illegally in the city;
- Israel's laxness in enforcing a closure of its borders in response to terrorist incidents; despite formal declarations to keep all non-Israeli Arabs out of the country, numerous Palestinians continue to enter Israel via dirt roads that skirt around the roadblocks;
- Israel's (as well as Arab) willingness to allow violent confrontation to occur at a low level (i.e., some but not many deaths) without escalating the conflict with the intention of ending it altogether. This chronic situation of no peace, no war has marked the situation in southern Lebanon, characterized the *intafada* in the West Bank and Gaza, and has appeared when the Israeli-Palestinian peace process has sputtered to a halt as a result of one or another side's claim that the other side had violated an agreement.

When Does Ambiguity Occur?

The reports of the State Comptroller do not answer this question conclusively. Like other bodies of its kind, the State Comptroller seeks to identify individual cases of faulty, misguided, inefficient, or corrupt administration. It does not seek to generalize about conditions or tendencies across time, or from one administrative unit or activity to another. However, individual reports, taken together, provide some backing for more general explanations as to conditions that promote ambiguity.

We have already seen that interested parties in the public sector exploit opportunities created when bodies with formal responsibilities for control do not allocate sufficient resources to these tasks. The case of unregulated changes in land usage suggests the problems inherent in a situation when two bodies (the Interior Ministry and the Lands Authority) have responsibility for supervising an activity but neither takes the lead. Supervision of public sector actors, especially those with political backing and national prestige like the kibbutzim, may not attract the aggressive oversight of public servants with agendas already crowded with other tasks. "Hear no evil, see no evil" is a safe alternative.

Political appointments in the public service and the casual assignment of purchasing contracts occur due to a lack of enforcement directed at the formal norms. Officials learn the informal rules but run the risk of being caught in violation of the formal rules. The State Comptroller began emphasizing inquiries into political appointments and favoritism in contracting only in 1987. Before then, it was common for ministers to exercise considerable freedom in making appointments and awarding contracts. Then the rules seemed to change, even though there was no formal announcement. The State Comptroller first reported on the appointment of grossly unqualified personnel to positions in government companies. The appointees singled out were family members, party affiliates, or hometown friends of the minister who initiated the appointments.[17] Subsequently the Comptroller reported on purchasing contracts given to political party colleagues of another minister.[18]

How Does Ambiguity Occur?

This question brings us to the styles shown by those who create and exploit ambiguity. The range extends from the crude to the artistic, and from countless small actions to substantial activities that affect huge resources and represent striking departures from what had been thought to be conventional procedures.

The crude and the small, which nonetheless accumulate into institutionalized mass actions and large sums, appear in the countless employees who profit from fictitious fringe benefits that are paid in a situation where the rules weigh against giving salary increases, *per se*. Also on the side of the crude exploitation of ambiguity is the widespread departure from salary limits supposedly imposed on local authorities. Municipal officials break the rules and get away with it. Like the payment of fictitious fringe benefits, these come to be institutionalized because authorities with responsibility for supervision routinely overlook their formal responsibilities.

Somewhat intermediate in sophistication are distorted municipal accounts that are occasionally identified by the State Comptroller. As might be expected, the tendency in these is to underreport income.[19] This trick seeks to exploit the cumbersome relationships between national ministries having overlapping responsibilities with respect to the supervision of local authorities, and the well-known failure of the Interior Ministry to make a thorough inspection of local finances.[20] The purpose of the underreporting of income by local authorities is to present an image of need and to qualify for larger grants of aid from the national government.

On the side of the grand and the sophisticated were two long-running episodes involving individuals at the peak of the nation's banking and government. One was the kiting of stock shares by virtually all of the major banks. This seemed to emerge from an agreement—some of which may have been left unspecified—that government officials in positions of economic control would support an increasing price for bank stocks as a device to encourage savings. The banks sold the shares to their clients, and lent money so their clients could buy more. Bank employees with the title of investment counselor assured customers that the government would not let the price of shares fall. The kiting began sometime in the 1970s and continued until prices collapsed in 1983. The government conceded some degree of responsibility by engineering a plan to assure investors the price of the shares before the collapse, plus interest and linkage to the cost of living, in exchange for the investors holding the shares for up to an additional ten years. The ambiguity surrounding the issue of responsibility allowed key politicians, ranking administrators with responsibility for overseeing the banks, and officials of the banks themselves to claim innocence. The police, the state prosecutor, and the courts spent more than ten years sorting out allocations of responsibility, imposing punishments, and hearing appeals. Efforts to privatize the banks whose shares the government acquired in the bail-out were still ongoing more than fifteen years after the bubble burst.[21]

The murky relations between municipalities and the Finance and Interior Ministries provided the setting for another artistic scheme that initially was reported by the media, then became the subject of a State Comptroller's report and a police investigation. The ambiguity in which the scheme developed reflected the joint responsibility of the two ministries for the expenditures of local authorities, and provisions for discretionary aid to be given at the behest of the Interior Minister. The State Comptroller described how the Interior Minister would offer aid allotments that had not been requested by selected municipalities, on condition that substantial portions of the aid be funneled to schools and other institutions affiliated with the minister's ultra-Orthodox political party whose members are largely Jews of North African and Asian origin. Prior to making the report public, the State Comptroller challenged the minister for allocating grants in ways that departed from the formal requirements of his own ministry. In response, the minister defended his actions in the name of corrective discrimination, or an Israeli version of affirmative action, in behalf of a group that claimed to have suffered discrimination. The State Comptroller condemned the minister for failing to establish the claim of discrimination and for awarding grants without respect to criteria meant to address such a claim. The report showed that grants were made disproportionately for the sake of party-related organizations and not programs for Jews of Asian and African origin, *per se*.[22]

Why Does Ambiguity Occur?

Our inability to plumb the motives of policymakers prevents a complete answer to this question. Yet without knowing for sure why a particular policymaker chose a particular formulation or a line of behavior, we can identify several conditions that seem to give rise to ambiguity. Some indicate a conscious decision to act ambiguously. Others suggest an innocence or an inability to act clearly. They provide some illustrations of non-decision making, or a failure to decide about a situation that seems to require a decision.[23] The conditions that produce ambiguity include the following:

1. An *inability* to define one's intentions clearly. This may result from an intellectual weakness, a lack of information, or disputes in a decision arena that cannot be resolved.

2. An *unwillingness* to define one's intentions clearly. This may result from an unwillingness to face reality, which in turn can be the result of disagreements about the costs in money or other values that are implicit in a clear definition of what is likely to ensue. It may be easier to let a program go forward with no up-front estimate of its costs and to explain budgetary "overruns" when they occur.

3. A desire to make awards for reasons of personal or political favoritism, and to mask the reasons for the appointment. This leads to ambiguity insofar as published criteria are not, in fact, used in making decisions.

4. A desire to buy time, perhaps to postpone a clear decision where there is disagreement, or a desire to avoid reckoning with the costs implicit in a situation. A desire to buy time can also reflect the calculation or the hope that conditions will improve and make it unnecessary to undertake undesirable activities.

5. A failure to recognize that one's actions are ambiguous. This explanation for ambiguity may reflect either the poor quality of policymaking or administration that gives rise to an ambiguous situation, or it may reflect the sensitivity of an observer who sees confusion where policymakers thought they were presenting a situation whose stages and implications were clear.

6. A lack of concern for the value of clarity. Policymakers and administrators get used to situations that are unclear and learn how to take advantage of them. The inconvenience of not knowing for sure may not be so important as to cause them to embark on a program of clarification and risk losing what they gain from the ambiguities.

Reports of Israel's State Comptroller include reference to several of these situations. Several reports dealing with political favoritism or the casual use of discretion have criticized decision makers for failing to make a systematic assessment of needs for personnel appointments, allocating resources, or providing services.[24]

Reports critical of poor planning in the use of the country's water resources cited policymakers for a failure to come to terms with policies of price and allocation that encourage great use and, sooner or later, would threaten the quality and viability of water supplies. The condition resulted, in considerable measure, from a failure to stand up to the demands of major users who wanted large quantities of water at low prices, and who were politically well placed.[25]

The State Comptroller's report on the research and development of the Lavi warplane cited policymakers for waffling over a period of several years between contrary specifications for the plane to be developed. As a result, they did not decide clearly between expansive desires and limited capabilities. The report concluded that the project failed to achieve any of the goals that were formally declared.[26]

The kiting of bank shares was partly a case of buying time in the hope that economic growth might facilitate a smooth exit from a situation where shares had been inflated in price substantially above conventional assessments of their market value.[27]

I once served on a committee appointed by the mayor of Jerusalem to plan for the city's future. Among our tasks were relations between the municipality and the national government. The majority of the committee wanted to simplify the numerous lines of authority and supervision between local and national offices. I argued for the merits of ambiguity. Other members of the committee agreed that the city had learned to exploit overlapping authority and confused lines of control. My colleagues conceded that, in practice, Jerusalem probably received a more generous share of national resources than other localities. But they thought that clarity was a good thing in its own right. It would lessen the struggles of local officials and make their work less unpleasant. The cochairs and most committee members disagreed with me. They could not accept the value of ambiguity. When I commented that the committee's recommendation would be adopted in principle but would not affect practice, they suggested by silence that I might be right. I will never know if I was interpreting their ambiguous response correctly. I was left with the feeling that I lost a point of principle among the members of the advisory committee, but that city officials would continue to cope successfully with uncertainties and ambiguities.

What Are the Effects of Ambiguity?

This is another question that can be answered in terms large or small, with perspectives that are narrow or wide. Most obvious is the assertion that the presence and exploitation of ambiguity represents departures from formal procedures. It is blatantly wrong in the eyes of people who ascribe to the clear allocation of resources, and it costs money. Some cases touch on issues of serious immoralities by virtue of violating principles of equal access to basic services, or equal protection from the sanctions imposed by the state. One example appears in a State Comptroller's report that focused on what Israelis call "black medicine." Physicians employed by government hospitals and publicly supported health maintenance organizations used the facilities of their employers to give priority in surgery and other procedures to patients who paid them privately.[28] Some issues are serious in a more immediate sense, as when responsible bodies slight schedules and criteria for inspecting sites and procedures for the disposal of dangerous substances. As a result there are no reliable records for the location or quantities of poisonous or combustible trash.[29] Some problems have implications for the near future, as in the case of pricing that encourages the use of more water than accumulates on an annual basis.

On the other hand, ambiguity and its exploitation provide the opportunities of flexibility and speed in responding to evolving conditions more rapidly than would be permitted by following the formal rules. There seems to have been considerable public support for departing from established land-use regulations in order to meet the needs of a massive wave of immigration for housing and other infrastructure. Formal decisions of the Cabinet and Knesset authorized shortened planning procedures for the period that was declared to be an emergency. Some of the profits accruing to collective agricultural settlements represented sales of land rights for admirable social purposes. Dwellings were provided for a wave of immigration that has so far exceeded 800,000 people. Within the framework of an emergency program, however, some actions represented the unregulated use of valuable agricultural land for upscale housing and commercial estates that brought substantial profit to organizations without making any contribution to the immigration.

Ambiguity continues as an unstated theme in negotiations and agreements in the peace process that began in Madrid in 1991. Declarations by all sides have promised a great deal more than has been achieved in practice. A secure peace continues to elude Israel, and the Palestinian economy has declined rather than prospered. According to a narrow view, leaders may be lying to their constituencies and creating conditions that bring frustration and violence. By a larger view, however, the fudging of the truth may allow stages in the negotiations to move forward, and agreements to be made that build a base for the eventual benefit of both Israelis and Palestinians. To be sure, the atmosphere is clouded by contrasting assertions that others have not kept all the agreements. Water, employment opportunities, and a halt of terror have been promised but not delivered to the satisfaction of all. Yet life goes on and some satisfactions are enjoyed despite these accusations.

Practitioners of ambiguity sacrifice a number of values esteemed by political philosophers. Clarity of goals and equality of treatment do not coexist easily with imprecision and vagueness. Along with a sacrifice of clarity there is also a loss of accountability as voters cannot be sure of the intentions pursued by elected officials. When openness or the transparency of government is not of highest priority, there is a risk to the values of equity, fairness, and justice.

Against these caveats it can be said that citizens who truly are aware of what happens in their democracies should know that accountability, equality, equity, justice, and fairness are elusive in any case. Accountability suffers from the length of officeholders' terms, and the probability that conditions will change between their election and the time when they must decide about issues that do not fit squarely with what they promised to the electorate. By the time of the next election, so many events will have transpired that voters will be unable to choose on the basis of any simple criteria such as unmet expectations.

Program implementation is likely to be imperfect in the best administered of large bureaucracies. Some clients will receive more or less than they deserve, and some citizens will escape their fair share of obligations.

As we have seen in previous chapters, the appeal of coping and ambiguity is not that they are ideal, but that they are practical. Judgments must be case specific. Among the questions that can guide an inquiry are:

- Was it possible to achieve additional increments of equity and justice and to plan more thoroughly in order to achieve a more efficient use of resources?
- Were further deliberations likely to be useful under the pressure of circumstances?
- Was program administration sloppy or admirably flexible in the presence of constraints?
- Was there a reasonable level of training provided to lower level administrators?
- Were cases of irresponsible behavior dealt with adequately in terms of discipline within the bureaucracy?
- Were there opportunities for appeal and compensation provided to individuals who felt they were treated unfairly?

The specific examples of ambiguity employed in this chapter have come from the reports of the State Comptroller and other Israeli sources. As such, they reflect peculiarities of one country's political culture and recent experiences. However, the typology used to array them has wider application. Ambiguity is widespread through public activities. It facilitates the good as well as the bad. Ambiguity provides a temptation for fraud and other abuses of public trust, and allows entrepreneurial policymakers and administrators to take shortcuts in order to benefit the public more quickly.[30] Ambiguity is no less pervasive throughout governance than are conflicting demands and insufficient resources. Ambiguity is a lubricant or a coverup for problems that are inevitable in the public activities of complex societies. A lack of precision and clarity, and the politics of which it is a part, allows governance to proceed.

5

Which Jerusalem?

Jerusalem is the place where Muslim, Jew, and Christian collide in their arguments about holy places and control.[1] Disputes of no less prominence set ultrareligious against secular Jews over behaviors to be allowed on the Sabbath and religious holidays, the rituals permitted to Jews at the Western Wall, food that can be sold, the care of ancient graves uncovered during construction projects, medical practices, and the modesty of women's attire. Disputes between Christians and Muslims in the twelfth century provoked the Crusades. In the nineteenth century conflict between Christian sects over Jerusalem sites played their part in the run-up to the Crimean War.[2] More recently the city's Muslims have disagreed about the roles that the royal families of Saudi Arabia and Jordan and the Palestine Liberation Organization (PLO) can play in refurbishing holy sites or selecting religious functionaries.

The most pressing of the present conflicts puts Israeli government demands for exclusive control over the entire city against Palestinian negotiators who insist on the return of the city to its 1967 boundaries, with a Palestinian state taking control over the eastern portion as a national capital, and perhaps the relocation of more than 130,000 Jews from neighborhoods created since 1967.[3] In other places the term "crusade" is used for a prosaic campaign, like cleaning the streets. The word was created for the earlier onslaught on Jerusalem[4] and refers to one of perhaps thirty-seven times when the city was invaded and control wrested from an existing regime.[5] In Jerusalem, "crusade" can still mean another invasion by excited hordes seeking blood, righteousness, and plunder.

The point of this chapter is to identify some of the most prominent variations in the meaning of "Jerusalem," and to extract from them some possible exits from postures that appear to be diametrically opposed. The discussion has significance not only for what occurs in and around one city, but for the importance of ambiguity as a tool in negotiations.[6] The chapter also says something about the nature of cities as evolving realities, whose name can append to various conceptions of a place.[7]

It is no easy task to reduce the discussion about Jerusalem from one conducted in hyperbole to a reasoned discourse. High emotion and uncompromising posturing behind different conceptions of historical justice is typical of the city. Neither Muslims, Christians, nor Jews can enter a plea of not guilty in this hysterical blot on intellectual fellowship.

Arab propagandists have sought to reshape history in order to give Palestinians a monopoly claim to Jerusalem, and to minimize the legitimacy of a Jewish foothold.

The native inhabitants, Christian and pagan, were descended from the original Carmel Man of Palestine, and from the Semitic Arab tribes of Amorites, Canaanites, and others who had entered the land from Arabia in migratory waves. . . . [The] Hebrews of the Old Testament were a limited group, [whose] rule in Jerusalem as a city-state was of short duration. . . . The invasions by Hittites, Hyksos, Hurrians, Persians, Greeks, and Romans were generally more extensive and lasted longer. . . . Despite Israeli propaganda, there are in fact no important Jewish monuments of religious significance in Jerusalem. It is true that there is a Jewish ritual of mourning at the Wailing Wall, but this in fact is a portion of the wall of the Haram Esh-Sharif, and is actually Muslim property.[8]

According to a publication of the Islamic Council of Europe:

. . . the Zionist usurpation and continued occupation of Jerusalem and Palestine . . . has perpetuated untold human misery and unleashed a seemingly unending reign of terror in a land held sacred by Moslems, Christians and Jews alike. As a result, more than a million men, women and children have been hounded out of their homes and forced to become refugees, while merciless Zionist persecution goes on throughout the length and breadth of their homeland.[9]

Jews are no less expansive. The 1967 victory has been described as "an act of God, providential, irreversible, final."[10] ". . . we could see the Western Wall, through an archway. . . . It was like new life . . . . I could see them, men who were too tired to stand up any more, sitting by the Wall, clutching it, kissing the stones and crying. We all of us cried. That was what we had been fighting for."[11] Some Jews assert the greater justice of their own claim on the city. "Jerusalem has a far more powerful corporate meaning for Judaism than for Christianity and Islam. Christians have Rome and Muslims have Mecca, but Jews have only Jerusalem."[12]

Jews emphasize that the Jordanians did not honor their 1948 commitments with respect to Jewish access to their holy sites, and claim that Arab Jerusalemites live better under Israeli rule than they did under Jordanian rule. Israel has renovated the Old City with new sanitary water and underground sewer systems, provided additional school rooms and library resources in Arabic, and improved medical facilities in Arab neighborhoods. Israelis claim that they have increased the literacy rates of East Jerusalemites, and offer more political liberty and press freedom, with more liberal voter qualifications than under the Jordanians. Some disparage the demand of Palestinians for a national capital in Jerusalem by noting that Palestinians never ruled the city. They assert that Palestinian nationalism developed from within the larger Arab community only in recent decades. They note that it was a Kurd, Salah al-Din, who took the city from the Crusaders in 1187, and that subsequent rulers came from Baghdad, Cairo, Constantinople, London, and Amman.

We can go back to the Crusades to capture the intensity of Christian acquisitiveness for Jerusalem:

Some of our men—and this was the more merciful course—cut off the heads of their enemies; others shot them with arrows so that they fell from the towers; others tortured them longer by casting them into the flames. . . . [Men] rode in blood up to their knees and bridle reins. Indeed, it was a just and splendid judgment of God that this place should be filled with the blood of unbelievers, since it had suffered so long from their blasphemies.[13]

An incident that occurred in 1990 serves to update the record of Christian possessiveness. When a group of Jews moved into a building near the Church of the Holy Sepulcher, they provoked a lawsuit by the Greek Orthodox Church and mass demonstrations that recalled stories from the nineteenth century of Christians who threw stones against Jews who dared walk by the church. Among the interchanges concerned with the 1990 incident was a public letter to the Greek Orthodox Church from Israel's President Chaim Herzog. Herzog's style in this letter differed from his usual temperate demeanor.

. . . the sight of a priest in clerical garments, standing on a ladder, ripping down a Star of David from a Jewish residence, cheered on by an enraged mob, is a horrible reminder of what our people lived through in history on many sad and tragic occasions.... I have been horrified to receive organized mail from the United States, in which it alleged that the Greek Orthodox Patriarch has been subject to physical assault by Israelis. This is a blatant lie which is being published abroad without any basis whatsoever. The issue centers on a dispute in a real-estate deal which is being contested in the courts of law in Israel and in respect of which over $5 million changed hands. For a Church to turn such a real-estate transaction, to which it is privy and a party, into a defamatory anti-Jewish campaign, is nothing short of disgraceful and despicable. . . .[14]

SYNONYMS FOR JERUSALEM

The numerous synonyms for Jerusalem provide some reason for optimism. They suggest a multiplicity of perspectives that offer the basis of finding common ground, the makings of a deal, or at least a continued muddling through without large-scale violence. They include Holy City, City of Peace, Spiritual City, Everlasting City, City on the Hill, Zion, Heavenly City, Jerusalem Above, and Jerusalem Below. Several of these entail messianic aspirations of a time to come, or an end of time when a messiah will come, or return, and put things right. Some are used as synonyms for Paradise. These names associate the city with holiness. However, not all of its holy sites are universally recognized as such, even within the major faiths. Christians differ as to the site of Christ's tomb, and Jews have not decided just where on the Temple Mount was the inner section of the Temple called the holy of holies. As a result, religious Jews are warned to avoid the Mount altogether, in order to avoid walking on ground forbidden to all but the high priest. Insofar as there is no high priest and no likelihood of an agreement on how such a person would be selected, there is reason to hope that religious Jews will forego any serious challenge to continued Muslim occupation of this holy place.

Loosely defined areas labeled East Jerusalem, West Jerusalem, New Jerusalem, Arab Jerusalem, and Jewish Jerusalem carry meanings that are more nationalistic and political than religious. East Jerusalem and Arab Jerusalem on the one hand, and West Jerusalem, New Jerusalem, and Jewish Jerusalem on the other hand, refer to areas that Jordan and Israel controlled during 1948–1967 between Israel's War of Independence and the Six-Day War. The same terms are used for Arab and Jewish residential areas of the present Israeli municipality, even though there are Jewish areas to the east of Arab areas, and Arab areas to the west of Jewish areas. The Old City is surrounded by a wall and seems to be well-defined. However the Jewish, Muslim, Christian, and Armenian Quarters within the Old City have been dynamic and are subject to different specifications. Some think of Mount

Zion as part of the Old City, even though it is outside the walls. And the walls themselves varied in their location several times between 1000 B.C.E. and their most recent reconstruction about 1540 C.E.

Not all of the city is holy. Only scattered sites seem to justify dispute at the highest level of intensity. This should work to insert some flexibility into thinking about the city's future. The Jordanian Prime Minister Dr. Abd-al-Salam al-Majali spoke about the several meanings of "Jerusalem" and hinted at what they offer to those who would determine its future. "The word Jerusalem is derived from sanctity or places of worship. . . . Political Jerusalem is different from the religious Jerusalem that is sacred to the three religions. Thus, a political solution is possible."[15] The novelist Amos Oz walked through the Old City soon after the battle that took it from the Jordanians. He was not as hopeful as he wanted to be. "With all my soul, I desired to feel in Jerusalem as a man who has dispossessed his enemies and returned to the patrimony of his ancestors. . . . Were it not for the people. I saw enmity and rebelliousness, sycophancy, amazement, fear, insult and trickery. I passed through the streets of East Jerusalem like a man breaking into some forbidden place. Depression filled my soul."[16] The honest and modest portrayals of al-Majali and Oz are not typical of Jerusalem. Propagandists with maximum territorial ambitions have applied the magic of the name "Jerusalem" far beyond the places with spiritual associations.

Jerusalem Below refers to the earthly here and now but is not defined precisely in terms of space. It features traffic congestion, crowded housing, local and international tensions involving authorities of the Israeli municipality and national government, as well as untold numbers of clerics, politicians, and political and religious activists from Jerusalem and abroad who want to influence what happens in the city. The range of participants reflects the international concern for what elsewhere would be prosaic disputes of a municipality or even a neighborhood: a change in municipal boundaries; the development of a vacant hillside; who moves into which apartment; and alterations to an existing building. They also indicate that Jerusalem is prominent among "cities of the world," even though it is unimpressive in the size of its population (550,000 in the present municipal boundaries and perhaps twice that in the metropolitan area) and its importance as a center of culture or commerce.

WHICH LOCALE OF JERUSALEM?

Jerusalem has ranged in size and population from the biblical City of David to the present metropolitan area. Remnants of David's City are about 0.06 unpopulated square kilometers of dusty archaeological dig outside the present walls of the Old City.[17] Presumably it was that tiny place which David captured from the Jebusites about 1000 B.C.E. Metropolitan Jerusalem or Greater Jerusalem lacks any official designation or published census. The outer boundaries of what planners speak of as the metropolitan area are defined by patterns of daily commuting and extend from Jericho in the east to the Modiin-Reut complex of new communities in the west, and from Ramallah in the north to Hebron in the south. This conception of the metropolitan area approximates 2,000 square kilometers. Part of it has already been turned over to the Palestine Authority, and additional parts of it seem likely to be assigned to a State of Palestine if negotiations underway since 1993 continue on their course. Smaller conceptions of the metropolitan area, amounting to about 1,000 square kilometers, go only as far as Ma'ale Adumim to the east, Bethlehem to the south, and Beit Shemesh to the west.[18]

In a country of Israel's small size and congestion, it is no surprise that two of the largest metropolitan areas overlap. The western extremes of the Jerusalem metropolitan area intrude into the eastern extremes of the Tel Aviv metropolitan area. Indeed, the closeness of the two core cities (approximately sixty-five kilometers) and considerable daily commuting indicate the presence of one megametropolis. The combined area would include some 30 percent of Israel's national population, and perhaps one-half of that in the Palestine Authority, as well as one-half of the Authority's land area, depending on final negotiations and a reliable census.

The ethnic picture throughout metropolitan Jerusalem is mostly Arab to the north, east, and south of the Israeli municipality and within the Israeli municipality in the neighborhoods to the east and north of the Old City; and mostly Jewish in the western and southern parts of the municipality. However, there are pockets of Jewish settlement in the area that is mostly Arab and pockets of Arab settlement in the area that is mostly Jewish. The metaphor of a Dalmatian dog is appropriate: some appear to be white with black spots, and some black with white spots. Critics of the Netanyahu government said that the development of a new Jewish neighborhood called Har Homa would insert a Jewish phalanx into the heart of Arab East Jerusalem. By another view, it would add just another spot to a map characterized by a mixture of patterns showing Jewish and Arab residential areas alongside and between one another.

Several Jewish settlements outside the municipality but within the metropolitan area abut Arab settlements. The pre-1967 Jewish settlements of Kyriat Anavim and Beit Nakofa sit alongside the Arab town of Abu Gosh. Post-1967 Jewish settlements of Givat Ze'ev and Betar appear on the map as Jewish outposts between Arab towns. The suburb of Ma'ale Adumim is in the Judean desert east of Jerusalem and west of Jericho. Since 1967 there has been no reliable census of that part of the metropolitan area in the occupied territories, and there is no agreed-upon definition of the boundaries of the metropolitan area. Various observers have estimated its population about evenly divided between Jews and Arabs, or tilted toward either Jews or Arabs in proportions of forty to sixty.[19]

Prior to the British Mandate, regimes in charge of Jerusalem did not worry about precise city boundaries. The outline of urban settlement shifted, contracted, and enlarged several times in a dynamism that continues. It was only in 1931 that the mandatory government gave Jerusalem the status of a municipality and defined its boundaries.

The long history and numerous changes raise the question of which map should be used in relation to demands about a return to Jerusalem as it was: The map based on the Armistice Lines after the 1948 war was no more permanent than the boundaries redrawn after the 1967 war, the latest extensions of the Israeli municipality in 1992, a map of the metropolitan area of today showing ethnic distributions, or any of the other points in a history of perhaps 4,000 years. Changes made in the shape of Jerusalem have included the following:

- Enlargements and contractions in the area included within the city walls occurred from ancient times to the latest construction during the reign of Suleiman the Magnificent from 1537 to 1541. Experts speculate about certain ancient developments. David's City (c. 1000 B.C.E.) is estimated at 0.05 to 0.06 square kilometer. City walls identified with his son Solomon (c. 965–927 B.C.E.) encompassed an area of 0.6 square kilometer. King Hezekiah's walls (c. 715–687 B.C.E.) added another 0.2 square kilometer. King Menassah (c. 687–642) extended the walls northward to enclose another 0.5 square kilometer. The biblical Books of Ezra and Nehemiah describe the problems involved in rebuilding the city destroyed by the Babylonians in 587 B.C.E. In the middle of the fourth century B.C.E. the city encompassed only about 0.12 square kilometers. It grew in stages to 1.6 square kilometers on the eve of its destruction by the Romans in 70 C.E. The walls that visitors see today include an area of about one square kilometer.[20] David's city, some of Solomon's addition, and much of Hezekiah's are outside the present walls.

- Expansions of urban settlement outside the walls began in the 1840s.[21] Early clusters of settlement built from the 1840s through the 1880s were within 0.5 kilometers of the Old City to the northwest, west, and southwest. More extensive building from 1890 through 1910 was mostly to the north and northwest, and reached two kilometers distance from the Old City. Building from 1910 to 1948 was also mostly to the northwest but occurred in all other directions as well.

- As the capital of the British mandated territory of Palestine, Jerusalem benefited from special emphasis in urban planning and development. The British offered various city plans during the urban growth and ethnic disputes that marked their reign: in 1918, 1920, 1922, 1930, and 1944. The area included in the earliest British plan was 17,900 dunams (1 dunam = 1,000 square meters), and 40,160 dunams in the last British Plan. Since 1948 the Israeli regime has put forward several additional plans.

- The British declared Jerusalem a municipality and fixed its boundaries in 1931.

- The prominent feature of the 1949 boundaries was its reliance on the cease-fire lines that ended the 1948 war. Then Israeli Jerusalem included the western three-quarters of the city defined as the municipality by the British in 1931, while Jordanian Jerusalem included the Old City along with an area to its north and east.

- Israel expanded its municipal boundaries westward in 1952 and 1963 to include developments for a population that grew by more than 96 percent between 1948 and 1967. The population of Jordanian Jerusalem grew by only 9 percent in the same period.

- Boundary changes of 1967 and 1992 illustrate the considerations used by recent generations of Israeli officials. Soon after the 1967 war, the Israeli government increased the municipal area from 38,000 to 108,000 dunams. Included within the new boundaries were the Old City, Arab neighborhoods to the north of the city walls and a number of Arab settlements immediately to the east of the Old City, as well as extensive open areas to the north and south formerly under Jordanian control but outside Jordan's boundaries for Jerusalem. The new city boundaries were crafted to include vacant areas that would lend themselves to housing for Jews and industrial development, as well as the airport north of the city. They stopped short of the Arab cities of Bethlehem and Beit Jalla to the south and Ramallah to the north and excluded a number of Arab settlements on the city's eastern boundary. In the north, the boundaries turned here and there to avoid Arab settlements. The point was to make Jerusalem more secure with a substantial Jewish majority. The most recent annexation in 1992 added another 13 percent to the city's area. It, too, was concerned with facilitating building for Jewish residents away from areas likely to provoke Arab opposition.[22]

- The Israeli government and the Jerusalem municipality have discussed an additional expansion westward in order to encompass Jewish suburbs and vacant land. The proposal has attracted the vocal opposition of Jewish surburbanites who do not wish to be reincorporated into a city they had left and of officials of suburban authorities who do not wish to lose their jobs and prestige. Also opposed are Palestinian authorities and a number of Western governments who see this as another Israeli move to fix the nature of Jerusalem in advance of negotiations with the Palestinians.

- Water, sewer, telephone, and electric lines can strengthen the dominance of a city beyond its boundaries. From 1967 onward, Israeli governments have expanded utility lines outward from Jerusalem to areas of the West Bank, seemingly to assure a central role for the Israeli city in a region heavily populated by Arabs.[23]

The controversies attendant on plans for Jerusalem may be judged by the experience of Mayor Teddy Kollek, who invited a panel of distinguished foreigners to comment on plans prepared in 1968. The mayor created The Jerusalem Committee from what he described as "distinguished architects, urban planners, historians, philosophers, theologians, artists and writers, concerned with the restoration and preservation of ancient sites, and the aesthetic, cultural and human needs of Jerusalem."[24] The mayor's own appointees roasted plans created by his municipality that featured monumental buildings and elaborate roadways. The themes emphasized by the Jerusalem Committee were modest and low profile, but its report has not dissuaded policymakers from approving several high-rise hotel, apartment, and commercial projects.

The record of the city's population provides a summary measure of its changing importance over the ages. In Table 5.1, the data shown prior to the 1920s are estimates, with those of the distant past being the least reliable. Despite their shortcomings, they provide the best record available for the city's changing fortunes.

Population peaks occurred prior to the destruction of the Second Temple, during the time when Jerusalem was the capital of the Crusaders' Latin Kingdom, and again after the onset of major Jewish immigration in the latter part of the nineteenth century. During most of the long period of Muslim rule from the seventh to the middle of the nineteenth century, Jerusalem had importance as the location of Islamic holy sites and religious institutions, but was politically and economically subordinate to the capitals of Cairo, Damascus, or Constantinople and never developed a large population. The most recent episode of population decline occurred during World War I. Jews of Russian origin were expelled as enemy aliens by Ottoman authorities. Now for the first time since Jerusalem's destruction by the Romans, post-1967 Jerusalem is again at the strategic heart of a country thickly settled by Jews. A book about the geopolitical importance of the city notes that it intrudes prominently into the center of Palestinian settlement on the West Bank. In what may be too final a conclusion, the author wrote that no Palestinian state can be viable without the Jerusalem that Israel will never concede.[25]

Table 5.1
Jerusalem's Population

1000 B.C.E.	2,500	
700	6,000-8,000	
600	24,000	(after the arrival of refugees from the north following the Assyrian conquest)
537	10,000	
0-70 C.E.	30,000	
1099-1187	30,000	
1200-1300	5,200	
1599-1600	4,700-15,800	
1800	8,000-10,000	
1834	22,000	
1840	15,000	
1860	20,000	
1876	25,000	
1900	70,000	
1913	75,200	
1928	62,700	
1931	93,100	
1946	164,400	
1961	243,900	(Israeli and Jordanian sectors)
1967	267,800	
1972	313,900	
1988	493,500	
1990	504,100	
1991	544,200	
1995	578,800	
1996	602,148	

Sources: Howard F. Vos, *Ezra, Nehemiah, and Esther* (Grand Rapids, Mich.: Zondervan Publishing House, 1987); Joachim Jeremias, *Jerusalem in the Time of Jesus: An Investigation into Economic and Social Conditions during the New Testament Period* (London: SCM Press, Ltd., 1969); (Yehoshua Ben-Arieh, *Jerusalem in the 19th Century: The Old City* (New York: St. Martin's Press, 1984); Amnon Cohen, *Jewish Life under Islam: Jerusalem in the Sixteenth Century* (Cambridge: Harvard University Press, 1984); Karl R. Schaefer, "Jerusalem in the Ayyubid and Mamluk Eras," Ph.D. Dissertation, Department of Near Eastern Languages and Literatures, New York University, 1985; U. O. Schmelz, *Modern Jerusalem's Demographic Evolution* (Jerusalem: Institute for Contemporary Jewry, The Hebrew University, 1987); F. E. Peters, *Jerusalem: The Holy City in the Eyes of Chroniclers, Visitors, Pilgrims, and Prophets from the Days of Abraham to the Beginnings of Modern Times* (Princeton: Princeton University Press, 1985); *Statistical Abstract of Israel, 1990* (Jerusalem: Central Bureau of Statistics, 1990); Statistical Yearbook of Jerusalem, 1988 (Jerusalem: Municipality of Jerusalem and Jerusalem Institute of Israel Studies, 1991); *Statistical Yearbook of Jerusalem, 1991* (Jerusalem: Municipality of Jerusalem and Jerusalem Institute of Israel Studies, 1993); *Statistical Yearbook of Jerusalem, 1992* (Jerusalem: Municipality of Jerusalem and Jerusalem Institute of Israel Studies, 1994); *Statistical Abstract of Israel, 1997* (Jerusalem: Central Bureau of Statistics, 1997).

THE POLITICAL SIGNIFICANCE OF NUMEROUS "JERUSALEMS"

There is no obvious or natural meaning of "Jerusalem" in this variety of concepts and geographical designations. However, the plurality presents opportunities as well as problems. Especially appealing is that most amorphous of concepts and places: metropolitan Jerusalem. Like other urban places, Jerusalem's core city draws workers, shoppers, and visitors from smaller cities, towns, and villages in its periphery. Some people commute back and forth on every working day, while others visit the central city occasionally for goods or services that are not available closer to home. Metropolitan Jerusalem spills over the as-yet unclear boundary between Israel and the Palestine Authority. The precise outline of the metropolitan area has not been defined by either Israeli or Palestinian officials.

The Palestinian Authority has begun to develop an administrative center in an area just outside the Israeli municipality that has already been assigned to it as a result of negotiations with Israel. Thus, the obvious question is, why not locate the capital of the emerging Palestinian State within the metropolitan area and allow the Palestinians to call it Jerusalem?

In the emotions aroused by Jerusalem, this solution is both too simple and too complicated. For Palestinian nationalists and Muslims it is too simple insofar as it overlooks the religious importance of what they call Haram Esh Sharif, located within the Israeli municipality. This is the site of the mosques Al Aqsa and Dome of the Rock, built in the seventh and eighth centuries, despoiled by the Crusaders, and sanctified again by the Muslims after the defeat of the Crusaders. Jews call the same place the Temple Mount. It was the site of the temple constructed by Solomon in the tenth century B.C.E. then destroyed by the Babylonians in the sixth century B.C.E., and the temple built by returnees from the Babylonian exile, reconstructed by Herod in the first century B.C.E. and destroyed by the Romans in the first century C.E.

The solution of identifying Palestinian Jerusalem in the suburbs of Israeli Jerusalem is also too simple because it does not deal with the more than 150,000 Palestinians living in the Israeli municipality. Most of these are concentrated in areas that the Palestinian Authority would separate from the Israeli city. Although Israeli officials insist that they are governing a united city, Israeli and Palestinian researchers agree that the unity is severely limited. Palestinians and Jews live in their own neighborhoods, read their own newspapers, send their children to their own schools, use their own bus lines and taxi companies. Palestinians in East Jerusalem academic high schools generally prepare for higher education in universities located in the West

Bank or other Arab countries. Intermarriages are discouraged in both Jewish and Palestinian communities and are rare.[26] Surveys show that substantial proportions of the city's Palestinians are severely critical of the Israeli regime and want their own state.[27]

The solution of calling part of the Arab share of the metropolitan area Jerusalem is too complicated for some Jews who object to the Palestinians using the name for their capital, even if it is located outside of the Israeli city. However, insofar as the Palestinians call their city of aspirations Al Quds (the Holy City), language may deal pragmatically with this Israeli sensitivity.

This is not the place to do all the work of the Israeli and Palestinian negotiators who sooner or later must deal with Jerusalem and/or its surroundings. Even the seemingly technical issues of accepting or rearranging existing water, sewage, and electric and phone lines provide their own political issues with high emotional potential. They are likely to occupy negotiators for many sessions.

Assertions about morality and blame for injustices of the past frustrate efforts to cope with present realities. Palestinian pragmatists will seek whatever potential for satisfying their concerns within the outline of what exists. It is unrealistic to expect the Israeli regime to abandon the neighborhoods built since 1967, to return Jerusalem to a status quo ante, whenever that might be dated, and move more than 130,000 Jews. It is no surprise that Israelis exploited their opportunities in the period since 1967. In the eyes of some this reflects Israelis' lack of concern for justice. In the eyes of others it is the result of legitimate concerns in the face of Arab threats against Jerusalem and its Jewish population, as well as Palestinian boycotts of the political opportunities offered them after 1967.[28]

Palestinian and Israeli assertions about the importance of Jerusalem as their individual national capital overlook the opportunities close at hand, as well as options that have been developed by other countries. It is not inevitable that a nation's capital be all in one place. The Federal Republic of Germany had its legislative chamber and key executive offices in Bonn, its supreme court 200 kilometers away in Karlsruhe, and its central bank and state audit office 100 kilometers from Bonn in Frankfurt. The united country of Germany is now engaged in a phased movement of some capital city functions to Berlin. South Africa has its legislative chamber in Capetown and executive offices 1,000 kilometers to the north in Pretoria.

There is also nothing inevitable about a city containing only one capital or the territory of only one national entity. Brussels is the seat of the European Union as well as the Belgian monarchy. New York City houses the headquarters of the United Nations. The territory and accredited personnel of the United Nations enjoy a form of sovereignty in New York without challenging national sovereignty over the remaining land. The situation is similar to that of the extraterritorial sovereignty granted to foreign governments' embassies, consulates, and diplomatic personnel in countries throughout the world, including Israel.

Israel also compromises its insistence that Jerusalem is its capital. It has kept the important Defense Ministry in Tel Aviv while moving other ministries to Jerusalem. The national telephone company plans to move its headquarters from Jerusalem to Tel Aviv for economic reasons. After proclaiming its move to Jerusalem, the Histadrut (Labor Federation) is moving back to Tel Aviv.

Israeli officials have often responded to nationalists by saying they will not let officials of the Palestine Authority receive foreign dignitaries at Orient House in the eastern part of the Israeli municipality, but they have backed down under pressures from major players like France, Great Britain, and the European Community. The implications for Palestinians are that they might develop a ceremonial site within the Israeli municipality, emphasize their spiritual affinity for the holy site of Haram Esh Sharif that has been controlled by Muslim clerics during the period of Israeli rule, and develop other governmental sites elsewhere in metropolitan Jerusalem, Gaza, and the West Bank.

Israeli planners are aware that they cannot ignore a metropolitan area that is binational. If all else goes well, negotiators may agree on some kind of designation of the metropolitan area that includes a forum for consultation between various local and national authorities. Metropolitan utility lines and sewage can be administered by organizations with representatives of both national entities, with a mandate to share development budgets, water allotments, revenues, and personnel appointments in a way to accommodate both communities. Within the Israeli municipality the following arrangements would represent slight if any extensions of what already exists. Some are specifically mentioned in a "secret" planning document prepared by a unit of the municipality and published by an Israeli newspaper.[29]

- Control of Christian and Muslim holy places by the religious authorities of each community. The present *de facto* arrangement can be formalized, perhaps (as suggested by former Mayor Teddy Kollek) embellished with a United Nations resolution that is adopted as Israeli law by the Knesset.

- Recognition of Orient House as a governmental seat of the Palestinian state, with a full panoply of flags, armed guards, and red carpets for visiting dignitaries.

- Devolution or consultations with respect to sensitive local services for the Palestinians living in the Israeli municipality.

- Choice by residents as to the authority in which they register, vote, pay taxes, and receive social welfare benefits. This provision can be sweetened by allowing Palestinians to vote in both Israeli and Palestinian elections, and to provide protection against double taxation. Their status would be an extension of the Israeli concession that Palestinian residents of East Jerusalem could vote in elections for the Palestinian Authority. It would also resemble the status of Israelis who also hold citizenship in countries, like the United States, that permit dual nationality.

The behavior of the Israeli Labor Party as recently as the election campaign of 1996 cautions that fears of voter backlash can overcome what appears to be a sober movement toward accommodation. Labor is the party of Yitzhak Rabin and Shimon Peres, who led the Israeli government to an accord with the PLO and Yassir Arafat. Much of the 1996 campaign featured charges by the Likud party that Peres sought to divide Jerusalem and permit the Palestinians to take part of it as a national capital. The response of Labor was to deny any such intention and to assert that it was committed to maintaining a united city under Israeli rule. Labor's minister for internal security announced that he would tighten control over Orient House and forbid the kinds of visits by foreign dignitaries that he had, in fact, permitted. What was missing from the Labor Party response was an effort to educate the Israeli public as to the complexity of the issues concerned with Jerusalem, the actions already undertaken by Labor officials, and the possibilities to be gained by recognizing the multiple meanings of "Jerusalem."

A PROPOSAL THAT COULD WORK, BUT THAT POLITICIANS CANNOT ARTICULATE

The most daring solution for Jerusalem is to *avoid* a solution. Both sides can consider the problem solved and leave things more or less as they are. The Palestinians of East Jerusalem could continue complying with some Israeli regulations and receive Israeli social benefits while continuing to resolve their internal problems with Muslim courts and Palestinian security personnel, as will be described below. Israel could insist that the city is united under its control as the capital of Jerusalem while continuing to overlook the connections of Palestinians to another authority.

A realist can appreciate the appeals of such a nonsolution but doubt that it will satisfy. Neither Labor nor Likud politicians from the Israeli side nor PLO leaders from the Palestinian side seem ready to describe in public the status quo or admit that it is satisfactory. Perhaps the essence of coping by way of ambiguity in the case of the most vexatious problems is just such an avoidance of truth. It works. But it may be able to continue only if it remains unarticulated.

A media flap in May 1998 revealed both the possibilities and problems of a finessed solution to the problems of Jerusalem. Israeli television broadcast pictures of a large structure being built alongside the boundary of the Jerusalem municipality. It took some days before Israeli authorities could agree that it was entirely outside of their jurisdiction. According to initial reports, it was to be the parliament building of the Palestinian State. For some Israeli officials, it was ideal. The Palestinians could say that they had a capital in Jerusalem. Israel could accept the new fact but would not have to concede the point. It was not in their Jerusalem. Right wing activists boiled. The building proved the duplicity of Netanyahu. The building was closer to the Western Wall than was the Israeli Knesset. The prime minister was dividing Jerusalem. Palestinians also had a problem with the building. Ardent nationalists saw it as betrayal. Arafat was agreeing on a capital only in the suburbs of Jerusalem and not in the city itself. Arafat waffled. PLO sources said that the building was not the parliament. It was a public facility, perhaps a university. Then it was said to be for Arafat's offices.

The possibility exists that Israeli and Palestinian actions represent the further working out of ambiguous and tacit agreements. Ambiguity does not work if the parties make clear their intentions. To accept this bit of optimism, it is necessary to overlook the centrality and intensity of the "Labor would divide Jerusalem" charge that Likud featured in its electoral campaign of 1996 and repeated in the campaign of 1999. Perhaps the true situation is that some Israeli and Palestinian policymakers are willing to cope with the benefits and problems of ambiguity, but others, or some of the same figures under the pressure of publicity, cannot depart from established policies and slogans.

ON THE ADVANTAGES OF COPING AND AMBIGUITY IN JERUSALEM

A neat or crisp solution for Jerusalem that deals with the demands of all the claimants appears unlikely. Coping is more appropriate than any effort to solve its complex problems once and for all time. The Israeli record in Jerusalem since 1967 shows a willingness to govern by managing ambiguity. The regime has insisted that it controls a united city but has accepted less than full sovereignty at sensitive points. Muslim and Christian religious authorities have been given *de facto* control over their holy places. Israeli authorities forbid Jewish prayers on what Jews call the Temple Mount in order to avoid offending Muslim sensitivities for what they call Haram Esh Sharif. Israeli officials have allowed Palestinian businessmen and professionals to practice under Jordanian licenses and the supervision of Arab associations, rather than force them to accept Israeli licensing and the rules of an Israeli Chamber of Commerce or professional societies. Municipal and national educational authorities have provided financial support to schools that teach according to Jordanian curricula and prepare their graduates for Arab universities.[30]

Events in Jerusalem since the signing of an Israeli-Palestinian accord in 1993 provide additional illustrations of governance via ambiguity. Israeli insistence on control over Jerusalem did not kept the government from agreeing that Palestinian residents of the city could vote in elections for the Palestinian Authority. Municipal and national education authorities fund schools in the Palestinian sector and formally appoint the teachers and administrators, but consult with representatives of the Palestinian Authority on issues of importance to them. Israeli health officials report that they limit their supervision over a major hospital in East Jerusalem that has been taken over by the PLO. The Israeli equivalent of the Red Cross (Red Star of David) operates ambulance services throughout the country. On account of its vehicles being stoned in East Jerusalem, it has begun negotiations to create an Arab subsidiary or to make arrangements with an Arab contractor to provide services in that part of the city.[31] Arabs living in East Jerusalem report problems among themselves to Palestinian authorities and bring disputes to traditional Muslim courts for adjudication. Israeli insistence that the Palestinian police not operate in Jerusalem are at odds with reports that Palestinian opponents of the PLO have been picked up in the city by Palestinian security operatives and transported elsewhere for detention and investigation.[32] A local newspaper headlined a report on Palestinian police activities in East Jerusalem with the claim that crime in the area was decreasing while it was increasing in other areas of Israel. The article assigned the credit to the concern of the Palestinian officers for the area, and the disinclination of Israeli officials to serve the city's Palestinians.[33]

Despite more shrill calls for a totally Israeli administration in Jerusalem, including the closure of Orient House and other institutions of the Palestinian Authority, Israeli authorities have looked the other way with respect to implementation. Hathem Abdel Kader, a member of the Palestinian Legislative Council, provoked an incident by receiving constituents in his Jerusalem home. To members of the Israeli Cabinet, this was a step towards a Palestinian capital in Jerusalem. The Israeli minister of internal security reached an accord in which Kader said that he would not conduct business of the Palestinian Authority, *per se*, in Jerusalem. The "policy" being followed seemed to resemble that of the U.S. military with respect to homosexuals: We won't ask; you don't tell.[34]

The stark choice about Jerusalem is clear borders and massive population transfers on the one hand or a continuation of ambiguity about borders and national affiliation on the other hand. The ambiguous situation would continue the present condition with a minimum of adjustment. It also surpasses by far on the criteria of humanity the option that would set clear lines and move populations in the interest of homogeneity.

The hope is that both Israelis and Palestinians will be able to continue coping with ambiguities. The city with a history of millennia is like others in being dynamic. People marry, change jobs, outgrow their flats and move. Businesses and other organizations prosper and fail. Traffic patterns change. Politicians argue about who promised what, and which elements of an agreement have been implemented. A city affected by religious and national aspirations and governed with more than a bit of ambiguity will not be easy, and it may be violent. Nothing else in the city's history has proved to be final.

JEWISH AMBIGUITIES IN JERUSALEM

Among the dynamics that can be expected to continue are developments within the Jewish sector that may spill over to influence Jewish-Palestinian relationships. By one scenario, Jerusalem's ultra-Orthodox communities are moving upward from perhaps 25 percent of the city's Jewish population. It is appropriate to describe them in the plural as "communities" because they are not unified in their religious doctrines or political inclinations, except perhaps when they are led to join one another in whatever is the season's campaign in behalf of enhancing the city's Judaic character against secular Jews.[35] Some of the ultra-Orthodox are nationalists, whereas others seem oblivious to the Jewish national struggle. As a result, it is difficult to decide whether they are likely to join with the city's Arabs in opposing a secular Jewish plurality or join with the Jews in seeking to maintain control of the city against the Arab minority. Other scenarios see Jerusalem's ultra-Orthodox growth peaking on account of individuals' economic needs to integrate themselves more fully into a wage-earning society. Substantial numbers of ultra-Orthodox Jews have already begun seeking housing in lower cost areas outside of the municipality.

Chapters 3 and 6 describe tensions between ultra-Orthodox and secular Jews. Each group in the population stereotypes the other as aggressive and encroaching, despite the lack of clear objective indicators that policy is moving in either the religious or secular direction. Religion and ethnicity make Jerusalem interesting and tense. Arabs and Jews, as well as religious and secular Jews, express discomfort about one another's presence and behavior in the city. Yet the nature of a city is heterogeneity. Jerusalem may present an extreme case where municipal officials and residents must cope with the cultural differences, but it is arguably not an outlier when compared with North American cities with substantial white, African-American, Hispanic, and Asian populations, or European cities with guest workers and immigrants (legal and illegal) from North Africa, the Balkans, and eastern Europe. There, too, officials and residents must cope with the present and are not sure about the future.

A NAME

> What's in a name? That which we call a rose
> By any other name would smell as sweet.[36]

Names are important, but the same name may convey different messages. There are different kinds of roses. Some smell sweeter, and the stems of some are less prickly than others. In the case at hand, there are different conceptions and geographical designations for Jerusalem. The name applies to sites with intense spirituality and to areas having the most prosaic of urban traits. Some meanings associated with the city's name convey discordant views of history and religious doctrine. Intense emotions get in the way of bargaining. Yet other associations and designations of Jerusalem are as new as the evolving metropolitan area. They are less encumbered by emotion and provide opportunities for creative and patient negotiators.

Nothing in this chapter should suggest that Jerusalem's future will be free of tension and perhaps violence. "Expectations" is too strong a word for a city with Jerusalem's history. Yet the dynamism that has marked its four millennia suggests that the future need not be entirely bad. The holding power of the Oslo agreement, despite several outbursts of violence since 1993, justifies some degree of optimism. It is not beyond the realm of possibilities that the very complexities inherent in the realities of Jerusalem may allow it to be the easiest to solve of the Israel-Arab problems and not the most difficult.

6

Assessing Israel

Judgments about policy are likely to be ambiguous. Seldom is it the case that a program receives applause from all parts of the political spectrum. Usually there are criticisms. Often the disappointments are apparent among program opponents even before activities get underway. Political dispute is not likely to stop with the victory of one or another side in an election or a vote in the legislature. Advocates and opponents prepare for the next round of voting, next year's budget debate, or the possibility of amending legislation by applauding or criticizing programs being implemented.

Ambiguity also affects assessments by virtue of technical complexities. Among the issues that are capable of provoking argument are:

- Which indicators and statistical techniques are most appropriate to judge a program?

- How should different findings be weighed when some indicators provide positive results while others are negative?

- What should be done about indicators that are positive but not as positive as program advocates seemed to be promising when they proposed the activities now being evaluated?

- If judgments are to be made comparatively about national or local activities, which other countries or localities should be chosen as the standard of judgment?

- If the assessment is to deal with the question of whether conditions have improved or deteriorated, which years should be used for the examination?

The assessments offered here may be especially ambiguous because they concern the performance of an entire country over a long period of time. Evaluations are typically focused on the accomplishments of individual programs or administrative units. Assessing Israel is likely to be viewed by experts in evaluation as too large a task to be done well. However, much of the world seems to be engaged perpetually in the judgment of Israel. Part of the Israeli experience is uncritical enthusiasm, regime apology, or severe censure by locals as well as outsiders. Extremes of apology and criticism seem to feed off one another. Much of the world seems to have drawn up sides either for or against Israel and what its government is doing.

Judaic traditions of self-examination and severe self-criticism have cultural roots that go back to the Hebrew Bible. Isaiah, Jeremiah, Amos, Hosea, and Nehemiah decried the actions of political and economic elites. Amos proclaimed that righteousness is superior to legality,[1] and thereby set a standard of criticism that is open ended: Actions can be proper in a formal sense, but not good enough.

Jewish radicalism is prominent in the history of Europe and North America as well as modern Israel. The intellectual movement labeled "post-Zionism" includes a number of Israeli intellectuals who emphasize uncomplimentary findings about the founding generation of national leaders, as well as more recent shortcomings. Israel's State Comptroller (equivalent to the U.S. General Accounting Office, the National Audit Office of the United Kingdom, and other supreme national audit bodies) is notable among its peers for having legal authority to criticize government units for failing to abide by the standard of "moral integrity," as well as the more conventional criteria of legality, economy, effectiveness, and efficiency. It is said that Jerusalem has more accredited foreign correspondents than any other city except Washington, D.C. Just as this claim is not thoroughly documented, however, so allegations about Israel's morality and immorality are more often proclaimed than subject to careful analysis.

Israel was designated politically incorrect even before Benjamin Netanyahu became prime minister. Until 1967, Israel was David to the Arab Goliath. Then the Six-Day War seemed analogous to the heroic denouement of the biblical conflict in the Valley of Elah.[2] The Jewish David won again. In recent years, however, Israel has carried the undesirable mantle of Goliath against the Palestinian David.

Students of ambiguity know that reality is often more complicated than image. We saw in Chapter 2 that Israel's status as a giant is fuzzy, at best. Palestinians' status as a heroic David is no less doubtful. The *intafada* that began in 1987 was anything but a glorious war of national liberation. There were ten times the number of Palestinians killed as Israelis, and some 40 percent of the Palestinian deaths were caused by other Palestinians.[3] Nonetheless, the *intafada* seems to have been a milestone of Palestinian pride on the way to national self-determination.

Actions that Israeli officials explain as taken in national self-defense, or within the country's own national aspirations, have been labeled by critics as the illegal occupation of territory, the repression of a conquered population, illegal detentions, torture, censoring the media, and piracy.[4] According to some ideological rituals, Israel's very existence is a threat to the security of its region. More reasonable critics describe a lack of opportunities for Israeli Arabs that reflect overt discrimination in hiring and insufficient government support for schools and local authorities in the Arab sector.[5]

It is common to find a tension between two themes in Israel's Declaration of Independence: that Israel shall be a Jewish country and that it shall not discriminate on the basis of religion, ethnicity, or sex. The 1948 declaration of equality was more lofty aspiration than concrete promise. In this respect, it resembled the U.S. Declaration of Independence that recognizes the right to "life, liberty, and *the pursuit of happiness*." The U.S. Constitution, drafted twenty-three years later, includes no such formula. The Fifth Amendment to the Constitution safeguards "life, liberty, and *property*" but indicates that a person may be deprived of them by due process. Insofar as rights of property are likely to translate into a preservation of differentials in wealth, the promise of the Constitution seems to stand against the social norms of the Declaration of Independence. Like Israel's Declaration, that of the United States seems in retrospect to have been more elevated sentiment than serious commitment.

Another issue that has provoked Israel's critics is religious tensions among Jews. Secular Israelis as well as overseas Jews concerned about the rights of the non-Orthodox see threats to the country's status as a democracy by virtue of sectarian demands supported by minority parties that exploit advantages in the machinations associated with coalition politics. Views to the future see high birth rates among ultra-Orthodox Jews as assuring them control of the Jerusalem municipality.[6] Speculations about the power of religious Zionists (i.e., Orthodox as opposed to the ultra-Orthodox) who are concerned primarily with enlarging Jewish settlements in the occupied territories see them as able to thwart the peace process, and even provoking a civil war between religious nationalists and secular Israelis willing to give up part of the Land of Israel for peace.[7]

In the emotions associated with Israel it is not easy to attempt a balanced assessment without risking the charge of being a committed critic or an apologist for the regime. Israeli officials at all levels of the government, in past and present administrations, have been heavy-handed with respect to the Arab minority. Israelis have missed opportunities for constructive accommodation. On the other hand, Israelis have suffered from chronic efforts at Arab terror, which give substantial reason to be suspicious of Palestinian gestures toward peace. In the realm of religious-secular conflict, there are ample examples of provocation as opposed to the pursuit of understanding from all segments along the spectrum of the ultrareligious to the antireligious. In fact, there is no calculus that can produce an evaluation of Israeli actions that is in perfect balance, much less one that is able to rank the country among Western democracies for the righteousness of its national leaders.

With all the reservations that are due such an enterprise, it is appropriate to seek some balance in the assessment of Israel's performance. We will focus on two significant issues: Jewish-Arab relations and religious-secular relations within the Jewish sector. Each is important as an indicator as to how Israel stacks up as a Western democracy. The first touches the domain of discrimination against an ethnic minority. The second involves several domains of individual freedom from sectarian dictates. Religious activists threaten free expression and the democratic selection of national leaders, as well as a host of other freedoms with respect to activities permitted on the Sabbath, food that may be purchased, occupations that may be pursued, the medical services of abortions and organ transplants, and the availability of non-Orthodox Jewish religious options.

There are no shortages of assertions about discrimination against Arabs or the achievements of religious and secular Jews at the expense of their rivals. What is lacking is any summary indicators of how well or poorly any of the groups actually fare alongside their claims of disadvantages. Not the least of the lessons from this exercise will be the complexity in assessing any country's treatment of an ethnic minority on the one hand or the demands of religious activists against those of antireligious activists on the other. The discussion that follows assesses some of the most prominent of these claims in the framework of international and historical comparison. The purpose is to show how well or poorly each Israeli claimant seems to be doing in comparison with its own recent past, as well as in comparison to countries that are widely viewed as appropriate standards of behavior among Western democracies.

We shall not deal with the evolving and important relations between the Israeli government and the Palestine Authority. This avoidance will provide ammunition to critics who will see this chapter as an apology for the Israeli regime. Israeli settlement activities in areas of the West Bank and Gaza are cited as Israeli violations of Palestinian rights. Yet the same behavior can be viewed as a fair instance of seeking advantages in a situation that is likely to move toward a final accord. Just as warring armies seek to improve their seizure of strategic territory towards a cease fire, Israeli as well as Palestinian authorities are seeking to improve their postures towards the final drawing of boundaries. Each is seeking to purchase land held by individuals of the other national group, and each is building rapidly in order to firm up its claim to territory.[8] While Israel has the advantage of government funds and those provided by Jewish nationalists overseas, the Palestinians call on donations from Arab states awash in oil.

Against the harassment of Arab villagers and the violence by Israeli settlers can be arrayed the behaviors against Israeli settlers by Arabs. And against Israeli land purchases and construction on what had been Arab land can be arrayed Palestinians' killing of Arabs who sell land to Jews. Ranking officials of the Palestine Authority have said that the killing has their support, while others deny that it is the work of the Authority. Neither Israeli nor Palestinian activities in the realm of land dealing would pass all the tests of morality. Both are tough actions taken as part of an evolving situation that features pressure as well as bargaining.

ALLEGATIONS AND ASSESSMENT

The allegations associated with Israel's performance on ethnic and religious issues are emotional and contradictory. Left-wing critics charge Israeli authorities with severe discrimination against Arab citizens, while right-wing critics charge that those authorities are not doing enough to combat Arab terrorism. And while antireligious Israelis assert that the ultra-Orthodox blackmail the state by means of political power and receive exaggerated allocations of financial support and other policy benefits, the ultra-Orthodox charge that state officials overlook their religious needs to the point of being anti-Semitic.

We cannot judge these allegations with conventional indicators of public policy. There are no summary measures of conditions in the fields of religious conflict or ethnic fairness. As a result, an assessment of Israel must be in part qualitative and judgmental. The following sections will summarize the allegations and assess some of them as far as possible in a manner that uses quantitative data and is comparative. The questions that should be addressed are: How does Israel compare with other societies in its treatment of ethnic and religious tensions, and are Israeli conditions getting better or worse?

It is important to seek a comparative perspective, both outward from Israel to other countries, and within Israel backward from the present. No social condition can be judged in isolation. Many situations are undesirable with respect to idealized conceptions of justice. However, a sophisticated assessment should inquire which of competing goals should receive additional portions of limited resources. In other words, how undesirable is each condition? One way of addressing this question is by comparison. If a condition in one country is said to warrant improvement, but is nonetheless better than comparable conditions in other countries to which the subject country may be compared, then policymakers in the subject country are best advised to look to other social problems when deciding where to put their limited resources.

Emotional campaigns that fail to compare one's situation with the outer world can produce a distortion of resource allocations. The results may be shortfalls in the accomplishments of other public policies that are not currently fashionable, or damage to the private sector as a result of taxes that are higher than in countries that are its competitors in international markets. Of course, social reformers who focus on a target issue may not be persuaded by such an argument. They can still demand maximum effort, even if a country's performance on an issue is the best in the world. However, such parochialism is less suitable for the real world than for a Paradise where resources are unlimited and where absolute justice is the ruling norm.

Those who criticize Israeli democracy are likely to identify the disadvantages of the Arab minority. No democracy is truly egalitarian, but Israel departs from that standard explicitly by proclaiming itself a Jewish state. Jews are approximately 79 percent of the national population, and they enjoy the major portions of political opportunities and policy benefits. Programs in Arab communities are less well financed than in Jewish communities or the Jewish neighborhoods of mixed cities. Non-Jews have reached positions as judges in lower courts and appellate courts, deputy ministers in government departments, and the rank of brigadier general with command over large units in the army.[9] It was only in 1996 that the first Israeli Arabs received appointment as ambassador in the country's foreign service and more recently an appointment to the Supreme Court. To date there has not been a non-Jewish minister in any Israeli Cabinet, or a non-Jew with the most senior rank of director general in a ministerial bureaucracy.

Israeli apologists are likely to explain these conditions with reference to Arab hostility, rejection of Israeli institutions, lack of preparation for key positions in the public sector, and Arab violence. They note that Arab citizens have traditionally voted for antiestablishment political parties, and that Arab local authorities tax their residents substantially less than the authorities of Jewish or mixed communities. While these assertions are partly true, they are also at least partly out of date. Political parties that won Knesset seats largely due to Arab votes supported the 1992–1996 government headed by Yitzhak Rabin and Shimon Peres, even though they did not formally join the coalition. In this ambiguous half-in-half-out posture, they resembled the actions that ultra-Orthodox parties have taken on several occasions: seeking government resources for their programs in exchange for support on key votes, without formally pledging their loyalty to the governing coalition. "Arab terror" is more likely to come from the territories occupied as a result of the 1967 war than from within Israel. Arab qualifications have increased substantially via education and experience in local authorities and nongovernmental institutions. Moreover, the claims of Arab hostility and the privileges associated with the Jewish character of Israel weaken in the face of charges brought against Jewish politicians for corruption, as well as pictures of ultra-Orthodox Jews who demonstrate against memorials to Israeli war dead and burn the Israeli flag on Independence Day.

Assertions that ultrareligious and secular (or antireligious) Israeli Jews make against one another resemble in some respects those heard about the Arabs of Israel: They convey some truth, but are drawn with a broad brush or in a way that does not lend itself to detailed reckoning.

- A conventional claim heard from religious Jews is that religiosity is the element that assured Jewish survival in the past and is most likely to assure the continued existence of the Jewish people.

- Against this, secular Jews ridicule the situation where large numbers of ultra-Orthodox Jews study in religious academies that avail them of exemptions from military service and do not provide modern education. As a result, ultrareligious Israelis do not to contribute their share to national defense, to the capacity of the economy to compete in international markets, or to the tax base that supports the military and domestic programs that aid, among other things, ultra-Orthodox religious academies.

- Secular Jews also worry about the dependence of the ultra-Orthodox on the leadership of aged rabbis who do not seem to express themselves clearly on matters of religious doctrine or politics. Secular Jews also worry about remarks by certain religious leaders that religious doctrine is more vital to Israel's future than democracy.

- Critics accuse the ultra-Orthodox of receiving unduly large allocations of public resources due to the leverage of their political parties in coalition politics, and point to the corruption of religious politicians. A leader of one ultra-Orthodox party drained resources from a family business and proclaimed bankruptcy without paying final compensation to the workers in a depressed town that had been dominated by his factory. Two leaders of another ultra-Orthodox party have been found guilty of fraud and other irregularities. One has served a prison term, and another is still involved in what may be the first of three judicial proceedings on separate charges.

- High birth rates cause the ultra-Orthodox neighborhoods to creep like a cancer through previously secular neighborhoods of Jerusalem. Blockbusting techniques familiar in mixed-race American communities see high prices paid for the first sales to ultra-Orthodox families, followed by a flood of additional families as secular families flee. Secular residents fear that the ultra-Orthodox will insist on the closure of neighborhood roads on the Sabbath, as well as harass neighbors who watch television, listen to secular radio stations, read secular newspapers, and do not dress according to ultra-Orthodox standards of modesty.

- Even outside of their neighborhoods the ultra-Orthodox seek to impose religious law on Israel. Their agenda has included a regulation of behavior permitted on the Sabbath and religious holidays, prohibiting the sale of nonkosher food, opposition to non-Orthodox rabbis and their congregations, and demands to use religious criteria in order to govern medical practices and the handling of ancient graves uncovered during construction projects.

- Religious politicians respond that they use their electoral power in ways that have been charted by the secular parties of Israel and that they are not the only parties whose leaders have been charged with corruption. On some of the charges levied against them, religious leaders respond that the liberal secular press and its political allies exploit every opportunity to stereotype the religious community. When newspapers published pictures of religious youth burning the Israeli flag, one religious leader claimed that the boys had been urged on by a journalist wanting a picture of scandalous behavior.

TESTING THE CLAIMS

There is more hyperbole than reasoned argument about the status of religion and ethnicity in Israel. Each side in perennial disputes asserts its points in ritualized fashion without addressing the points being made by antagonists.

Religion

Disputes about religion are the most difficult to assess systematically. In part this is because of the overtly doctrinaire and uncompromising positions that the ultra-Orthodox take in keeping with their faith. Their argumentation resembles what has been written about religious activists elsewhere, whose "special problem has been the other-worldly orientation of these deeply religious people."[10]

One factor that hinders a systematic inspection of the claims made by the ultra-Orthodox or their opponents derives from a biblical episode concerned with King David. As reported in II Samuel 24: ". . . the anger of the Lord was kindled against Israel, and he moved David against them to say, Go, number Israel and Judah. For the king said to Joab the captain of the host, which was with him, Go now through all the tribes of Israel, from Dan even to Bersheva, and number ye the people, that I may know the number of the people." The story goes on to report that 70,000 people died of a pestilence that the Lord sent by way of punishment for a census that God himself had initiated. Commentators have wrestled with this story over the centuries. One explanation is that David's census was to be taken in preparation for apportioning taxes, work levies, or military recruitment involved with conquests or plans to build the Temple. Popular opposition to the levies, as described by the metaphor of a plague, may have been the factor that dissuaded David from going forward with the Temple.[11]

On account of this story religious Jews have been wary of counting people. At a personal level, they may evade a friendly inquiry that other people use as a conversation starter: "How many children do you have?" When Israel's Central Bureau of Statistics was preparing the national census in 1995, the Rabbinical tribunal of one congregation, Edah Ha-Haredit, ruled that counting Jews was against religious law and would cause a plague, as in the case of David's census. Other ultra-Orthodox rabbis also opposed the census, but accepted a proposal by the Central Bureau of Statistics to remove a question of religious affiliation from the questionnaire. This would turn the census into a counting of Israelis and not a counting of Jews. For the rabbis of Edah Ha-Haredit, this was not sufficient. They continued in their opposition to any census. As in years past, the census appeared likely to undercount ultra-Orthodox Israelis who would refuse to cooperate due to the experiences of King David.[12] Because of David's problem, there are no official statistics about the number of ultra-Orthodox Jews or other social indicators that are typically derived from government questionnaires: their levels of income and education, housing congestion, or the spatial spread of their communities.

Other problems preclude any systematic efforts to assess the ultra-Orthodox share of public resources. A variety of Israeli government offices provide aid to ultra-Orthodox communities, but there is no central recording of what is given to the ultra-Orthodox. The culture of Israeli political competition may have something to do with this lack of record keeping. Those asking for aid do not relish the target of the request being able to know the full resources available to the requester. Similar postures are taken by other groups that receive government allocations: municipalities, minorities, non-Orthodox religious congregations, poor families, and discharged soldiers. The givers of aid cooperate in creating this ambiguity. In a situation where all governments have been coalitions because no party has ever won a majority of Knesset seats, each minister owes allegiance to a political party more than to the government as a whole. Ministries provide as little information as possible to the Ministry of Finance. In this way they weaken the Finance Ministry's capacity to scrutinize their activities or to control their ability to help those groups that support their party.

There are several governmental sources of aid to the ultra-Orthodox communities:

- The Ministry of Construction and Housing builds subsidized housing and infrastructure suitable for religious communities, often allocated to congregations for resale to their members. In keeping with the economic and demographic conditions in religious communities, the housing typically involves apartment blocks designed for a maximum number of children and built at a high level of congestion in order to save on land costs. Many secular as well as ultra-Orthodox Israelis support the principle of voluntary housing segregation in order that each community can live according to its lifestyle.

- The Ministry of Finance and the Bank of Israel authorize government-supported lending programs and set interest rates that affect the mortgage options of ultra-Orthodox families.

- The Ministry of Education aids primary and secondary schools as well as religious academies operated by ultra-Orthodox congregations.

- The Ministry of Welfare provides direct aid to low-income individuals as well as funding to institutions that provide services to the ultra-Orthodox. Ultra-Orthodox politicians have been creative in their efforts to support religious communities, many of whose members have low incomes and large families. Secular critics of a rabbi who served as Minister of Welfare uncovered financial aid given to a library associated with a religious institution in Jerusalem. When questioned about the appropriateness of the welfare ministry aiding a library, the minister replied that the library served aged and handicapped readers.[13]

- The Ministry of Religions is one of the least open and systematic of Israel's bureaucracies. It is a honey pot of patronage and a frequent target of media accounts and State Comptroller reports about irregular appointments and the lack of clarity in the financial records. It supports religious academies, cemeteries, ritual baths, synagogues, and other institutions associated with religious communities.

- Several ministries not only both provide direct aid to ultra-Orthodox individuals and institutions, but also funnel additional aid through local authorities. For their part, municipalities use their own tax revenues plus funds received from the ministries to aid ultra-Orthodox institutions. Local authorities also provide sub-

stantial discounts on local taxes and water bills to ultra-Orthodox families due to
their income levels and family size.

Aside from these governmental sources, ultra-Orthodox institutions
typically raise voluntary contributions in Israel and overseas. While some
donations move through formal organizations and are officially reported,
others move in the gray areas of individual emissaries who receive a percentage of the donations they solicit, as well as money lending and currency
exchanges outside of established banks.

From both religious and antireligious activists, one hears claims of losses
and gains in what seems like an ongoing tug-of-war. On some occasions,
each can claim both victory and defeat, as when authorities have enacted
measures that seem to favor one side, but fail to implement them. We saw in
Chapter 3 the ambiguities with respect to Sabbath observance, "indecency"
in advertising and at the Yad Vashem Holocaust memorial, nonkosher food,
and the "monopoly" of Orthodox rabbis in performing marriage, divorce,
and conversion.

A comprehensive account would have to reconcile the irreconcilable;
groups both gain and lose but on different issues. How many restaurants,
coffee houses, bars, and discotheques that are now open on the Sabbath (i.e.,
victories of the secular) are equal to how many blocks of roads that are
closed on the Sabbath (i.e., victories of the religious)? Also, how many
non-Orthodox synagogues, supported with public funds (i.e., victories of
the non-Orthodox) are appropriate compensation for the failure of the Israeli Rabbinate to recognize marriages performed by non-Orthodox rabbis
in Israel (i.e., victories of the Orthodox)? And how does one judge the
power of the Rabbinate to refuse sanction for non-Orthodox marriages
while the Interior Ministry and the courts recognize such marriages when
they are performed outside of Israel?

In arraying a final score about incommensurate issues, it seems fair to say
that the competition has been tied, more or less, or that a number of issues
remain open to continuing dispute. Resolutions to date do not provide any
final determination of religious or secular winners and losers.

Israel's perennial coalition politics has something to do with the continued tensions between religious and secular Jews and ambiguous outcomes
without final resolution of major issues. Religious political parties are
likely to maintain some degree of power in Israel's politics of proportional
representation. However, all the religious parties together have never been
able to amass as many as 25 percent of the Knesset seats. Secular politicians
within Israel and Diaspora activists of non-Orthodox religious movements
have employed their leverage in the Knesset, the Supreme Court, govern-

ment ministries, and international Jewish organizations against the efforts of Orthodox and ultra-Orthodox activists. Moreover, the Israeli religious bloc itself is likely to split on issues of trading parts of the Land of Israel for peace, or the concern for applying religious law against the opposition of nonreligious Jews. The result is that secular politicians are reluctant to impose total defeat on the religious, out of concern that they will need their support in the Knesset sooner or later. And with less than 25 percent of the Knesset, religious parties are in no position to dictate on matters staunchly opposed by secular Israelis.[14]

Equally problematic are efforts to determine if religious activists are more prominent, or if their power is greater in Israel than in other Western democracies. As measured by responses to surveys, religious believers seem to be about as well represented in Israel as in other Western democracies. About 20 percent of Israelis define themselves as ultra-Orthodox or Orthodox, and 79 percent place themselves on a continuum between "strictly observant" and "somewhat observant."[15] A compilation of surveys from twenty-one countries that did not include Israel found clusters in the same ranges. Between 2 percent and 82 percent of national samples reported that they attend church weekly; 24 percent to 81 percent feel religious; and 39 percent to 96 percent express a belief in God. The twenty-one-country averages were 25 percent attending church regularly, 58 percent feeling religious, and 74 percent expressing a belief in God.[16]

The prominence of religious symbols in Israel also resembles the situation in other countries. The use of a religious emblem on the national flag puts Israel in a group along with Australia, Denmark, Finland, Greece, Iceland, New Zealand, Norway, Sweden, Switzerland, and the United Kingdom. The flag of the United States is secular, but coins and currency, as well as the pledge of allegiance, proclaim the importance of God. The national holidays of many democracies are heavily affected by religion. Most of Israel's national holidays come from the Jewish religious calendar, while those of other countries include Christmas, Easter, and Good Friday, plus whatever might be said about the residue of religion attaching to the New Year, St. Patrick's Day, St. Valentine's Day, and Halloween.

The prominence of religious issues on Israel's national agenda also resembles the situation in other countries. Israel is not clearly more or less preoccupied by religious issues than countries that are debating abortion, euthanasia, prayer in schools, the teaching of evolution, the wearing of religious garb in schools or the military, the display of religious symbols in public buildings or on public land, ritual slaughter of animals, the rights of homosexuals, provisions for divorce and birth control, and the status of children born out of wedlock.

On the dimension of government support for religion, Israel also finds itself in company with numerous other countries where aid flows from public authorities to religious bodies in several ways. Even in the United States, alongside a claim of separation of church and state, substantial benefits flow to religious organizations via tax exemptions, as well as direct public support for hospitals, schools, and other institutions affiliated with religious bodies. While there is no established church in the United States, religiosity appears to be the national creed. In Utah it is Mormon authorities who speak out prominently on issues of policy and occasionally seem to influence the decisions of government officials. Elsewhere it may be a Cardinal of the Roman Catholic Church who is prominent in New York, Boston, Chicago, or Philadelphia or the preacher of a Baptist megachurch in a southern city. Like the rabbis of Israel, however, none of these Christian authorities can be assured of influencing government on a matter of religious importance.

Ethnicity

The sorting out of claims with respect to Israel's treatment of ethnic minorities is somewhat more conclusive than claims dealing with religion. Arguments about ethnicity involve more indicators that lend themselves to assessments that are quantitative and comparative. Alongside of them, to be sure, are arguments involving feelings of deprivation that do not always correspond with indications that conditions are, in fact, improving or are better than they are in the case of ethnic tensions in other countries. The information included in Tables 6.1 to 6.3 deals with several of the allegations about Israel's treatment of its non-Jewish minorities. Table 6.1 shows the government's financial treatment of Jewish and Arab local authorities in 1982 and 1993. Table 6.2 shows the relative family incomes of Israel's minorities, alongside a parallel comparison of African-American and white families in the United States. Table 6.3 employs another measure that has been used to judge living standards: the infant mortality of majority and minority populations in Israel and the United States. While these data do not resolve all the issues, they do put the assertions in the context of what exists now, in comparison to Israel's own past and experience in another country that is heterogeneous socially and is widely cited as a standard of judging democracies. The years chosen for comparison are those for which comparable data is available, that show changes over ten- or twenty-year periods to the early 1990s.

Table 6.1
Relative Advantages of Jewish and Arab Local Authorities

	Governmant grant/capita	Government grant as a percentage of local authority
1993		
Arab	401	35%
Jewish	403	17%
Arab/Jewish ratio	0.99	2.09
1982		
Arab	925	59%
Jewish	2,834	52%
Arab/Jewish ratio	0.33	1.14

Sources: Local Authorities in Israel: Financial Data, 1993 and 1981/82 (Jerusalem: Central
   Bureau of Statistics, 1996 and 1983). With respect to grants/capita, a change in Israeli
   currency is responsible for smaller numbers in 1993 than 1982.

Table 6.2
Family Income Differentials, Israel and the United States

	1991	1970
Non-Jews monthly family incomes as a percentage of the Jews in Israel	72%	68%
African-American annual family incomes as a percentage of the whites in the United States	60%	61%

Sources: Statistical Abstract of Israel, 1992 (Jerusalem: Central Bureau of Statistics, 1992),
   Table 11.4; *Statistical Abstract of Israel, 1982* (Jerusalem: Central Bureau of Statistics,
   1982), Table XI-13; *Statistical Abstract of the United States, 1993*, CD-ROM edition
   (Washington, D.C.: U.S. Government Printing Office, 1993), Table 712.

Israel's non-Jewish local authorities have improved substantially with
respect to their receipt of government aid. The Ministry of the Interior provides a grant to local authorities that is meant to compensate for a lack of local resources. Most local authorities receive a grant under this program,
except for the most well-off Jewish communities. Grants of Jewish and

Table 6.3
Infant Mortality Differentials, Israel and the United States

	1990	1970
Non-Jews infant mortality in relation to that of Jews in Israel	1.97	1.96
African-American infant mortality in relation to that of whites in the United States	2.21	1.83

Sources: Statistical Abstract of Israel, 1992 (Jerusalem: Central Bureau of Statistics, 1992), Table 3.11; *Statistical Abstract of Israel, 1982* (Jerusalem: Central Bureau of Statistics, 1982), Table III-2 and III-3; *Statistical Abstract of the United States,* 1993, CD-ROM edition (Washington, D.C.: U.S. Government Printing Office, 1993), Table 121.

non-Jewish recipient authorities were almost identical in 1993: an average 403 New Israeli Shekels (NIS) per capita for the Jewish local authorities and 401 NIS for the Arab local authorities. As a proportion of their total budgets, however, the grants received by Arab local authorities were more than twice those received by Jewish authorities. In 1982 the condition of Arab local authorities was substantially less desirable. Their per capita grant was only one-third that of the Jewish local authorities. In 1982 the Interior Ministry gave to the Arab local authorities a larger percentage of their total expenditures than in the case of the Jewish local authorities, but the differential was 1.14 to 1 (non-Jewish in relation to Jewish local authorities) in 1982, compared to 2.09 to 1 in 1993.

It is still true that Arab local authorities are less assiduous than Jewish local authorities in taxing their residents. A ratio of the total local budget in relation to the mean income of local families was an average 0.49 in the Arab sector during 1993 and 0.68 in the Jewish sector.[17]

With respect to family incomes, Israel's minority scores better in relation to the majority than a comparable measure involving African-Americans in the United States. Changes over the 1970–1991 period are too small to support strong conclusions, but they suggest improvements in the minority-majority ratios in Israel and a worsening of conditions in the United States. The family incomes of non-Jewish families have increased slightly in relation to Jewish families over the period 1970–1991: from 68 percent of the average for Jews to 72 percent. African-American family incomes in the United States were 62 percent of white incomes in 1991, down slightly from 63 percent in 1970. These findings resemble other indications that Israel's "social gap," as measured by income differentials between the wealthy and poor, is not as wide as in several countries chosen as a comparison group, despite claims to the contrary by Israel's own social critics. According to various measures that take account of per capita income and national GNP, Israel appears more egalitarian than Australia, Canada, Denmark, France, Italy, New Zealand, Norway, Sweden, Switzerland, United Kingdom, United States, and West Germany.[18]

Infant mortality rates in Israel and the United States have dropped over the 1970–1990 period, testifying to medical advances and their availability to the population. Infant deaths (i.e., infants up to the age of one year) declined in the United States from 20.0 per 1,000 live births in 1970 to 9.2 in 1990. In Israel the decline was even more pronounced: from 24.2 to 9.8. The Israeli differentials between Jews and non-Jews remained about the same between 1970 and 1990, while the gap between African-American and white infant death rates in the United States increased. In 1990, the rate of infant mortality among non-Jews was 1.97 times greater than the rates among Jews in Israel, while the rate among African-Americans in the United States was 2.21 times that among whites.[19]

IS THE GLASS HALF EMPTY OR HALF FULL?

There are no simple resolutions for the accusations that local and overseas critics level at the Israeli society. It is a country with substantial social cleavages and serious problems of security, as well as a tradition of moralizing with roots in the Hebrew Bible. The assessment of Israel remains ambiguous, thanks to the complexity of competing measurements, as well as some allegations that do not lend themselves to systematic analysis.

Part of the modern Israeli travail began with a Declaration of Independence that both proclaimed the creation of a *Jewish* state and said that there would be no discrimination on account of religion, ethnicity, or sex. The sentiments were noble but promised a number of clashes involving Jewish religious law about sex roles, as well as the preferences to be given Jews with respect to immigration and other privileges. At the time the declaration was drafted, much of the non-Jewish population opposed the creation of Israel and for several years was subject to the formal limitations of a military government in their areas of residence. Against those who assert that Israel exploits the claim of defense to justify repression are records of terrorism from the early years of the twentieth century to the present and promises to eradicate the Jewish country proclaimed by governments and organizations that reject the Middle East peace process. Even now, when economic development and other opportunities have proceeded considerably in the non-Jewish sector, the Declaration of Independence is best viewed as setting forth ideal aspirations rather than clear lines of public policy designed for implementation in the near future.

It may be fair to cite Israel for paying more attention to the majority rule features of democracy than to the provisions of minority rights. If the United States may again be used as a model of comparison, the minority African-American population has only recently achieved equal access to voting rights and even more recently won significant representation in elective and appointive positions in government. While Israel's non-Jewish minority has had longer access to voting opportunities, it lags in access to prestigious appointed positions in administration and the judiciary. On the summary indicators of family incomes and infant health, the non-Jews of Israel do relatively better than African-Americans.

There is no comparable summary for the Israeli Jews who are ultrareligious against those who are secular or antireligious. Spiritual demands, convoluted financial records, and a great deal of hyperbole get in the way of dispassionate research. Each side has gained and each suffers on account of their antagonists. The country endures a *kulturkampf* that is chronic and noisy, but perhaps no more so than in other Western democracies where religion and secularism have battled one another off and on since the Enlightenment moved across Europe in the eighteenth and nineteenth centuries.

A question that remains is, why the severity of charges against Israel—from critics both domestic and foreign—when religious and ethnic conditions are not all that different from countries to which Israel may be compared? Although the comparisons detailed here are limited, they suggest that the religious Jews of Israel do not threaten domestic peace or democratic values more than intensely religious activists in other Western societies. And while Israel's Arab minority enjoys fewer benefits than the Jews, it seems no worse off and perhaps is even better placed than the African-American minority of the United States. Some indicators about the economic situation of Arab cities and towns in Israel and the incomes of Arab families have improved over the most recent decades with respect to those of Jews, whereas a comparable measure of African-American family income indicates a worsening situation relative to American whites.

The noise about Israel may reflect disappointment in the ideals associated with the Bible. The People of the Book have not created a Paradise on Earth, and the failure disappoints many of them as well as others who expected better. The criticism by Jews against other regimes, seen in the incidence of Jews among radicals on several continents, may incite some of their antagonists to criticize the Jewish state. Also to be taken into account is the campaign against Israel by Arab governments and other countries whose governments wish to demonstrate support. European and Third World governments may expect economic or political benefits in exchange for supporting Arab claims against Israel. Israel's victories in the wars of 1948, 1956, and 1967, plus the failure to defeat it in 1973 and its invasion of Lebanon in 1982, provide all that is needed for those who would assert that it is expansionist as well as bankrolled, equipped, and supported politically by the United States in international forums. Leftists in well-to-do countries cannot but participate in the chorus. That equality and democracy are far from Israeli standards in Arab and other Third World countries does not silence the campaign.

7

Ambiguities of the Peace Process

There is nothing more prominent on Israel's agenda than the peace process, and there is nothing more affected by uncertainty, ambiguity, and ambivalence. The importance of the peace process is relatively new. It began formally with a conference in Madrid during 1991 that brought together ranking officials from Israel with representatives of the Palestine Liberation Organization (PLO), Syria, Lebanon, Jordan, Egypt, Saudi Arabia, plus the United States and Russia as joint organizers, and a number of other countries that wanted a piece of Middle Eastern peace. The major breakthrough in the event was the sitting down together, in a public forum, of representatives of Israel, the PLO, Syria, and Saudi Arabia. The proximate cause that allowed such a meeting was the success of the United States in forging a united front with Egypt, Syria, and Saudi Arabia in the Gulf War, and the concern of the United States to exploit the momentum to produce a change in relations between Israel and its neighbors.

The peace that now is at the top of Israel's agenda represents a shift in emphasis from the issue of security that had been Israel's major concern since the 1948 War of Independence. It has often been a time of war in Israel's modern existence, but since 1991 it has been a time of peace. Yet the presence of both war and peace on the same intellectual spectrum appears in the several interruptions of the peace process by violence. Uncertainty about the present and future has alternated with cautious optimism and bursts of euphoria.

During the whole time of peace, neither Israeli nor Palestinian communities have been united in euphoria or optimism. In both camps there are those who see the changes as superficial, or as working against what they perceive as the justice of their national cause. The extremes appear among those Palestinians and Israelis who have killed. Some incidents of violence appear to be the work of individuals expressing their own rage. Some have been carrying out personal acts of revenge for the suffering of acquaintances or family members in earlier episodes. Some violent individuals have been marginal personalities lacking in mental capacity or mental health. But some have been associated with large or small political or religious movements, purposeful and trained in order to perform acts with the strategic goal of frustrating efforts at peace. Since 1991 there have also been statements and actions by Israeli and Palestinian authorities that seem more designed for a time of war than a time of peace.

To describe the period since 1991 as a time of peace is to recognize a prominent theme in a complex mixture. There has been significant movement toward peace between Israel and a Palestine Authority, albeit with delays and outbursts of violence. On the Syrian-Israeli front, the situation since the Madrid conference has been mostly stagnant. And violence continues to be the principal theme in southern Lebanon, where an average of two Israeli soldiers per month have died as a result of small unit engagements with one or another Shi'ite movement, supported to one or another degree by Iran and Syria.

The purpose of this chapter is to illustrate the themes of ambiguity and coping where they have been most prominent. It is not the purpose to condemn one side or another. By emphasizing the ambiguity and coping on both sides of the Israeli-Palestinian divide, the purpose is to show the relevance of ambiguity and coping in a most difficult political situation. As this chapter is being drafted, it is more clearly a time of peace than war between Israel and the Palestinians, but mistrust, mutual recrimination, and violence compete with optimism. Each side accuses the other of violating signed agreements, yet neither side has renounced the agreements it has signed. There may be no better demonstration of the usefulness of ambiguity and coping than a process that has been saturated with them, and that survives despite mutual dissatisfaction. What exists is far from perfect, but it seems better than the alternative of declaring that violence will bring a complete solution to the problem.

We shall not provide a complete history of the Israeli-Palestinian conflict, or the larger Israel-Arab conflict of which it is a part. Nor shall we detail what has occurred since the Madrid conference of 1991, or the signing of the accord between Israel and the PLO in 1993. However, an outline of major events will help in the analysis.

MULTIPLE DISPUTES

The starting point of the Israel-Arab disputes is a matter of contention. The Jews of Israel describe roots in their land that extend back some 4,000 years, and the Arabs claim no less. It is conventional to begin the modern history of Israel-Arab disputes with the onset of secular Jewish migration to Palestine in the 1880s. Older communities of religious Jews already comprised a majority of Jerusalem's population, and there were communities of religious Jews in the towns of Hebron, Safed, and Tiberias. The ethos of homeless Jews with a yearning for their Holy Land had long prompted some Diaspora Jews to migrate. A larger movement began with pogroms in eastern Europe and was turned into a mass movement by the Holocaust and pressures against Jewish communities in Arab lands after Israel gained its independence in 1948. The prospect of an end to the Israel-Arab conflicts has come with the collapse of the Soviet Union. Arab rejectionists of accord with Israel no longer have a major power providing weapons and political support for their attacks on an Israel described as America's neocolonial stooge. And Israel can no longer count on American aid as the Middle Eastern bastion against communism.

Pessimists will insist that the picture remains cloudy. While the Soviet Union is no more, oil-rich extreme states like Iran, Libya, and Iraq can still finance the arming of Arab movements that reject peace. There is no shortage of arms and willing merchants in the former Soviet Union, North Korea, and China.

Basic elements of the Israel-Arab conflict are different religions and cultures, as well as clashing nationalisms. Israelis perceive that many Muslims want no Jewish state in the Middle East, or no Jews who are not subordinate and obsequious with respect to Arab governments and ruling classes. Arabs, for their part, speak in terms of Western neocolonialism in an Arab region, with the Jews of Israel serving as the tools of foreign governments and economic elites. Table 7.1 notes major episodes in the Israel-Arab conflict.

Amidst the verbiage of religion, ethnicity, nationalism, and a resilient Marxism, the concrete issues are land, boundaries, and settlements. Jewish settlements in the territories occupied in the Six-Day War have played a central role since 1967.[1] The 1967 war itself resulted from tensions associated with Arab resistance to Jewish settlement in Palestine beginning in the 1880s, as well as issues left unsettled by wars of Israel's War of Independence in 1948 and the 1956 war when Israel joined with France and Great Britain against Egypt, plus numerous incursions from Arab countries, the killing of Israeli civilians, and Israeli retaliations.[2]

Table 7.1
Chronology of Israel-Arab Conflict

c. 1880	Onset of modern Jewish migration to the Land of Israel, or Palestine, then part of the Ottoman Empire.
1917–1922	Balfour Declaration indicated the support of the United Kingdom for the establishment of a Jewish homeland in the Land of Israel; British conquest of Palestine; and the establishment of a British mandate for Palestine under the authority of the League of Nations.
1947	United Kingdom returned the problem of Palestine to the United Nations after failing to control Arab uprisings against Jews, to satisfy Jewish demands for immigration, or to win acceptance from both sides for a division of the land.
1948	United States decided to divide the British mandate into Jewish and Arab states. The Jews declared their acceptance of the decision and established Israel. Arabs rejected the United Nations decision and invaded Israel. As a result of the war, Israel expanded into parts of what the United Nations had assigned to an Arab state, and Jordan annexed parts of Jerusalem and areas on the West Bank of the Jordan River. The Gaza Strip remained under the control of Egypt, but was not annexed to Egypt.
1967	Six-Day War resulted in Israeli occupation of the Sinai Peninsula, the West Bank, and parts of the Golan Heights.
1977–1982	Signing and implementation of the Israel-Egypt peace treaty, including Israeli withdrawal from the Sinai Peninsula.
1982–?	Israeli war in Lebanon, which peters out with staged Israeli withdrawal and continued occupation of a "security zone" in southern Lebanon.
1987–?	Palestinian *intafada*.
1991	Madrid conference formally begins peace process.
1993	Signing of Israel-PLO accord which provided for continuing negotiations to deal with a number of outstanding problems.
1994	Signing of Israel-Jordan peace treaty.

The setting within Israel in June 1967 was euphoria at the extent of the military victory and optimism with respect to the prospects for a political solution. The war that was launched in the face of Arab threats to liquidate

Israel ended in six days with the Israelis in control of what had been the Egyptian Sinai, the Syrian Golan Heights, the Jordanian West Bank, and the Gaza Strip. Less than a week after the fighting ended, the Israeli Cabinet indicated its willingness to return to the prewar international borders with Egypt and Syria, except for the Gaza Strip. That area had been a chronic source of terror attacks, and the Israeli cabinet decided that it should remain within Israeli control. A quarter century later, it was the Gaza Strip that Israel was most anxious to assign to some other authority. In the case of the Jordanian border, the 1967 cabinet chose to remain silent.[3]

Security and religious issues made the Jordanian border more problematic than the others and kept the several parties in Israel's government coalition from reaching agreement among themselves with respect to the Jordanian border. The entire West Bank was within the biblical Land of Israel. To many religious Jews, it should not be returned to an enemy after being taken in a defensive war. The Old City of Jerusalem with its Western Wall sacred to Judaism had been closed to Jews since 1948. Moreover, the West Bank presented sizable Arab populations close to Jewish cities, and the history of Palestinian attacks against Jewish civilians made the area a security threat.

The Khartoum Declaration of September 1967 became the definitive Arab statement. There would be no negotiations, no peace, and no recognition of Israel. Violent forays against Israeli civilians from Jordan in the years after 1967 and then from Lebanon in the 1970s and 1980s added to Israeli distrust of Arab intentions.

Israel's cabinet alternatively pursued an active policy of establishing Jewish settlements, avoiding an outright proclamation of annexation outside of Jerusalem, and minimizing further settlement activity in the occupied territories. One reason for the lack of clear policy was the impossibility of reaching consensus on the issue within cabinets divided between parties and factions. Some officials hoped that a fluid, undecided situation would permit an appropriate response to an Arab willingness to negotiate. Against outright annexation was the lack of desire to absorb the Arabs living in the territories as part of Israel's citizenry, and the international opposition likely to be provoked by further annexations.

Israel enlarged the boundaries of Jerusalem to include what had been Jordanian East Jerusalem and considerable vacant land in what had been the Jordanian-controlled West Bank. In contrast to other sections of the West Bank, Israel annexed the area added to Jerusalem. More than 130,000 Jews lived in neighborhoods created in these areas by the mid-1990s. Only the government of Israel formally recognized these neighborhoods as part of Jerusalem or as part of Israel.

Jewish settlers initially wanted to establish themselves in the heart of Hebron. A Jewish neighborhood there had been abandoned after a bloody Arab riot in 1929. The city has significance to religious Jews for the Cave of the Patriarchs, the burial place of Abraham, Isaac, Jacob, and their wives. The same cave also has religious significance for Muslims. During the long years of Muslim and British domination, Jews had been denied entry or relegated to a subordinate part of the mosque that was built over the site. The Labor-dominated government that served until 1977 compromised with the settlers and authorized construction of a new settlement called Kiryat Arba, just outside of Hebron. The relations of the Arabs and Jews in and near Hebron have featured Arab violence against Jews and Jewish violence against Arabs.[4]

The elections that occurred in May 1977 were different from previous Israeli elections. For the first time, it would be the nationalist Likud Bloc and not the Labor Alignment that would lead the coalition. The cabinet lifted the ban against private land purchase by Jews in the occupied territories. The new settlement policy emphasized suburbs connected by fast roads to Tel Aviv or Jerusalem instead of small villages with a minimum of urban facilities. The Likud government also gave in to settler demands to establish a Jewish presence in the old Jewish neighborhood close to the center of Hebron.

The 1977–1981 period was a time for making peace with Egypt. However, it was also a time of violence. Lebanon had become the focus of Israeli security concerns. Palestinians who had moved there after a bloody expulsion from Jordan turned Lebanon into a base for attacks against Israel. Israel retaliated periodically and mounted a substantial operation in 1978. Operation Peace for the Galilee, began in June 1982, was a major war. Israeli forces entered Beirut and drove the PLO leadership from the city but soiled their international reputation by being identified with a slaughter of Palestinian civilians carried out by Lebanese Christians. As of this writing, Israeli forces, together with Lebanese mercenary units allied with Israel remain in the extreme south of Lebanon. They engage periodically with Lebanese Shi'ite Muslims, who have now become Israel's greatest security worry in Lebanon.

A wave of violent demonstrations began in Gaza and the West Bank during December 1987 and came to be known as *intafada*. Palestinians blocked roads and threw stones and homemade fire-bombs. The Israeli army greatly increased its patrols by regular and reserve units in the cities and villages of the territories. At various times it employed wooden truncheons, tear gas, rubber or plastic bullets, and lethal gun fire against the demonstrators. Israel also took social and economic measures against the uprising, including periodic denial of entry to Israel, and the closing of Palestinian schools and universities. In December 1993, an Israeli human rights organization reported that 1,095 Palestinians had been killed by Israeli security forces since the onset on *intafada*, 771 Palestinians had been killed by other Palestinians, 109 Israelis had been killed by Palestinians, and 76 Palestinians had been killed by Israeli civilians.[5]

Some Israelis asserted that the security forces were reacting too aggressively to Palestinian demonstrators. Others demanded a more speedy and thorough repression of Palestinian violence. They charged that the government's policy was too moderate, that it was sending ambiguous signals that Palestinians read as Israeli weakness and an encouragement to further rebellion. Some spoke of ending Israel's Palestinian problem by moving the hostile population over the Jordan River or into Lebanon. Some threatened civil war if the Cabinet decided to withdraw from the territories.[6]

The Palestinian uprising dominated the 1988 election campaign. The Labor Party's candidate for prime minister, Shimon Peres, advocated international negotiations in which Israel would be willing to withdraw from parts of the occupied territories in exchange for peace. The Likud Bloc, under the leadership of Yitzhak Shamir, opposed any withdrawals.

The outcomes of the election reflected the close division within the country. Likud barely outpolled Labor, forty seats to thirty-nine. A group of small parties inclined to an alliance with Labor won ten seats.[7] A group of small parties inclined to an alliance with Likud also won ten seats.[8] Religious parties won another eighteen seats. The five seats won by the National Religious Party might be assigned to the Likud side of the controversy about the future of the occupied territories. Yet many of the voters who supported the other religious parties, as well as some of those voting for the National Religious Party, are likely to have cast their ballots for religious issues (e.g., the application of laws governing the Sabbath and kosher food, or financial support for religious education) rather than for occupied territories or international relations.

Israeli politicians responded to the close division of the vote by forming a Government of National Unity with representatives of both Likud and Labor in key positions. As the new government was in the process of formation, the PLO moved in stages to meet what the U.S. government defined as the minimum demands for PLO participation in a peace process. First there was a meeting of the Palestine National Council in Algiers that produced an ambiguous renunciation of terrorism and recognition of Israel, plus a declaration of an independent Palestinian state. The initial American response was to reject the PLO statements as insufficient and to deny a visa to Yassir Arafat that would have allowed him to address the U.N. General Assembly in New York. This forced the General Assembly to sit in Geneva so the PLO chairman could address it. Within a few days, the United States announced its satisfaction with clarifications that Arafat made and initiated its first open and formal discussions with his organization.

Complicating the issue was the refusal of PLO factions to support the policy of settling the dispute with Israel by peaceful means. Armed bands continued to attempt infiltration into Israel with plans to seize civilian hostages. When the mayor of Bethlehem suggested ending the *intafada* as an expression of good faith, Yassir Arafat threatened to kill him.

The leaders of both major Israeli parties refused to accept the PLO's new statements and insisted that the organization was still committed to terrorism. Labor leader Shimon Peres, who became minister of finance in the new government, left open the prospect of changing his position. A number of Israelis indicated that the PLO's statements merited a more serious response and demanded that their government begin talks with that organization. The Labor Party left the government coalition in 1990, and the Likud minister of housing and construction began a new wave of expanding Jewish settlements. After the 1991 Gulf War, U.S. Secretary of State James Baker prodded Israel, Jordan, the Palestinians, Syria, and Lebanon to begin negotiations.

The results of Israel's 1992 elections were not a dramatic victory for one perspective or another. Likud and right-of-center parties won forty-nine seats in the Knesset, Labor and the left-of-center Meretz parties won fifty-six seats, Jewish religious parties without clear postures on territorial issues won ten seats, and Arab-dominated parties won five seats. However, the government that emerged from parliamentary negotiations was much different from its predecessor. Yitzhak Rabin put together a coalition of Labor plus Meretz, with off-and-on participation by the Sephardi religious party SHAS, plus amorphous commitments from the Jewish religious party Torah Judaism and Arab parties. With a central theme to emphasize the peace process, the new government achieved an accord with the PLO in its first year and a peace treaty with Jordan in its second year.

The 1996 election operated for the first time with Israeli voters casting two ballots: one for the direct selection of the prime minister, and one for a party list of Knesset members. The election produced a narrow victory for Likud's candidate for prime minister, Benjamin Netanyahu. His campaign rhetoric and his statements as prime minister signaled another change in Israel's relations with its neighbors. He emphasized the increase in Israeli casualties from terrorism after Israel signed an accord with the PLO in 1993 and promised to elevate Israeli security in contrast to the emphasis on accommodation by the Labor government. He asserted that he would not divide Jerusalem or allow the Palestinians to create their capital in the city and that he would not accede to Syrian demands for a complete withdrawal from the Golan Heights. The Palestine Authority and Arab governments charged that Netanyahu was abandoning the principle of returning land for peace and that he was endangering the entire peace process.

As of 1997, between 145,000 and more than 300,000 Jews were living on what others persisted in calling Arab land. The exclusion or inclusion of the Jerusalem neighborhoods in the estimates produces, respectively, the lower or higher figure.[9] Israeli security forces have been able to ensure these Jews a fair measure of physical security. Yet the domestic and international controversies that rage about their homes deprive them of quiet certainty as to their future.

AMBIGUITIES

The environment has been charged with enough emotion to affect even simple features of discourse. Should territory at issue be labeled "conquered," "seized," "occupied," or "administered"? Should places be named according to the ancient Hebrew terms of Yehuda and Shomron (Judea and Samaria), which are favorites of the Israeli right wing; Palestine as preferred by Arabs; or the more neutral West Bank (i.e., the geographical designation as the west bank of the Jordan River)?[10]

There are contrasting pressures on negotiators for each side. May Israelis raise issues of prior Arab aggression in order to justify the actions of Israeli security forces and the construction of settlements for Jews? May Arabs recall that Israelis expelled Arab villagers during the wars of 1948 and 1967 and that Israel has generally refused permission for Palestinian refugees from those wars to return to their homes? It may be necessary to avoid each of these questions in order to move forward with negotiations. Dissatisfied Israelis and Palestinians continue to demand more justice and thereby endanger the achievements represented by signed agreements.

Ambiguities reflect a viewer's perspective. What one person sees as clear, another can see as imprecise. Many Israelis see the present as clear and fixed. They are willing to accept the past and negotiate from the present. However, many Palestinians see past actions as unsettled and demand a return to settlement patterns of 1967, 1948, or even earlier. Each side sees ambiguities in the expressions and actions of the other. Each accuses the other of violating written agreements or the spirit of the agreements. (While it is conventional to speak about the "spirit" of an agreement, that concept ensures ambiguity and questions the words of a written accord.)

It is helpful to array ambiguities perceived by Israelis and Palestinians separately, even though there are considerable overlaps. That is, elements of each national community share some perceptions that are prominent in the other. Leaders of both nations have achieved one of the conditions for successful negotiations: that is, they understand the perspectives of the other. The portrayals that follow are, to some extent, stereotypes presented for purposes of analytic simplicity. They overlook the complexities in each community. We should recall that the peace process has been successful in large measure despite continued dispute about what has been accomplished and what remains to be done.

Israeli Perceptions of Ambiguity

Israelis worry about the intentions of the Palestinians. While it is clear that many Palestinians accept the idea of living in peace with Israel, many of these also expect an Israeli pullback to the lines of 1967 and substantial concessions within lands occupied since 1948. It is not clear what the Palestinian leadership is willing to accept. Israelis are impressed favorably by what seem to be an increasing incidence of articulate Palestinians who speak about peace, often in Hebrew, which some of them learned while in Israeli detention.

While some Palestinians speak about their regime as a democracy, or aspire to a democracy, that is an ambiguity that Israelis are willing to accept. Israelis seem to view with dispassion reports describing the authoritarianism within the Palestine Authority and the violence that officials use against Palestinians who criticize their regime. Israelis worry more when Palestinian authorities encourage or tolerate the killing of Palestinians who have sold land to Jews or cooperated in other ways with Israel. Israelis also do not know what concessions to Israeli demands the Palestinian leadership is willing or able to impose on its population. Adding to the ambiguities that Israelis do not appreciate are statements from ranking Palestinians about compensation for the lands taken in 1948 and demands for a Palestinian Jerusalem that will be their national capital.

Some of these uncertainties are natural in any negotiations. Each side guards its plans and the details of the ultimate concessions it will make, and expects the same from its antagonist. Indeed, each side may not define its ultimate terms but allow them to emerge during the process of negotiations. Or each may work with flexible scenarios, with the extent of its concessions on territories, for example, dependent on the other side's concessions on another dimension, such as financial arrangements, water, commerce, commitments about security, or cooperation in international forums.

The most worrying signs are those cases of violence that are encouraged or tolerated by the Palestinian leadership. They provoke questions as to whether there might be a reasonable measure of peace at the end of the process or just a series of Israeli concessions against a bottomless pit of Palestinian demands, with the Palestinian leadership returning to violence at each pause in Israeli concessions.

Palestinian Perceptions of Ambiguity

Palestinians see ambiguities in Israeli expressions and actions that parallel the ambiguities perceived by Israelis in Palestinian expressions and actions. Israelis talk peace but continue taking land that Palestinians claim as their own and expanding Jewish settlements in the area whose future is still the subject of negotiations. Even left-of-center secular Israelis seem to adhere to the outlines of the plan conceived after the Six-Day War by the late Minister of Foreign Affairs Yigal Alon, according to which Israel must maintain control over the Jordan Valley and points of access between the Valley and Israeli centers of population. Palestinians have learned a great deal about the workings of Israeli democracy, but they do not know any more than the Israelis about the influence wielded by Jewish settlers and other religious Zionists who seem intent on maintaining control over what the Jews describe as the Land of Israel.

Palestinians aspire to a state, but they are not sure that the Israeli government will make that concession. And they are not sure what kind of state they can expect. Even left-of-center Israelis who have accepted the idea of a Palestinian state have spoken of severe limits on the armaments that such a state can acquire and an Israeli veto over the international alliances that such a state can enter. Israelis are concerned that the future Palestine not enter alliances that might act against Israel militarily. In such statements by Israelis who view themselves as accommodationists, Palestinians see insulting limitations on their as-yet-to-be-achieved national sovereignty.

Ambiguities that Israelis Perceive in the Expressions and Actions of Their Own Government

Prominent among the overlaps between Israeli and Palestinian perceptions of ambiguity is the lack of clarity that Israelis see in the expressions and actions of their own government. This is a topic that exposes the multiple ambiguities of democratic politics. While left-of-center Israelis criticize their government's failure to make more concessions to the Palestinians, right-of-center Israelis wonder why there have been so many concessions and why Israel has not been more forceful in dealing with Palestinian violence.

The government of Prime Minister Benjamin Netanyahu represented the ambivalence that Israelis as well as Palestinians perceive. Some blamed Netanyahu himself, and it may be correct to conclude that a clumsiness in several aspects of his administration affected the peace process. Commentators with an inclination to be generous toward the prime minister note that his behavior may have reflected a lack of experience. Unlike most previous prime ministers, he did not climb slowly through the ranks of governmental activity but moved quickly and reached the prime minister's office without having a previous position that trained him in administration close to the summit of policymaking. Within a year after becoming prime minister, Netanyahu's actions had caused two long-time Likud activists to resign ministerial positions and to join other Likud members of the Knesset in denouncing the prime minister as untrustworthy.

The ambiguity about the peace process began before the election of 1996. While Yitzhak Rabin was still prime minister, then after his assassination when Shimon Peres was prime minister, the Israeli government reacted strongly to an escalation of violence in southern Lebanon and to a series of suicide bombings carried out by Palestinians in Israel. In southern Lebanon Israel responded with an operation called Grapes of Wrath that involved extensive bombardments and caused thousands of Lebanese to flee their homes. Israel responded to the suicide bombings by closing itself to access by Palestinian workers from Gaza and the West Bank and increasing the use of foreign workers from the Balkans and the Far East. The result was to deepen the economic hardship that already marked the areas controlled by the Palestine Authority. A number of Israeli Arabs viewed Grapes of Wrath and the closures as overreactions to violence and withheld their votes from Peres's candidacy as prime minister. Their actions provided an example for our argument against political activity that is thoroughgoing in its pursuit of ideal solutions. In rejecting Peres because he did not meet all their requirements, Israeli Arabs who withheld their votes helped to elect a government that was even less inclined toward the Palestinian cause.

Netanyahu campaigned against the accommodations that the Rabin-Peres government had made to the Palestinians. He waffled with respect to his acceptance of the 1993 agreement developed at Oslo and signed in Washington, but he eventually indicated that he would accept the steps already taken by Israel. However, other Knesset members of his Likud Party, as well as leading members of parties that joined his coalition, continued to express the view that the Oslo accords were not legitimate.

Israelis argue about whether the Netanyahu government made a difference with respect to the peace process. After taking the difficult step of agreeing to deal with the PLO, Rabin and Peres took the easiest steps. They transferred to the Palestinians areas that were centers of Palestinian population with no Jewish settlements. They fell behind the agreed timetable for transferring to the Palestinians the problematic city of Hebron with its Jewish neighborhood and history of Arab-Jewish enmity, and they did not implement the secure land route for Palestinian traffic between Gaza and the West Bank.

Under both Peres and Netanyahu, Palestinian security forces were allowed to operate in the Palestinian sectors of Hebron, and Israeli security forces concentrated their activities in protecting the Jewish neighborhood. After several months in office, Netanyahu took the formal step of transferring control of the non-Jewish areas of Hebron to the Palestine Authority. Palestinians and many Israelis blamed Netanyahu for problems in the peace process. They point to renewed building in Jewish settlements and the beginning of a new Jewish neighborhood in an area of Jerusalem said to be Arab. Netanyahu's supporters say that Jewish settlements continued to expand under the previous Labor government. The prime minister's opponents on the Israeli right wing accused him and his ministers of not doing enough to develop the settlements.

At the transition between the Netanyahu and Barak governments, Israel and Syria had not resumed formal contacts that were suspended during the Peres administration. The two sides disagreed as to whether substantial progress had been made earlier: whether Israel had agreed to a substantial or complete withdrawal from the Golan Heights, and what Syria was willing to promise in return.

COPING WITH OUR NEIGHBORS AND OURSELVES

There is no final solution in sight for the conflict between Israel and the Palestinians. There is low-level, chronic violence, with substantial complaints from both Palestinians and Israelis about the other. The problem of Jerusalem, ostensibly the most sensitive, has not yet reached the point of formal discussions. Israelis themselves did not decide clearly in the elections of 1988, 1992, or 1996 on the course they wanted to take. There is no sign that the 1999 election will have an outcome that is strikingly more clear.

While there is no final peace, there is also no war. Casualties are unpleasant, but the danger is at the level of individuals and the families of victims. Currently there is no overt threat to the survival of either the Jewish or the Palestinian people. Readers in North America and Europe might not sense the importance of the difference between no peace and no threat to national survival. However, it is crucial for Israelis with memories of the Holocaust and the wars of 1948, 1967, and 1973. Disturbing this optimism are persistent reports about Iran's pursuit of nuclear weapons and long-range missiles, and Syria's armament with chemical weapons plus missiles that can strike Israeli cities.

Palestinians suffer no less than Israelis from the current situation. Palestinians and Israelis would also share suffering if the two nations embarked on an all-out campaign to settle the issues once and for all time, and to achieve the justice denied them by obfuscating politicians. Israelis learned the frustrations of seeking complete solutions in Lebanon during the 1982–1985 period of heavy military involvement and heavy losses. Palestinians had a similar lesson at the same time. While Israel did not solve its northern problem, its military inflicted profound losses on the Palestinian areas that had been the source of terror attacks. Another Palestinian lesson about the futility of violence may have come with the *intafada*. While that spurt of violence may have exhausted the Israelis and won the beginning of a peace process, it also cost the Palestinians heavily in lives lost, as well as in schooling that was denied a generation of students by the closure of institutions and economic decline caused by workers denied access to Israel. Now the Palestinians have an Authority that might become a state. However, each spurt of violence has resulted in the further shrinking of labor opportunities in Israel. The economic record of Palestine to date has been one of annual *declines* in gross national product.

What to some appear to be ambiguities in relations between Israel and the Palestinians may be the evolution of informal rules of the game. Each side appears to tolerate certain violations of the written agreement, even though protests may be made when they are revealed. Israel appears to accept a certain level of governmental activity in the Palestinians' Orient House, even though it compromises the Israeli insistence that Jerusalem will be the capital of Israel alone. Israel also tolerates the presence of Palestinian security forces in Arab sections of Jerusalem. An article in a Jerusalem newspaper expressed the ambiguity of policing with headlines that described "Joint Patrols [almost] of the [Israeli] Border Police and the PLO in the Eastern Part of the City" and "Full Coexistence Even if Not a Formal Coordination."[11] Israeli undercover forces have also operated in areas presumably assigned to the Palestinians. The operatives of each side have seized individuals in the jurisdiction territory of the other and carried them off to their own territory.[12] An article in the prestigious newspaper, *Ha'aretz*, cited an Israeli government report that Palestinian security forces "kidnapped" 39 individuals from Jerusalem in 1997 and 21 in 1998, and that they "arrested" 89 persons in Jerusalem during 1997 and 50 in 1998.[13]

Other actions are no less perplexing. Ranking leaders of each side alternately express sentiments that sound aggressive and conciliatory. The Municipality of Jerusalem and the Israeli national government agreed to move forward with the construction of a new Jewish neighborhood on one site said to be Arab land (Har Homa), but work has moved sporadically in response to protests from Palestinians, international sources, and Israeli opponents of the project.

Prime Minister Netanyahu was the target of scathing criticism from ranking members of his own party. Accusations that he practiced duplicity and dissimulation were polite ways of saying that he lies, that he hides his real intentions behind artful ways of seeming to agree with all sides, or that he is simply an opportunist without any firm intentions.

Perhaps there is a message in these criticisms for the theme of this book. Netanyahu's avoidance of straightforward openness and honesty may have reflected the contrary demands upon him. On the one hand Palestinians and their Arab supporters demanded further concessions of territory. Not always clear messages from high U.S. officials seemed to support those demands. Numerous Israelis agreed. They saw promise in a continued implementation of the Oslo Accords. Yet other Israelis, among them leading figures in the blocs that support Netanyahu, opposed any further concessions of territory to a Palestinian Authority that they equate with terrorism.

We can speculate as to how Netanyahu coped with the contrasting demands:

- Avoid laying out a clear set of intentions.
- Keep options open.
- Try to avoid an open break with any of the forces that are threatening hostility, violence, or a withdrawal of support.

The agreement hammered out during a nine-day seige of negotiations at Wye Plantation, Maryland, in October 1998, provides its own lessons about ambiguity and coping. Critics of the agreement were quick to point out that it did little more than reaffirm the Oslo Accords of 1993. Why was it necessary to agree to what had already been agreed upon? The answer is that both sides had found it convenient to violate important provisions of the earlier agreement. Each could claim it was not fulfilling its promises in order to withhold benefits from antagonists who were not fulfilling their promises. Who was the greater violator? The question could not be answered with mutual satisfaction due to the ambiguities of multiple provisions, each dealing with different normative values. The Palestinians had not done what they could in stamping out rejectionists of peace and their terrorist organizations. The result was violence and a greater incidence of death and injury among Israelis than before the Oslo accords. Israelis had not provided the

Palestinians with easy access between the various parts of the territory ceded to them, had sharply limited the access of Palestinian workers to Israel, and taken other steps to limit Palestinian economic opportunities.

The *Washington Post* headlined one report about the Wye Plantation agreement, "Clinton Ambiguity Proves a Strength." It referred to a dispute as to whether the president had promised to release Israeli spy Jonathan Pollard as part of the agreement. The *Post*'s description of the issue illustrates the utility of ambiguity in moving negotiations forward, as well as the dangers of misleading partners who might be intense about the issue at stake.

President Clinton had not exactly said yes, but he had not decisively said no. As the Wye River peace summit reached its closing hours Friday, Clinton's bottom line was shrouded in ambiguity. It was not clear until the end whether this haze of language and intentions would ruin the day—or save it. . . .

Israeli officials maintained afterward that Clinton had clearly left the impression Thursday that he was willing to release Pollard immediately. U.S. officials insisted that Clinton told Netanyahu this was not the case. But one Clinton adviser acknowledged that Clinton had been encouraging enough about the Pollard case in a vague way that the Israelis could have heard a pledge that was never precisely made. . . .

The Monica S. Lewinsky controversy, in the view of Clinton critics, has revealed the president as a rhetorical contortionist who often misleads as he tells people what he thinks they need to hear. At Wye River, however, participants said Clinton's ability to soften the edges of disputes with his personal presence and to recast old issues in new language helped the parties narrow their gaps at critical moments.[14]

Immediately after the ceremonial signing of yet another round of agreements that looked much like their predecessors, optimists expressed the hope that these provisions would hold more firmly. The new agreements included several provisions to specify more concretely the commitments of both parties and put into place mechanisms to monitor compliance. Pessimists had trouble overlooking the continued existence of Palestinians committed to violence, and Israelis pledged to expand Jewish settlements in what remained under Israeli control of the disputed territory. Representatives of both sides proclaimed contrary and confusing interpretations of what was agreed upon. Some of this seemed directed at soothing opposition within the speaker's camp. But it also portended difficulties for anyone who expected smooth implementation.[15]

The ambiguous peace process has a dual message. On the one hand, unfulfilled promises wound both national communities. On the other hand, neither national leadership has abandoned it. Imperfect peace is desirable over war. Optimism may be unwarranted. An explosion may result from the frustration of Palestinians or Jewish settlers, or from the response of the Israeli military to Palestinian violence.

FINALITY, LIKE CONSISTENCY, IS THE PREOCCUPATION OF SMALL MINDS

The peace process involving Israelis, Palestinians, and other Arabs illustrates the utility of ambiguity in a condition of high drama. There are few more prominent challenges to policymakers than bringing peace to the Holy Land after so many years of bloodshed. The process underway does not promise clear and final victories for the peacemakers. Palestinian and Jewish extremists are likely to feel cheated by whatever is agreed to, and some of each may use violence in the hope of keeping the door open to a more complete victory. Yet the very fact that the peace will not be final renders it more humane. The intermingling of Israeli and Palestinian settlements and neighborhoods diminishes any prospects of clear separation between potentially hostile populations. Israel's need for labor and Palestinians' need for work will insure daily commuting. The especially intense problems of Jerusalem may be dealt with, as at present, by unstated autonomy. Palestinian authorities cannot concede Israel's control over the entire city, and Israeli authorities have little desire to settle disputes involving Palestinians. The result is the Palestine Authority's involvement in East Jerusalem, without Israeli officials openly conceding the point.

The Israeli-Palestinian disputes are not the only cases of muddled no peace–no war. The ambiguous relationships involving mainland China, Taiwan, the United States, and other countries is another model of how to avoid disaster by living with unresolved problems. Governments in both Beijing and Taipei officially ascribe to a fiction that they are responsible for all of China. The mainland government says that it would not tolerate a Taiwan that declares its independence, and Taiwan has so far avoided that provocation. A result is that the United States and some other countries parse their relationships so that they have official diplomats on the mainland but only trade missions on Taiwan. Yet the United States continues to commit itself to the defense of Taiwan. Both Beijing and Taipei authorities have invested considerably in militaries ostensibly concerned with the other China. Neither recognizes the other officially, but there have been on-again off-again negotiations involving high-level officials. There are programs that allow visits and substantial investments by Taiwanese on the mainland. One straw in the wind is that Taiwanese authorities will accept reunion when the mainland becomes democratic. But an opposing theme is that a democratic China, based on the mainland, is at least several generations in the future. Cynics can say that democracy will solve the problem of two Chinas about the time that an agreed-upon messiah will solve the problems of the Holy Land.

It is not only the dramatically insoluble issues that invite ambiguities. Even the pedestrian details of managing orderly societies demand a bit of fudging. Legislators and chief executives who are political rivals usually squabble over the details of the government budget. Over the years they have devised routine evasions of clear solutions that allow all sides to claim some victory. They are more subtle than demanded by the ideal norms of management, but they allow government to proceed. One study of budgeting described the tactics in the following terms. A reader interested in the details can consult the citation in the notes. The names of the tactics provide us with enough indication that the intention is to produce what might be called acceptable deception.

- cut the popular programs
- cut the less visible items
- alter the form
- shift the blame
- when cuts mean increases
- inch ahead with existing programs
- the wedge or camel's nose
- just for now
- so small
- look, no hands
- spend to save

What is common to these labels, and the tactics they denote, is a continuing effort to obfuscate, to hide what is really about to occur in government spending, or to label X as Y.[16]

The editorial writers of the *Washington Post* winked at one set of arrangements they titled, "Cheating Around the Edges."[17]

One hallowed way of getting around the rules is to declare an expenditure an emergency, which means it doesn't count against the normal caps. . . . Timing changes are another way of avoiding the rules. You mask the cost of a program by postponing it. . . . A third alternative is simply to look the other way. A proposal to sweeten military pensions would be financed by such blinking, as would a proposal to let the states keep the full amounts that they recover from tobacco companies for past tobacco-related Medicaid expenditures, even though the feds are by law entitled to roughly half.

Yet other examples of cheating around the edges are the flexibility granted to traffic police and tax inspectors who find it easiest to allow a bit of leeway to violators, and the daily shortcuts in the workplace that facilitate interactions. Sanctions called "work to rule" indicate that improprieties may benefit the organization as well as the employee. A threat to work according to the book may bring the bosses to their knees.

Political disputes and public policies are not the only place where one finds incomplete agreements imperfectly implemented. Private individuals and business firms change their minds after they agree to deals, and interpret their commitments to suit their needs. If the world was orderly and agreements were sacred, there would be far less work for attorneys and courts.

If Social Science Is Ambiguous, Can Governance Be Different?

There is no room for final solutions or higher principles when democratic polities decide about divisive issues. Both final solutions and higher principles demand too much from policymakers and are likely to harm citizens. Politics is a happy science, and it is also a messy science. Those who object to the term "science" can substitute "art" or "skill" in the previous sentence. When arguments are intense and the population closely divided, democratic policymakers are not likely to decide clearly about the best policy alternatives for the least cost. There are too many irreconcilable disputes about what is good and too many complications in defining benefits and costs. A democratic polity does not, in practice, aspire to agreement about such issues. More important is deciding with a minimum of friction. For this, coping mechanisms of accommodation, indirection, improvisation, avoidance, and above all ambiguity are appropriate tools of governance.

It is by no means the case that all who aspire to rational decisions are fascists or authoritarian. Many well-meaning democrats want their governments to take everything into consideration when making policy decisions, to choose the alternative that is most efficient, is most cost-effective, and provides the greatest benefits to the greatest number. However, it is impossible to achieve these criteria in the case of issues mired in serious dispute. "The final solution" was a slogan for the ugliest of policies pursued by a regime that elevated discipline and the national interest to the highest of values. By ridding itself of the Jews and other undesirables, the Nazi regime claimed that it would put right the German economy and society that were troubled by an array of problems having little to do with the Jews or other minorities. The duplicity and horrors associated with the final solution suggest that while the coping, ambiguity, and related messiness of democracy are problematic, they are of human dimension and more likely to be humane than aspirations to deal with a society's problems once and for all time.

The argument of this chapter is that ambiguity also appears prominently in fields of social science that aspire to precision and exactitude. The irony is that the work claiming to be most exact is often too complicated to produce findings that are clear and useful to policymakers. If social science is ambiguous, can governance be different?

In order to develop this argument, we adopt a historical perspective on a wide conception of what is now called *policy analysis*. Policy analysis is concerned with appraising social conditions that might become the object of public action and assessing the costs and effects of proposed and ongoing public activities. Included within this are cost-benefit analysis; program evaluation; audit reports that assess governmental activities with respect to the values of effectiveness, economy, efficiency, and equity; plus assessments of regime traits likely to impinge on policy (e.g., widespread corruption).

There are numerous varieties and perspectives of policy analysis,[1] as well as claims asserted for each.[2] Our inclusive view of policy analysis has advantages to compensate for whatever nuances it overlooks. It permits comparisons of many activities over a long time span in different contexts and a consideration of what may be the outer limits of policy analysis.

The historical perspective differs from a history of policy analysis. The concern here is not to represent all historical periods and types of policy analysis, but to establish the longevity and multifaceted character of the activities involved and to identify policy-relevant implications of prominent varieties. The survey illustrates ancient concerns with the character of government and skips to modern developments that began with the collection and analysis of statistics pertaining to economic and social conditions. Our critical review cites works that seem to have been concerned with shaping public policies in certain directions but that have been used to justify other policies. It also considers researchers who have lessened their own effectiveness by specifying their limited usefulness or whose work has been so complex as to have lent itself to numerous and different interpretations. It also considers works of literature, journalism, and social commentary that have been relevant for public policy, as well as research done by social scientists, *per se*.

The implicit question is: Have the gains from increasing sophistication been worth the effort? The answer is positive, but not entirely so. Some of the most sophisticated analyses seem to be inherently limited in realizing their aspirations to affect policy. The record suggests that their influence is more likely to be intellectual than operational. They produce an understanding of how social processes operate more than they support a selection of policy alternatives. Of greater policy utility may be studies that are simple conceptually and methodologically but that describe extreme conditions that demand public response. Their authors choose targets with a daring to go beyond issues that are conventional, but with a care not to depart from the imprecisely defined range of acceptable reform.

The implication of this chapter is that traits of policy analysis and policy-making operate parallel to one another. Both are affected by complexities that hinder the application of simple solutions for difficult problems. Both aspire to clarity, but usually remain ambiguous.

POINTS IN THE HISTORICAL RECORD

Early varieties of what we may call policy analysis are apparent in the Hebrew Bible. The Books of Samuel, Kings, and Chronicles detail the successes and failings of monarchies over a span of some 500 years. Assessments reflect criteria of acting wisely, military and political success, personal stability, regime maintenance, as well as doctrinal correctness. The Books of Amos, Hosea, Isaiah, and Nehemiah criticize authorities and economic elites for a lack of justice shown to those who cannot look after themselves. The Book of Jeremiah details the failings of several kings at a crucial stage of Israelite history, not only for injustice and heresy, but also for the problems inherent in a foreign policy that tilted toward Egypt rather than Babylon. The skepticism that appears throughout the Book of Ecclesiastes has public administration as one of its targets. "If you witness in some province the oppression of the poor and the denial of right and justice, do not be surprised at what goes on. . . ."[3]

The problems of policy analysts also appear in the Hebrew Bible. While the Israelite regimes were notable for allowing some prophets to criticize the economic and political elites, the Bible describes the prophets' lack of influence. A typical scenario is severe criticism by a prophet and a continuation of the activity that is criticized, until a great destruction occurs that is identified as the punishment wrought by the Lord against a regime that did not listen to the prophet.

We could fill the premodern period of policy analysis with further discussions of numerous commentators from various periods and locales. Aristotle and Plutarch dealt with the traits of regimes and styles of governance; Thucydides with the precursors, the conduct and results of war; Josephus with the causes and consequences of civil strife; St. Augustine with regime decay. Machiavelli advised how a ruling elite should look after its own power and the welfare of its population; Montesquieu assessed features most likely to assure liberty; and Adam Smith and Edmund Burke made detailed criticisms of mercantile policies. Burke's pleas for the interests of North American colonists must also be put in the same category with policy analyses that did not succeed in overcoming interests of greater political saliency. His speech to the electors of Bristol in 1774 is a landmark of pragmatic reasoning and a plea for moderation, but the British government and the American colonies continued on their fateful courses.[4]

There were numerous developments in the eighteenth and nineteenth centuries with respect to the collection and analysis of statistics relevant to social and economic issues. Items in the British experience include:

- criminal data collected to establish patterns of crime, their cause, and appropriate policies;
- the recording of births, deaths, and marriages designed to estimate population growth relevant to food supplies and to meet the concern of insurance societies for actuarial information;
- information on education collected as part of what was termed moral statistics, sometimes mixed with records about the incidence of Bibles, church attendance, and flower growing, and linked to poverty, disease, crime, and illegitimacy;
- records of diet, climate, and work collected in order to reduce the noncombat deaths of soldiers and sailors.

Researchers working with this information were sensitive to problems about cause and effect or the lack of symmetry between correlation and cause, and they controlled primary relationships for elements such as age, season, sex, and location.

Data collection and analysis were not free of patronage and sacred cows. Cause of death was added to official record keeping partly to provide positions for physicians, and the Anglican Church blocked for a time the registration of births, deaths, and marriages by civil authorities. Among the accomplishments linked to statistical analyses were sharp reductions in the incidence of death among British naval personnel: from one death out of eight personnel in 1779, to one in thirty-two in 1811, and one in seventy-two in 1830–1836.[5]

Upton Sinclair's *The Jungle* (1906) is prominent among the many examples of fiction that have dealt with issues of public policy. Sinclair's novel also illustrates the lack of fit between the most prominent focus of a work and its policy impact. Sinclair's novel is credited with advancing the case of food inspection, but the filth of packing houses was only the background for a novel whose primary concern was social conditions. "Ah, God, the horror of it, the monstrous, hideous, demoniacal wickedness of it! He and his family, helpless women and children, struggling to live, ignorant and defenseless. . . ."[6] America might have eaten more hygienic sausages as a result of Sinclair's book, but the workers in packinghouses and other industries did not so readily achieve safer working conditions, better housing, or programs of health and income security.

Journalists and popular commentators may be the most prolific suppliers of material to the public's agenda of policy discussion. Lincoln Steffens's *The Shame of the Cities* (1906) did as much as any other volume to advance the causes of election and civil service reform. The strength of such work lies in the exposure of horrible cases. No sophisticated methodology is necessary, beyond an author's capacity to describe conditions that contrast sharply with popular norms. When Steffens wandered into more complicated issues, the public was disinterested or hostile. His commentary on the biblical Joseph and Moses, which lionized Lenin and the Russian revolution (*Moses in Red*, 1923), had limited impact on Western intellectuals and may have isolated Steffens as a writer who had left the reservation of acceptable discourse.[7]

Good description can expose excessive subtlety as well as gross shame. A book about the muddled statements and actions of the U.S. Government toward the Panamanian strongman Manuel Noriega depicts the complexity of a policy machine with too many heads and too many goals to offer a clear statement of intent. The same quotation reminds us about the ambiguity in politics that is at the core of this book. "U.S. officials began incorporating a new anti-Noriega line in press briefings. They gave a stiffer spin to a semitough speech by Assistant Secretary Elliott Abrams. . . . Abrams . . . did not mention Noriega by name, but the briefers called the speech the 'strongest' and 'harshest' signal to date of Washington's growing 'impatience.'[8] According to the book quoted here, an important element in the ambivalent relationship between the U.S. Government and Manuel Noriega was a clash in values and assessments within the U.S. Government: between an appreciation of Noriega's help with United States activities with respect to Nicaragua and recognition of his control over Panama on the one hand, and frustration at his drug trafficking and human rights abuses. Among the lessons of the book being quoted are that the subtleties in ambiguous messages are not likely to be perceived by their targets in the ways intended by those who send the messages (in this case Noriega) and may even be misperceived by the various elements in the government that produces them (in this case the United States).

THE OUTER REACHES OF POLICY ANALYSIS: JAMES S. COLEMAN AND OTHERS

The outer reaches of policy analysis are those studies that venture beyond description and into systematic efforts to explain or to demonstrate relationships between variables that serve as proximates for cause and effect with respect to social problems or public policies. The nature of the work requires assumptions of how the social system operates and choices from a variety of measurements and statistical techniques. Insofar as the analysis is likely to be costly, it is also necessary to select time frames, locales, and populations to represent larger entities. The sum of the choices made, and those foregone, provides skeptics ample opportunity to cast doubt on the findings and to limit their impact on policy. The points can be illustrated with the record of projects dealing with the factors related to educational achievement, linkages between guaranteed income and work incentives, plus the reports of one of the most sophisticated units that assesses government programs, the U.S. General Accounting Office.

On Educational Achievement

Published in 1966, *Equality of Educational Opportunity* was the product of a team financed by the U.S. Government and headed by James S. Coleman.[9] It examined numerous measures likely to be linked with racial integration and educational achievement in various regions of the United States. The study probed interactions among traits of schools, teachers, pupils, and families in surveys that accumulated almost 650,000 questionnaires. Its findings dealt directly with several issues of political sensitivity: linkages between race, class, the qualitative traits of schools and teachers, and school achievement. Prominent findings included the following:

- race, *per se*, seems less important for pupils' achievement than region or residence in an urban or rural locale;
- race and social class segregation in school magnifies the disadvantages of minorities;
- several widely used indicators of school quality (e.g., expenditures per pupil, credentials of teachers, class size) do not show strong relationships with measures of pupil achievement; and
- stronger relationships with measures of pupil achievement are shown by educational achievements of parents and attitudes toward education shown by student peers.

Coleman's report suffered both from the pressures of policymaking and the criticism of fellow social scientists. The Johnson administration issued a summary of findings which emphasized those points that bolstered support for its policy of integration. The Nixon administration, in contrast, soft-pedaled the report's findings that could be read to support integration and championed implications for its policy of cutting education expenditures.[10]

Despite its extent and expense, Coleman's project did not do enough to avoid all the potential faults. It was a gold mine for the academic industry and stimulated the production of numerous reanalyses and anthologies of commentary.[11] Critics assert that Coleman's project:

- did not test for extreme differences in school qualities;

- was a one-time, cross-sectional analysis;

- was limited in its capacity to expose the ways that various measures of school quality or family traits might affect educational achievement; and

- did not test for the possibility that while total expenditures might not affect achievement as measured by cognitive tests, the right mix of budget items might teach skills to many children that enable them to live richer lives.

Scholars also criticized Coleman's choice of statistical analysis, as well as his lack of theory. The lack of theory means that Coleman did not fully specify how each independent variable was expected to work on his dependent variables. As a result, a relationship could really be the opposite of what he concluded. High personal efficacy, for example, might be caused by achievement rather than achievement caused by high personal efficacy.[12] Coleman answered that his study was explorative and open to findings that could then guide theory. If the theory was complete, he wrote, there would be no need for the research.[13]

Coleman's response is technically correct but also points to an inherent problem in policy analysis with sophisticated aspirations. The findings cannot possibly define once and for all time the relationships between potentially relevant variables. One or another critic or skeptic is likely to assert that some other variable, measurement, population sample, statistical analysis, theoretical perspective, or time period might indicate different conclusions and support for different policy options.

On Work Incentives

Responses similar to those given Coleman's analysis were offered to an experiment designed to test the impact of guaranteed income on work incentives.[14] The U.S. Office of Economic Opportunity financed the project.

It involved outlays of $8 million, 1,300 families, and a time frame of three years. None of that was enough to satisfy sophisticated critics. They indicated that:

- a different combination of tax rates and income definitions, as well as a longer experiment, may have produced other findings;

- the temporary nature of the experiment may have affected the behavior of participants;

- limited samples and an emphasis on economists in the research team limited the utility of the experiment to shed light on noneconomic behaviors;

- the results may have been limited by the social conditions and the cultures of the communities investigated;

- changes in welfare provisions applicable to nonparticipants during the experiment may have affected calculations and behaviors of participants; and

- subsequent changes in welfare provisions may limit the application of the findings.

As in the case of the Coleman Report, the politics of policymaking also affected the impact of the income study. The findings did not find marked declines in work incentives among families who were offered a guaranteed income. These were championed by policy advocates who argued for a simplified incomes policy, without complex program requirements or a huge welfare bureaucracy to test needs and supervise recipients. Although President Richard M. Nixon occasionally seemed sympathetic to these policy implications, the prospect of his personal support and the fate of the reform was lost amidst political maneuvers between different camps in the administration and Congress.[15]

In response to Coleman's work on equality of educational opportunity and the income experiment, there have been numerous specialized analyses of income, education, and other variables, along with summary assessments of the detailed studies. Some summaries qualify as policy analyses in their own right, given their detailed concern with the limitations and policy implications of others' work, and their effort to assemble and assess numerous findings that differ in detail. Of particular note is a weighty volume by Christopher Jencks and associates, and subsequent commentaries and reanalyses of Jencks's work. Like other sophisticated policy analyses, their role in ongoing policy disputes may lie more in what they detract from simplistic expectations of cause and effect than what they add by way of clear findings.

Jencks and his colleagues began with a focus on income equality as a value in its own right, which might allow greater equalities in other social goods. However, their review of numerous policy analyses did not produce much evidence that *any* social policy pursued by American governments contributed significantly to the equality of income. They also found little evidence for the proposition that equality of income is likely to produce an overall improvement in job satisfaction, increased education, a decline in social tensions, or improved health.[16]

Government Auditors

Sophisticated policy analysts are not only familiar with the conventional criticisms of research, but sometimes supply potential critics with a full list of reasons to doubt their conclusions. This represents an admirable level of scientific honesty but is likely to restrict the applicability of the findings.

The point is illustrated by the work done by one of the most well-endowed organizations that deal in policy analysis, the U.S. General Accounting Office (GAO). The training catalog of the GAO duplicates the offerings of social science faculties at respectable universities in research methods, statistics, and computer science.[17]

GAO auditors have been honest about their research.

- An audit study of education reform conceded that the gains in pupil achievement found were not isolated from programs to teach testing skills as opposed to substantive improvements.[18]

- A study of freight trucking identified some variables useful in predicting high levels of risk but admitted that it did not assess the costs of using those variables in a policy of enforced compliance.[19]

- A study of enterprise zones found some increase in employment in certain zones but admitted that the increase could not be attributed to the zones, *per se*.[20]

- A study of employee stock ownership plans conceded that its time frame of five years was not sufficient to establish the reliability of its findings.[21]

- Studies of fatality rates associated with certain types of vehicles that controlled for numerous variables that might have intervened in the findings admitted that it did not take into account all such variables, and therefore its policy implications ought to be viewed with caution.[22]

- A review of Defense Department training simulations found that the department examined only a limited number of factors for their reliability. The subtitle of the audit report reveals its central criticism: "Improved Assessment Procedures Would Increase the Credibility of Results."[23]

Other audit reports illustrate that policy analyses of modest sophistication can describe severe problems and gain a place on the public agenda. The Philippine Commission on Audit added to the criticism of the Ferdinand Marcos regime even while Marcos appointees were heading the audit body. The country's newspapers provided coverage to audit reports showing "glaring discrepancies in the financial transactions" of government-owned and controlled corporations and exposing one government minister who supplemented his base salary equivalent to U.S. $5,000 with additional payments amounting to U.S. $129,000 from government corporations.[24]

An audit report by Israel's State Comptroller illustrates how a policy analysis can have a direct impact on the decisions of policymakers. The issue was Israel's development of an advanced military plane, whose planners initially specified a number of operational goals and cost targets they expected to achieve.[25] The timing of the report and the political context were prominent in its success. It reached the Cabinet just as that closely divided group was about to vote on the project's future. The audit report was sharply critical of the project's capacity to attain its operational and economic goals. The subsequent decision to end the project was decided by a margin of one vote.

ON THE BASIC ASSUMPTIONS IN POLICY ANALYSIS: WHAT DOES IT ALL MEAN?

Integral to a historical perspective on policy analysis are the ideas of Michel Foucault in his *Discipline and Punish: The Birth of the Prison*.[26] The book is poorly organized, repetitious, indirect, and might deserve censorship for its graphic depiction of violence. Yet it emphasizes an idea that is profound as well as simple: prevailing ideas about the state, morality, personality, theology, psychology, and other underlying concerns affect conceptions and expectations of policy issues. Foucault illustrates this point with the history of criminal justice in France, Great Britain, and the United States since the seventeenth century. He argues that the controls exercised explicitly in prison are like those of factories, schools, hospitals, the military, and much else in society. He implies that we are all in prisons made up of procedures that teach us to accept society-imposed conceptions and discipline. Our social prisons reinforce themselves with constraints and rewards just as penitentiaries transmit crime from older to younger inmates and assure themselves a steady supply of repeat offenders.

We can find the truth time and again in the history of policy issues of Foucault's basic idea about the importance to policy analysis of widespread conceptions.[27] The development of British incomes and employment policies shows an incremental growth from the confinements and other humiliations of Poor Laws, which viewed poverty as largely the fault of the poor and encroached on individual freedom without seeming to recognize the encroachment. Then poverty came to be viewed as a problem rather than a phenomenon. Conceptions broadened to recognize that social and economic forces limit the free choice of many individuals. Early programs nibbled away at principles of individual responsibility and private property by offering state protection to categories of workers perceived as inherently weak, like children and women. Eventually the locus of responsibility moved from the individual, family, or neighborhood to local public authorities, and then from local authorities to central governments. Involved in the changes of public conception were descriptive studies that fit within this chapter's conception of policy analyses, dealing with the numbers of people affected by poverty and characteristics of their deprivations.[28]

A consideration of policy analysis in the United States should not overlook the cultural priorities that seem to focus on the costs more than the benefits of government programs. American debates show the importance of individualism and *laissez-faire*, reinforced by the federal system, all of which make the United States an outlier among Western democracies on social policies.[29] In recent years, moreover, attitudes and policy seem to have moved backwards toward those of the early twentieth century. Conservatives or neoconservatives like Peter Drucker, Nathan Glazer, and Thomas Sowell have asserted that modern governments are good only at waging war and inflating the currency and that social policy cannot compensate for weaknesses in the traditional mechanisms of family, ethnic group, neighborhood, and church.[30] Involved in the scene are policy analyses that detail bureaucratic clumsiness and the waste involved by providing government aid to people who can take care of themselves.[31] Perhaps related to the conservative drift is Tom Wolfe's *The Bonfire of the Vanities*.[32] It offers fictional contrasts with Harriet Beecher Stowe's *Uncle Tom's Cabin*. Wolfe depicts blacks who moved from misery in the plantation South to misery in northern ghettoes, and owe their repression partly to black representatives in welfare politics who claim to advocate their interests.

One field of research that reveals the tensions on the borders of acceptable policy analysis is that dealing with relationships between race or social class and intelligence. The work of Arthur Jensen, Richard J. Herrnstein, and Charles Murray provokes discomfort and ill temper both among those who assert its validity but distance themselves from certain policy implications, as well as those who challenge its validity. One commentator describes "a conspiracy of silence about the deep roots of policy issues,"[33] but the discussion hardly seems silent.[34]

The finding that African-Americans tend to score lower than whites on I.Q. tests has been examined time and again, in different settings, with a variety of control variables. Jensen's own summary of the findings argues that race accounts for 8 percent of individual differences in intelligence after controlling for the important variable of social class. However, he pointedly refrains from policy implications that might lead to a renewal of racial segregation or discrimination. He accepts a major reservation about his work: that findings about groups (i.e., African-Americans) cannot predict the success of individuals and must not be used to limit the opportunities made available to individuals. Jensen also writes that racial integration plus compensatory education have strong moral justifications independent of their impacts.[35] One of the volumes Jensen coedited begins with a quotation and a dedication to Martin Luther King, Jr. ". . . we must reaffirm our belief in building a democratic society, in which blacks and whites can live together as brothers, where we will all come to see that integration is not a problem, but an opportunity to participate in the beauty of diversity."[36]

An observer can only wonder at the situation that Jensen and his colleagues have created. They pursue their research avidly, yet distance themselves from policy implications that seem to follow from their findings. Critics lump the researchers along with racists and others who seize on their findings to argue against social programs.

There is no standard response to the question about what may increase the influence on policy of policy analysis. Methodologically simple depictions of horrible situations and sophisticated analysis of cause and effect have found supporters among policymakers. They have also been read selectively or ignored by policymakers who either do not comprehend the findings, or decide to overlook them in the interest of issues that to them are more pressing. Political interests and alignments have a lot to do with who sees what as well as who gets what. The formulation and timing of a study's findings, as well as the early preparation of potential supporters may aid its influence. However, those who oppose the findings also have access to the political process and have learned how to supply their allies with criticisms of the analyses offered or their own counteranalyses.[37]

This chapter seeks to place recent policy analyses in the context of an age-old concern with the actions and inaction of government. Against this background, the most sophisticated analyses stand out by virtue of their concern to go beyond the description of conditions that invite attention. They add the dimensions of sophisticated explanation, typically by virtue of statistical analysis of variables seen as proximates for cause and effect.

Several analyses are prominent by virtue of the financial investments made in the research, the variables considered, and the time frames employed for social experimentation or data collection. However, the richness of their techniques attract an equally rich variety of criticism. It is as if the more sophisticated methodologies assure themselves limited acceptance because of each assumption built into their choice of sample, time frame, locale, questionnaire item, social or economic measurement, theoretical perspective, and statistical technique. Those who question each assumption on its scientific ground or oppose the policy implications of the findings supply material for ongoing academic deliberations and lessen the prospects of any direct impact on public policy. In such conditions policymakers are tempted to see ambiguity. If the scientific experts cannot agree, why should politicians adapt the findings in making policy?

There is also no shortage of examples indicating that the literature about policy analysis has had limited impact on elite education. Against the work of professional analysts that seeks to sort out the many influences on the results of policy was Michael Dukakis's self-interested claim in his 1988 presidential campaign. He took personal credit for the "Massachusetts miracle" of economic growth that coincided with his tenure as governor, overlooking the likely impacts on the growth from economic conditions that had developed in the nation and region. Another example of overly simple conclusions appeared in a *New Republic* article that described a debate about state government policy and student achievement scores. It suggested that a decline of four points in South Carolina students' scores could be attributed to the policies of a governor who had served for three years.[38]

An item in the *Washington Post* about "road rage" focused on the lack of clarity in a popular notion that enraged drivers have become a major factor in highway carnage. Public opinion polls showing a perception of rising danger on the highway may reflect media reports stemming from a few bad incidents, an enthusiastic response from police officials, and the invention of a catchy label: road rage. Reporters noted that their own paper had used the terms "road rage" and "aggressive driving" in more than 200 articles. Yet there is no evidence of an epidemic. Official records show declines in the rates of crashes, injuries, and traffic deaths. Several experts have commented on the lack of agreed-upon definitions for road rage or aggressive driving. They criticize one advocate who has classified aggressive driving as any behavior that "endangers or is likely to endanger people or property," including drunken driving and nearly all bad driving except that caused by fatigue or inattention. In the view of a critic, "If we don't know exactly what we're talking about, how do we compare it to anything?" Another says that "it's bogus," and "the more people read in their papers about road rage the more they think they see it."[39]

This chapter directs its warnings explicitly to social science. To some extent, all science may be affected by an awareness of so many variables that may affect outcomes at issue and the problems in defining the components measuring the influence of any one in its various combinations with others. However, it is social science that most clearly suffers from this condition. Comments in a review of a book that identified the problems of research in psychiatry in comparison with other fields of medicine are relevant here. Psychiatry is a field of medicine with a heavy emphasis on social as opposed to physical notions of cause and effect: ". . . scientific psychiatric research is very hard to do. Experiments involving behavior present many more 'confounding' variables than experiments involving conditions such as pneumonia or cancer. Furthermore, 'endpoints' and 'outcomes' are hard to measure, and can take an inordinately long time to reach."[40]

For policy analysts concerned with shaping social policy, it may be best to choose targets from among extreme conditions that invite reform, use simple methodologies, and describe well the most horrid examples of policy failure. However, one finding of this historical perspective on policy analysis is that many pitfalls separate any analyst from a policy impact. Policymakers may not notice the message that the analyst intends to convey or extract backing for their own postures, even if that is at odds with the analyst's interpretation of the work in question.

Having an impact may be more difficult now than in the past. Even research techniques that are transparently simple and produce dramatic findings suffer from the increasing sophistication about the policy process. The knowledge we have acquired includes the many elements that interact in shaping policy impacts and the variety of ways they may be conceived and measured, as shown by Coleman. It also includes insights attributed to Foucault that underlying social conceptions shape what we ask about society and how we interpret the answers. Perhaps we know too much and are too skeptical for even the most dramatic findings to generate crusades that will produce significant changes in policy. We can find ambiguity in any policy analysis, and thereby limit its capacity to influence policymaking.

9

Coping with the Downside of Coping

The ideal of policymaking is to solve problems, but vexatious problems resist solution. An insistence on solution in these cases may do more harm than good, insofar as it is likely to threaten the vital interests of intense contenders. In these cases, coping and its variants, like accommodation, avoidance, ambiguity, indirection, and improvisation, may be more suitable than the pursuit of solution. Whereas these approaches to a problem do not end tensions, they may keep them moderate and without violence. Coping allows some programming to go forward or a maintenance of existing programs, where that is the most that can be achieved.

The essence of coping and related approaches to policymaking is to avoid, blur, or postpone a direct encounter with sensitive issues that engender distrust and conflict. While they may succeed in minimizing conflict, they also distract policymakers from achieving goals that are more far reaching. Detours, zigzagging, standing in place, and treading water are epigrams used by critics of policymakers who avoid desired achievements even while they evade determined opposition.

THE DOWNSIDE OF COPING

Coping, ambiguity, improvisation, avoidance, and indirection are not only ways of dealing with vexatious problems. They also contribute stresses that add to the problems of policymaking. Israeli and Palestinian authorities, as well as ultrareligious and antireligious Jews proclaim goals for Jerusalem that appear to be irreconcilable. Activists on either side accuse their

leaders of compromising basic aims. The problems associated with policy
or administrative improvisation that goes bad resemble those of improvisation that is pursued by an unskilled speaker or musician. They range from
minor snafus in program administration and undisciplined or irresponsible
behavior to major organizational chaos or policy that is wasteful of resources and productive of more social and economic harm than benefits.
While supporters may claim that an improvisation has saved time and resources, opponents link it to a waste of time and resources. Terms like "dil-
ettante" and "opportunist," as well as "amateur," are directed against an
improviser who does not succeed in accomplishing goals or in convincing
doubters. The writings of Yehezkel Dror express both positive and negative
assessments of improvisation. He has praised creative inspiration as an es-
sential trait of policymakers who must deal with new and challenging conditions.[1] He has also condemned "hand to mouth" policymaking as a futile
way of responding to events without adequate planning.[2] The situation is
similar to that in sports. A player who departs from the expected may be
cheered as brilliant. If the same action goes wrong, the player may sit on the
bench and suffer the boos of the crowd.[3]

The late Prime Minister of Israel Yitzhak Rabin spoke out against a culture of improvisation, or what he termed "rely on me." He described it as
sloppiness and irresponsibility. His own death was due partly to the slov-
enly way that security personnel handled assignments. Their lack of disciplined attention to the rules allowed a number of unchecked civilians,
including Rabin's assassin, to congregate in the area where the prime minister's vehicle was to meet him after a rally.

Another example of clumsy improvisation occurred in response to the
killing of two Israeli civilians in December 1996. Meeting a few days after
the event, the Israeli Cabinet voted to expand government subsidies for Jewish settlements in areas whose future was still to be negotiated with the Palestine Authority. Immediately after the decision was announced, two
Cabinet members dissociated themselves from the decision and said that it
could not be implemented. Palestinians, several Arab governments with
whom Israel had secured formal relations, the White House, leaders in
Europe and elsewhere, and left-of-center opposition parties within Israel
condemned the decision as a threat to the peace process. When the Israeli
government began to back down and stressed the limitations in its decision,
right-wing Jewish settler organizations criticized the government for yet
another case where it promised support but failed to deliver. The government made some clumsy efforts to defend itself from domestic and international attacks from the right and the left, yet nothing but frustration and
anger seemed to remain.

Again when 2 suicide bombers killed 13 and injured more than 170 in a Jerusalem market in July 1997, the government seemed to move decisively but soon issued confusing messages. Acting a few hours after the explosion, the Cabinet proclaimed a series of draconian measures focused on pressuring the Palestine Authority into acting against Islamic organizations that practice terror. There would be a closing of Israel to the territory of the Authority, as well as a freeze of revenue owed to the Authority and a jamming of broadcasts by an Authority radio station that had incited violence. Within a day, however, the minister of interior indicated that the closure was temporary and would not justify the entry of additional foreign (i.e., non-Palestinian) workers as demanded by Israeli employers. Other officials announced that the closure would not be imposed against humanitarian cases involving the transfer of foods or medicines or the travel of physicians, lawyers, or members of the Palestinian Legislative Assembly.

A story of failed ambiguity appeared in the Israeli press shortly after the opening for tourists of an ancient tunnel alongside what Jews call the Temple Mount and Muslims call Haram Esh Sharif. Israeli authorities said they had offered a package deal to Muslim religious authorities: development of an area of Haram Esh Sharif called Solomon's stables as a mosque in exchange for acceptance of Israel's opening of the tunnel. Israelis who attended one meeting perceived that Muslim officials shook their heads in apparent agreement. The tunnel's opening in September 1996 was associated with an outbreak of violence and perhaps 100 deaths. Muslims denied that any agreement had been achieved.

Once the crisis occurred, there were assertions by Israelis of "we told you so" and "you did not consult with us" between officials of the municipality, the national government, the military, police, and other security services.[4] There were conflicting claims among present and former Israeli ministers, the mayor of Jerusalem, and police officials with respect to whether the "package deal" was one-sided without the agreement of the Muslims, whether Muslim authorities had sent a letter rejecting the opening of the tunnel, and whether the former police minister had transmitted such a letter to the government.[5]

It is not only the Israeli cases where coping and ambiguity are useful but leave policy activists frustrated. Americans suffer from uneven legislation and flawed implementation with respect to illicit drugs and sex, as well as from a lack of clarity in court decisions about abortion and government support for religious observances. The dithering of foreign policymakers in Europe and the United States gave a chance to the residents of the former Yugoslavia to settle their own problems and caused great suffering to individuals who found themselves ousted from their homes or worse. Human rights activists in China, Burma, Nigeria, and other countries have been led to express themselves when intellectuals and officials in Western democracies indicated their support. Third World activists then pay the price of being outspoken when those Westerners fail to back up their words with any persuasive actions.

Even the best intentions of ranking policymakers can be frustrated by the problems caused by inept or callous officials further down the hierarchy. A story from ancient Jerusalem has its modern parallels. During a time when Roman governors were pursuing a policy of accommodation with the city's Jews, Roman soldiers insulted Jewish sensitivities by baring their bottoms in the vicinity of the Temple.[6] The riots and repression that followed such incidents made the regimes seem anything but accommodating. In our own day, critics of regimes that administer hostile populations cite cases of middle- and lower-echelon officials who insult the people being administered either because of their insensitivity or intended meanness. The charge has been made about Israeli soldiers in the territories occupied after the 1967 war, Europeans sent to administer colonies, Canadians seconded to U.N. units in Africa, and American police officers working in ethnic ghettoes.

POLITICAL PERSPECTIVES AND THE JUDGMENT OF COPING

Coping in the midst of vexatious political problems is not for the innocent. Its techniques involve subtle distinctions, well-crafted appeals to individuals with different perspectives, plus guile, trickery, mendacity, and outright deception. Judging coping is also not for the innocent. It is incumbent on an observer to separate symbolic from substantial actions, sense the true strategy that lies behind the tactics, as well as to admit that strategy may be rendered secondary to the accumulation of tactical accomplishments. The person coping may be led astray from original goals in the process of doing what seems necessary.

It should be no surprise that individuals with different perspectives make contrasting judgments about policymakers' coping. The Palestinians of Jerusalem have, for the most part, expressed their feelings about the Israeli administration by condemning its policies and boycotting political opportunities. When asked if they were satisfied with the services rendered by the Jerusalem municipality, 86 percent answered "No," or "Not at all." When asked, "If confronted with a choice, which would you choose: Palestinian state, economic well-being, family and community, or religion?" almost 90 percent chose "Palestinian state." Less than 40 percent reported that they have some relationship with an Israeli institution.

Israelis might have found cause for optimism in the finding that 26 percent of the Palestinian respondents indicated their support for an open city of Jerusalem where residents could move freely between Jewish and Palestinian sectors. Yet 55 percent responded to the same question by saying that the city should be divided east (Palestinian) and west (Jewish).[7] Palestinian participation in local elections between 1967 and 1993 (available to local residents regardless of their citizenship) has never been higher than 22 percent of those eligible and has been substantially below 10 percent. An Arab politician created a movement that he named Second Jerusalem and ran as a candidate for the municipal council in 1998. He gained less than 2 percent of the vote, less than necessary to win a seat. On election day, PLO monitors circulated in Palestinian neighborhoods to enforce a boycott against voting. According to one news report, the city's Palestinians prefer to tolerate crowded schools, sporadic garbage collection, and unpaved streets rather than grant the recognition to the Israeli regime involved in taking part in local elections. They forfeit the power to be gained by more than 25 percent of the city's voters against the hope of extracting their neighborhoods from the Israeli municipality.[8] Few Palestinians included in the city as of 1967 have taken the Israeli citizenship required for voting in national elections.[9]

Jerusalem is a symbol of both hope and frustration. Residents of all communities suffer from being denied sole control over their Holy City and sacred sites within it. Rivalries among Christian sects, among Muslim religious authorities, and between secular and religious Jews are not clearly less intense than disputes between Muslims, Christians, and Jews. Jerusalemites who are Palestinian nationalists are frustrated by having to live in Israel's capital. Jews are nervous about the world's respect for Palestinian claims. Jews must be alert to an abandoned package that may be a bomb or a Palestinian who shouts "God is great" and stabs Jews. After an act of Palestinian terror has succeeded, Palestinians must worry about Jews seeking revenge.

Israelis with a long record of support for accommodation are frustrated by the incidence of Arabs who reject the accommodations that seem possible. The bitterness is prominent among academics. They have led the national movement in the direction of concessions, yet potential colleagues among Arab intellectuals remain the most staunch opponents of peace. As I was preparing this book, I happened upon a review in Arabic about an earlier book that I had published about Jerusalem. Its comments on my book were descriptive rather than critical. What was worrisome was that every mention of Israel was in the equivalent of quotation marks, as if the country was a temporary, illegitimate intrusion in the Middle East.[10]

Just as both Jews and Palestinians suffer on account of the ambiguities in Jerusalem, religious and antireligious Jews both suffer throughout Israel. Religious Jews suffer because the state does not enforce religious law strictly enough, and antireligious Jews because their religious antagonists have succeeded to some extent in having the state enforce religious law.[11]

We have seen ambiguity and coping employed to deal with issues much less dramatic than the future of Jerusalem and conflict about religion among the Jews. Prosaic items of salary and fringe benefits muddy the picture of wages in Israel and cause discomfort among workers who have not yet discovered a potential fringe benefit that they can use to persuade employers to increase their take-home pay. The bizarre picture caused by so much fiction on the wage slips may produce some discomfort among those who want good government. Israeli "googoos" (the label given to good government advocates by snickering antireformers in the United States) also suffer from ministers who evade the civil service law and regulations about competitive bidding in order to distribute jobs and contracts to favored individuals, from the employees of local authorities who receive higher salaries than have been approved by national government ministries, and from a host of other shortcuts through a structure of government that formally is closely regulated from the center.

COPING WITH THE PROBLEMS OF COPING

Coping with the problems of coping will not be neat or tidy. We have already seen the lack of clarity in results and the problems of policymakers in achieving declared goals in a situation of sharp rivalries. To be sure, there is the equally troubling issue of knowing what goals truly are sought and which are merely put up to confuse one group of observers or to boost the morale of another group. If a situation has been difficult enough for policymakers to call on coping mechanisms, as opposed to a straightforward pursuit of declared goals, then dealing with the problems of coping will call forth yet another version of coping!

If the major problem at issue is a perceived loss of direction, then the answer is hardly likely to be a public declaration of true goals. If such a statement were accepted by the skeptics in one's own camp, it might also be seen as a threat by adversaries. A leader concerned about the problems of coping can employ a staff to anticipate the problems of wandering from highly esteemed goals. However, there are ample stories in the literature of policymaking—from the ancient Greeks to modern presidents and prime ministers—of leaders who do not suffer critics from among their advisers. Some leaders may be capable of learning from criticism, but openness at the highest levels cannot be assumed. Pragmatic activists accept the limitations of serious problems and adjust their aspirations accordingly. Where they do not see the possibility of an immediate and far-ranging solution, they exploit opportunities to achieve marginal improvements.

Several homilies stand ready to serve policymakers, but they are limited against the complexities of serious problems and entrenched opposition.

- Define policy goals clearly, and keep them simple (of limited utility in the case of complex problems).

- Seek to educate policymakers and the public to accept aspirations that are realistic in terms of available technology, the resources available, and the values that are widely held (of limited utility in the case of entrenched opposition that is not amenable to persuasion).

- Monitor program evolution, and be prepared to respond to problems as they emerge. The responses that may be required include more money, additional personnel, changes in the legislation, or the generation of public support (of limited utility if there is strong opposition to the policy).

These homilies must be viewed in the context of what is possible. They cannot make up for poor judgment in the initial selection of policies. It is useless to seek public support for programs that are hopelessly flawed on other dimensions. Occasional declarations of war against domestic problems seldom produce lasting public support for poorly described goals. The acronym for a Moral Equivalent of War—(MEOW)—does not suggest a high likelihood of success.

Another homily urges those who would formulate policy to deal with a social problem to *ask the right questions*. One set of questions that might be recommended is:[12]

- What is happening?

- What is expected in the near and more distance future?

- Is our intelligence reliable?

- What is the history of the problem? How is it viewed by those with different perspectives (e.g., what are "their" perspectives as opposed to "our" perspectives)?

- What changes in attitudes and behaviors should we expect from the public as a result of continuing developments? What should we expect from the domestic groups or foreign governments currently viewed as supporters or opponents of our policy?

- If there seems to be a *similarity* between this event and past events, what *differences* between this and past events ought to be taken into account?

- How will planned actions look in the future? Are we embarking on something that will make a positive impression on our successors, or are we setting a precedent that will be viewed as an undesirable departure from tradition?

These questions may not be great help against the intense pressures associated with serious problems and a situation of crisis. We must admit that there are limits to the usefulness of coping, ambiguity, and all the other recommendations that political scientists can suggest to policymakers. While cynicism should be avoided, skepticism appears to be healthy. The coping methods described by psychologists may help the individual experiencing stress deal with the problem even if they do not banish the stress. Likewise, ambiguity and other ways of coping appear widely in the activities of politicians and policymakers not because they are ideal, but because they are more desirable than the alternatives of complete, fulsome, thoroughgoing, and final solutions to difficult problems.

Some forms of ambiguity are so widespread as to be lumped under the popular curse, "that's politics!" Disinformation, trial balloons, the obfuscation of diplomats, and the assurances of campaign promises are the stuff of public life. We believe what we perceive in a message, which may be different than the explicit words, even though individuals of other perspectives perceive something else in the same message. For these ambiguities, there may be no other remedy than the skepticism that should be in the armory of any intelligent citizen or public official.

WHEN IS COPING WORTH THE COSTS?

The workability of ambiguity and other forms of coping requires a mutual willingness to profit from them. All sides must be willing to take some chances and to make some concessions in order to convince their partners and adversaries that the results are worth the risks.

There is no absolute answer to the question as to the worth of coping. All who participate will lose something, and all will gain. Individuals of different perspectives will reach contrasting conclusions as to the balance between losses and gains, or whether the losses that are suffered are worth the gains that are achieved. To paraphrase the Book of Ecclesiastes, there is a time for coping and a time for heroic decision, a time for clarity and a time for ambiguity.[13]

The outsider's response is that coping is worth the costs as long as the participants continue with their partial losses and gains, and do not throw over the process and seek a more fulsome solution to the problem. The experienced observer expects a continuing barrage of complaints and threats from both sides. In the case of an issue with especially high stakes, like the Israel-Arab dispute or religious-secular conflicts among Israeli Jews, there are likely to be outbursts of violence along with the complaints and threats.

The insider's calculation is more complicated. Participants must assess their own feelings as well as those of their comrades and antagonists. The gains of coping will be worth its losses as long as one's calculations indicate that a critical mass of colleagues and antagonists are willing to continue. How much is a critical mass? And how does one read the signs of support for the process amidst the complaints, threats, and violence? These are questions to be judged by experience. It requires subtle analysis and a capacity to assess with one's fingertips. There are seldom clear signs, even though competing observers seek political support by asserting that their judgment is certain.

Judgment of coping is surrounded by the noise of competing assessments. It is, in the final analysis, political. Participants must persuade their rivals or be persuaded by them. The stakes are high. Some losses cannot be tolerated by oneself, one's colleagues, or one's adversaries. A time of peace via coping may become a time of war. Individuals who prefer peace at almost all costs will strive to hold back the onslaught. To succeed, they must be good judges of tolerances as well as persuasive leaders.

The most difficult issues in other societies are not the same as Israel's. To the extent that they are long lasting, they are likely to be affected by a history of coping, imperfect solutions, and residues of frustration. Many Israelis and Palestinians have tired of violence that leads only to more violence. Religious and secular Jews look backward 2,000 years to civil wars that opened their nation to conquest and dispersal. Optimists in each of these camps perceive that a lack of clear resolution of major problems is better than concerted efforts at a just solution.

Notes

CHAPTER 1

1. "Latest Church-State Divide: Bible Week," *Christian Science Monitor,* November 24, 1998, Internet edition.

2. Herbert Simon, *Administrative Behavior* (New York: Free Press, 1976).

3. Chester A. Crocker, "South Africa's Defense Posture: Coping with Vulnerability" (Beverly Hills: Sage Publications, 1981); Deborah Pellow and Naomi Chazan, *Ghana: Coping with Uncertainty* (Boulder, Colo.: Westview Press, 1986); Jeffrey Gale Williamson, *Coping with City Growth During the British Industrial Revolution* (Cambridge: Cambridge University Press, 1990).

4. Daniel P. Moynihan, *Coping: On the Practice of Government* (New York: Vintage Books, 1975).

5. George V. Coelho, David A. Hamburg, and John E. Adams, eds., *Coping and Adaptation* (New York: Basic Books, 1974); Jack T. Tapp, "Multisystems Holistic Model of Health, Stress and Coping," in Tiffany M. Field, Philip M. McCabe, and Neil Schneiderman, eds., *Stress and Coping* (Hillsdale, N.J.: Lawrence Erlbaum Associates, Publishers, 1985), pp. 285-304. Some writers perceive engagement coping as leading to more effective adaptations to situations of crisis. See Rudolf H. Moos and Jeanne A. Schaefer, "Life Transitions and Crises: A Conceptual Overview," in Moos in collaboration with Schaefer, eds., *Coping with Life Crises: An Integrated Approach* (New York: Plenum Press, 1986), pp. 3–28; S. Folkman and R. S. Lazarus, "Coping and Emotion," in A. Monat and R. S. Lazarus, eds., *Stress and Coping: An Anthology* (New York: Columbia University Press, 1991), Chapter 10. Some researchers make the point that the psychology literature has yet to confirm any strong linkage between types of coping and the outcomes of stressful situations. See Susan Folkman, "Personal Control and

Stress and Coping Processes: A Theoretical Analysis," *Journal of Personality and Social Psychology*, 46, 1984, 839–852.

6. See, for example, Folkman, "Personal Control and Stress, 839–852.

7. Meron Benvenisti, *Jerusalem: The Torn City* (Minneapolis: University of Minnesota Press, 1976).

8. Dr. Yair Zalmonovich has contributed greatly to my understanding of improvisation.

9. J. M. Lee, "The Reorganization of the British Council: Management Improvisation and Policy Uncertainty," *Public Administration* (London), Vol. 75, No. 3 (Autumn 1995), 339–355.

10. Aaron Wildavsky, *The Politics of the Budgetary Process* (Boston: Little, Brown, 1964).

11. William E. Connolly, *Politics and Ambiguity* (Madison: University of Wisconsin Press, 1987).

12. *New York Times*, fax edition, June 21, 1997, p. 7.

13. National Environmental Protection Act Section 101, Section 4331 (a).

14. U.S. Code, Title 16, Section 706.

15. On "fuzziness," see Bart Kosko, *Fuzzy Thinking: The New Science of Fuzzy Logic* (New York: Hyperion, 1993).

16. James C. Scott, *Comparative Political Corruption* (Englewood Cliffs, N.J.: Prentice-Hall, 1972).

17. Michael Lipsky, *Street Level Bureaucracy: Dilemmas of the Individual in Public Services* (New York: Russell Sage Foundation, 1980); and Steve Herbert, "Morality in Law Enforcement: Chasing 'Bad Guys' with the Los Angeles Police Department," *Law & Society Review*, Vol. 30, No. 4 (November 1996), 799–818.

18. "Tax Exempt Organizations: Activities and IRS Oversight" (Washington, D.C.: General Accounting Office, June 13, 1995).

19. Eric Bates, "Private Prisons," *The Nation*, Internet edition, January 5, 1988.

20. See my *Wither the State? Politics and Public Enterprise in Three Countries* (Chatham, N.J.: Chatham House, 1979).

21. Carl Von Clausewitz, *On War* (1833) (London: Penguin Books, 1968).

22. *New York Times*, fax edition, July 29, 1997, p. 2.

23. *Ha'Aretz*, December 10, 1997, p. 3 (Hebrew).

24. Martha L. Henderson, "Geography, First Peoples, and Social Justice," *The Geographical Review*, Vol. 86, No. 2 (April 1996), 278*ff*.

25. Barbara W. Tuchman, *Bible and Sword: England and Palestine from the Bronze Age to Balfour* (New York: Ballantine Books, 1956), p. 3.

26. Richard E. Neustadt and Ernest R. May, *Thinking in Time: The Uses of History for Decision Makers* (New York: The Free Press, 1986).

27. David J. Lee, "Class as a Social Fact," *Sociology*, Vol. 28, No. 2 (May 1994), 397*ff*.

28. Floyd Jackson Fowler Jr., "How Unclear Terms Affect Survey Data," *Public Opinion Quarterly*, Vol. 56, No. 2 (Summer 1992) 218*ff*.

29. Terence Penelhum, "Response to Chappell," *Religious Studies*, Vol. 33, No. 1 (March 1997), 115.

30. See, for example, Peter J. Tanous, *Investment Gurus* (New York: New York Institute of Finance, 1997).

31. Peter L. Bernstein, *Against the Gods: The Remarkable Story of Risk* (New York: John Wiley & Sons, Inc.,1996).

32. Joel F. Handler, *Down from Bureaucracy: The Ambiguity of Privatization and Empowerment* (Princeton: Princeton University Press, 1996).

33. *New York Times*, fax edition, August 31, 1997.

34. *Statistical Abstract of Israel, 1992* (Jerusalem: Central Bureau of Statistics, 1993), Table 21.14; *Statistical Abstract of the United States, 1993* (Washington, D.C.: U.S. Government Printing Office, 1994), Tables 300, 303.

35. *Oxford English Dictionary,* CD-ROM edition, Version 1.02 (Oxford: Oxford University Press, 1992).

36. Harold D. Lasswell, *Politics: Who Gets What, When, How?* (New York: McGraw Hill, 1936).

37. Richard Rose and Guy Peters, *Can Government Go Bankrupt?* (New York: Basic Books, 1978).

38. Said to be a principle followed in the Ottoman Empire. Abraham Ashkenasi, *Israeli Policies and Palestinian Fragmentation: Political and Social Impacts in Israel and Jerusalem* (Jerusalem: Hebrew University, Leonard Davis Institute, 1988), p. 15.

39. For discussions of rational decision making and its critiques, see Yehezkel Dror, *Public Policymaking Reexamined* (San Francisco: Chandler Publishing Company, 1968); Dror, *Policymaking Under Adversity* (New Brunswick, N.J.: Transaction Books, 1986); E. S. Quade and Grace M. Carter, *Analysis for Public Decisions* (New York: North-Holland, 1989); David Dery, *Data and Policy Change* (Boston: Kluwer Academic Publishers, 1990); Dery, *Problem Definition in Policy Analysis* (Lawrence: University of Kansas Press, 1984); Charles E. Lindblom, *The Policy-Making Process* (Englewood Cliffs, N.J.: Prentice-Hall, 1968); Lindblom, *The Intelligence of Democracy: Decision-Making Through Mutual Adjustment* (New York: The Free Press, 1965); Lindblom and David K. Cohen, *Usable Knowledge: Social Science and Social Problem Solving* (New Haven: Yale University Press, 1979); Wildavsky, *The Politics of the Budgetary Process*; Ira Sharkansky, *The Routines of Politics* (New York: Van Nostrand Reinhold, 1970); and Deborah A. Stone, *Policy Paradox and Political Reason* (Glenview, Ill.: Scott, Foresman and Little, Brown, 1988).

40. Richard H. Thaler, *The Winner's Curse: Paradoxes and Anomalies of Economic Life* (Princeton: Princeton University Press, 1992).

41. Arturo Sangalli, "Vote, Vote, Vote for Fuzzy Logic: Adoption of Fuzzy Logic for Making Outcome of Referendums More Accurate," *New Scientist*, Vol. 144, No. 1951 (November 12, 1994), 51*ff*.

42. Scott, *Comparative Political Corruption*; Arnold J. Heidenheimer, ed., *Political Corruption: Readings in Comparative Analysis* (New York: Holt, Rinehart & Winston, 1970).

43. John W. Kingdon, *Agendas, Alternatives, and Public Policies* (Boston: Little, Brown, 1984).

44. Daniel A. Mazmanian and Paul A. Sabatier, *Implementation and Public Policy* (Glenview, Ill.: Scott, Foresman and Company, 1983); Robert T. Nakamura and Frank Smallwood, *The Politics of Policy Implementation* (New York: St. Martin's, 1980).

45. See, for example, Eleanor Chelimsky, *Program Evaluation: Patterns and Directions* (Washington, D.C.: American Society of Public Administration, 1985).

CHAPTER 2

1. "Adherents of All Religions by Continental Areas, Mid-1990," *The World Almanac and Book of Facts,* Microsoft CD-ROM Bookshelf 1992.

2. *Jerusalem Post*, September 30, 1994, p. 5.

3. *World Almanac and Book of Facts, 1992,* Microsoft Multimedia Viewer Version 1.00a.358.

4. Flavius Josephus, *The Jewish War*, translated by G. A. Williamson (New York: Penguin Books, 1970).

5. See the author's *The Political Economy of Israel* (New Brunswick, N.J.: Transaction Books, 1987).

6. Joseph Heller, *God Knows* (New York: Dell Publishing Company, 1984), p. 256.

7. For a view that sees a growth of regionalism in Israel, see Y. Gradus, "The Emergence of Regionalism in a Centralized System: The Case of Israel," *Environment and Planning D: Society and Space*, 2, 1984, 87–100.

8. A series of "Basic Laws" require extraordinary majorities to change them. To date, there is no comprehensive bill of rights for individuals.

9. Chaim Kalchheim, "The Division of Functions and the Interrelationships between Local and State Authorities," in Daniel Elazar and Chaim Kalchheim, eds., *Local Government in Israel* (Lanham, Md.: University Press of America, 1988), pp. 41–82.

10. Kalchheim, "The Division."

11. *Ha'Aretz*, July 13, 1997, p. 7.

12. Ronald Storrs, *Orientations* (London: Ivor Nicholson & Watson Ltd., 1939), p. 456.

13. Details in this section come from the author's "Mayor Teddy Kollek and the Jerusalem Foundation: Governing the Holy City," *Public Administration Review*, July/August 1984, 299–304; *Kal Ha'ir*, May 17, 1991 (Hebrew); and Supplement for the 25th Anniversary of the Jerusalem Foundation, *Kal Ha'ir*, May 24, 1991 (Hebrew).

14. *Kal Ha'ir*, November 27, 1998, p. 15 (Hebrew).

15. *Kal Ha'ir*, December 4, 1998, p. 41 (Hebrew).

16. This section relies on joint work underway with Dr. Reuven Schwartz of the University of Haifa.

17. Jameson W. Doig, "If I See a Murderous Fellow Sharpening a Knife Cleverly . . . The Wilsonian Dichotomy and the Public Authority Tradition," *Public Administration Review*, 43, 1983, 292–304.

18. For example, Marilyn Taylor, "Between Public and Private: Accountability and Voluntary Organizations," *Policy and Politics*, Vol. 24, No. 1 (January 1996), 57–72; Kevin Kearns, "The Strategic Management of Accountability in Nonprofit Organizations: An Analytical Framework," *Public Administration Review*, Vol. 54, No. 2 (March/April 1994), 185-192; Diana Leat, "Voluntary Organizations and Accountability: Theory and Practice," in Helmut K. Anheier and Wolfgang Seibel, eds., *The Third Sector: Comparative Studies of Nonprofit Organizations* (Berlin: Walter de Gruyter, 1990), pp. 141–153.

19. Paul C. Light, *Thickening Government: Federal Hierarchy and the Diffusion of Accountability* (Washington, D.C.: The Brookings Institution, 1995); and Rathgreb Smith and Michael Lipsky, *NonProfits for Hire: The Welfare State in an Age of Contracting* (Cambridge: Harvard University Press, 1993).

20. *Survey of Income and Expenditure of Non-profit Institutions 1980–1996* (Jerusalem: Central Bureau of Statistics, 1998).

21. *Annual Report #47* (Jerusalem: State Comptroller, 1997), pp. 590–603 (Hebrew).

22. *Annual Report #40* (Jerusalem: State Comptroller, 1990), p. 49 (Hebrew).

23. *Annual Report #48* (Jerusalem: State Comptroller, 1998), pp. 322–325; *Annual Report #47* (Jerusalem: State Comptroller, 1997), pp. 311–325, 366–375; *Annual Report #46* (Jerusalem: State Comptroller, 1996), pp. 549–559 (Hebrew).

24. *Annual Report #47*, pp. 412–424.

25. "Tax Exempt Organizations: Activities and IRS Oversight" (Washington, D.C.: General Accounting Office, June 13, 1995). For social science research on American Third Sector organizations, a reader may begin with B. Gideron, R. Kramer, and L. M. Salamon, eds., *Government and the Third Sector* (San Francisco: Jossey Bass, 1992); L. M. Salamon, *Partners in Public Service: Government-Non-Profit Relations in the Modern Welfare State* (Baltimore: Johns Hopkins University Press, 1995); and Smith and Lipsky, *NonProfits for Hire*.

26. "International Organizations: U.S. Participation in the United Nations Development Program" (Washington, D.C.: General Accounting Office, April 17, 1995). For social science research, see Thomas J. Weiss, *Humanitarian Challenges and Intervention: World Politics and the Dilemmas of Help* (Boulder, Colo.: Westview Press, 1996); Robert J. Berg and David G. Gordon, eds., *Cooperation for International Development: The United States and the Third World in the 1990s* (Boulder, Colo.: Lynne Rienner, 1989).

27. Eliezer Don-Yehiya, "Does Place Make a Difference? Jewish Orthodoxy in Israel and the Diaspora," in Chaim I. Waxman, ed., *Israel as a Religious Reality* (Northvale, N.J.: Jason Aronson Inc., 1994), pp. 43–74.

28. *The Jerusalem Post*, January 17, 1992, p. 1B.

29. Charles S. Liebman and Elihu Katz, eds., *The Jewishness of Israelis: Responses to the Guttman Report* (Albany: State University of New York Press, 1997).

30. *The Jerusalem Post*, February 23, 1955, p. 1.

31. *Ha'Aretz*, April 13, 1995, p. 9 (Hebrew).

32. *The Jerusalem Post*, February 9, 1996, p. 6.

33. *The Jerusalem Post*, January 22, 1996, p. 1.

34. *Statistical Abstract of Israel, 1996*, Table 16.1.

35. "Water and Peace in the Middle East: A Roundtable Discussion," *Economics Quarterly*, 43, November 1996, 433–453 (Hebrew).

CHAPTER 3

1. See, for example, John Dart, *The Jesus of Heresy and History: The Discovery and Meaning of the Nag Hammadi Gnostic Library* (San Francisco: Harper & Row, 1988), especially Chapter 18.

2. Baruch Halpern, *The First Historians: The Hebrew Bible and History* (San Francisco: Harper & Row, 1988), Chapter 11.

3. Genesis 18:23–33.

4. Exodus 32:10–14.

5. Exodus 13:17: "And it came to pass, when Pharaoh had let the people go, that God led them not through the way of the land of the Philistines, although that was near; for God said, Lest peradventure the people repent when they see war, and they return to Egypt."

6. Job 38–41.

7. Deuteronomy 17:14–20.

8. I Samuel 8:10–18.

9. Judges 21:24–25.

10. Ecclesiastes 2:16.

11. Ecclesiastes 3:1–8.

12. Ecclesiastes 2:13; 3:12; 4:6; 7:11–17.

13. Ecclesiastes 3:11.

14. Ecclesiastes 1:4.

15. Ecclesiastes 8:13.

16. Ecclesiastes 12:13–14.

17. Ecclesiastes 12:12.

18. On the contrasting views see R.B.Y. Scott, *Proverbs and Ecclesiastes* (*Anchor Bible*) (New York: Anchor Books, 1965), pp. 191–207; and Robert Gordis, *Koheleth: The Man and His Work: A Study of Ecclesiastes* (New York: Schocken Books, 1968), p. 73.

19. Scott, *Proverbs and Ecclesiastes*, p. 196.

20. Exodus 20:13.

21. Numbers 35.

22. Genesis 4:8.

23. John Henry Cardinal Newman as quoted in Aaron Wildavsky, *The Nursing Father: Moses as a Political Leader* (University: University of Alabama Press, 1984), p. 11.

24. Robert M. Grant with David Tracy, *A Short History of the Interpretation of the Bible* (Philadelphia: Fortress Press, 1984), p. 28.

25. *The New English Bible* (New York: Oxford University Press, 1970), *Isaiah*, 53:4–5.

26. Amos Hacham, *The Book of Isaiah* (Jerusalem: Mossad Harav Kook, 1984), pp. 567 *ff.* (Hebrew).

27. Ronald Williamson, *Jews in the Hellenistic World: Philo* (Cambridge: Cambridge University Press, 1989), p. 146.

28. Gershom Scholem, *Sabbatei Sevi: The Mystical Messiah*, translated by R. J. Zwi Werblowsky (Princeton: Princeton University Press, 1973), p. 117. Jonathan Z. Smith makes a similar point when he writes that a preacher's interpretation of sacred text resembles a pagan witch doctor divining meaning from the arrangement of sacred objects. See his *Imagining Religion: From Babylon to Jonestown* (Chicago: University of Chicago Press, 1982), p. 51.

29. Nahum N. Glatzer, ed., *The Dimensions of Job: A Study and Selected Readings* (New York: Schocken Books, 1969), pp. 287–288.

30. II Samuel 5:21.

31. I Chronicles 14:12.

32. Louis Ginzberg, *The Legends of the Jews* (Philadelphia: The Jewish Publication Society of America, 1911).

33. Brad H. Young, *Jesus and His Jewish Parables: Rediscovering the Roots of Jesus' Teaching* (New York: Paulist Press, 1989), p. 130.

34. Dart, *The Jesus*, Chapter 18.

35. I Corinthians 15:13–14.

36. Daniel J. Harrington, S.J., "The Jewishness of Jesus: Facing Some Problems," *The Catholic Biblical Quarterly*, 49, January 1, 1987, 1–13.

37. Haim Cohn, *The Trial and Death of Jesus* (London: Weidenfeld and Nicolson, 1972).

38. Anthony J. Saldarini, "Reconstructions of Rabbinic Judaism," in Robert A. Kraft and George W. E. Nickelsburg, eds., *Early Judaism and Its Modern Interpreters* (Philadelphia: Fortress Press, 1986), p. 457.

39. Hugh J. Schonfield, *The Passover Plot* (London: Corgi Books, 1967), p. 270.

40. Herman C. Waetjen, *A Reordering of Power: A Sociopolitical Reading of Mark's Gospel* (Minneapolis: Fortress Press, 1989), pp. 1–2.

41. Matthew 3:7.

42. Matthew 15:14.
43. Matthew 23:1.
44. Luke 23.
45. Matthew 28:11.
46. Acts 14.
47. Acts 24–25.
48. See, for example, Leonard Dinnerstein, *Anti-Semitism in America* (New York: Oxford University Press, 1994).
49. George W. E. Nickelsburg with Robert A. Kraft, "Introduction: The Modern Study of Early Judaism," in Kraft and Nickelsburg, eds., *Early Judaism*, pp. 1–30.
50. For readers interested in pursuing a point where the ambiguities of religion, history, and science intersect, they might prepare themselves to be skeptical and read Holger Kersten and Elmar G. Gruber, *The Jesus Conspiracy: The Turin Shroud and the Truth About the Resurrection* (Shaftesbury, Dorset: Element, 1992).
51. See, for example, Mordecai Zar-Kavod, "Introduction to Kohelet," in *The Five Scrolls* (Jerusalem: Mossad Harav Kook, 1973, Hebrew), p. 26; and John L. McKenzie, S .J., *The Two-Edged Sword: An Interpretation of the Old Testament* (Garden City, N.Y.: Image Books, 1966), p. 104. For the development of the concept of God, both before and after the biblical period, from Jews as well as non-Jews, see Karen Armstrong, *A History of God: The 4,000–Year Quest of Judaism, Christianity and Islam* (New York: Ballantine Books, 1993).
52. Meir Tamari, *"With All Your Possessions," Jewish Ethics and Economic Life* (New York: Free Press, 1987), p. 110.
53. *Ha'Aretz*, July 7, 1997, p. 1 (Hebrew).
54. Tim Chappell, "Rationally Deciding What to Believe," *Religious Studies*, Vol. 33, No. 1 (March 1997), 105-109.
55. Gadi Wolfsfeld, *The Politics of Provocation* (Albany: State University of New York Press, 1988); and Sam Lehman-Wilzig, *Stiff-necked People, Bottle-necked System: The Evolution and Roots of Israeli Public Protest, 1949–1986* (Bloomington: Indiana University Press, 1991).
56. Charles S. Liebman and Elihu Katz, eds. *The Jewishness of Israelis: Responses to the Guttman Report* (Albany: State University of New York Press, 1997).
57. Charles S. Liebman and Eliezer Don-Yehiya, *Civil Religion in Israel: Traditional Judaism and Political Culture* (Berkeley: University of California Press, 1984).
58. Jacob Neusner, *Death and Birth of Judaism: The Impact of Christianity, Secularism, and the Holocaust on Jewish Faith* (New York: Basic Books, 1987); and Calvin Goldscheider and Jacob Neusner, eds., *Social Foundations of Judaism* (Englewood Cliffs, N.J.: Prentice-Hall, 1990). This book uses B.C.E. (Before the Common Era) and C.E. (Common Era) as equivalent to the Christian B.C. and A.D.

59. Neusner, "Judaism in America: The Social Crisis of Freedom," in Gold-scheider and Neusner, *Social Foundations*, pp. 130–133.

60. Norman F. Cantor, *The Sacred Chain: The History of the Jews* (New York: HarperCollins, 1994).

61. *The Jerusalem Post,* May 10, 1993, p. 2.

62. *The Jerusalem Post,* December 3, 1993, p. 1.

63. *The Jerusalem Post,* November 12, 1993, p. 2.

64. *The Jerusalem Post,* December 9, 1993, p. 14.

65. *The Jerusalem Post,* July 17, 1992, p. 1B.

66. *The Jerusalem Post,* February 8, 1993, p. 2.

67. *The Jerusalem Post,* February 5, 1993, p. 1.

68. *The Jerusalem Post,* February 5, 1993, p. 1.

69. *The Jerusalem Post,* February 8, 1993, p. 2.

70. *Ha'Aretz,* May 3, 1995, p. 1 (Hebrew)

71. *Ha'Aretz,* November 13, 1995, pp. 1, 7 (Hebrew).

72. See the author's *What Makes Israel Tick? How Domestic Policy-makers Cope with Constraints* (Chicago: Nelson Hall, 1985), Chapter 4.

73. F. E. Peters, *Jerusalem: The Holy City in the Eyes of Chroniclers, Visitors, Pilgrims, and Prophets from the Days of Abraham to the Beginnings of Modern Times* (Princeton: Princeton University Press, 1985), p. 521.

74. On the competing allegations about the contribution of holy sites to the Crimean War, see Norman Rich, *Why the Crimean War? A Cautionary Tale* (Hanover, N.H.: University Press of New England, 1985); and Brison D. Gooch, ed., *The Origins of the Crimean War* (Lexington, Mass.: D. C. Heath & Co., 1969).

75. Colleagues at both universities, as well as countless other people in Utah, earned my thanks for their friendship and guidance. This section relies heavily on my "Religion and Politics in Israel and Utah," *Journal of Church and State*, Vol. 39, No. 3 (Summer 1997), 523–542.

76. Robert A. Campbell and James E. Curtis, "Religious Involvement Across Societies: Analysis for Alternative Measures in National Surveys," *Journal for the Scientific Study of Religion*, Vol. 33, No. 3 (1994), 215-229. See also Stephen D. Johnson and Joseph B. Tamney, eds., *The Political Role of Religion in the United States* (Boulder, Colo.: Westview Press, 1986); Robert Wuthnow, *The Restructuring of American Religion* (Princeton: Princeton University Press, 1988); R. Laurence Moore, *Selling God: American Religion in the Marketplace of Culture* (New York: Oxford University Press, 1994); and Michael J. Lacey, ed., *Religion and Twentieth-Century American Intellectual Life* (New York: Cambridge University Press, 1989).

77. Kenneth D. Wald, *Religion and Politics in the United States* (Washington, D.C.: CQ Press, 1992); and David C. Leege and Lyman A. Kellstedt, eds., *Rediscovering the Religious Factor in American Politics* (Armonk, N.Y.: M. E. Sharpe, 1993).

78. James Ault, "Family and Fundamentalism: The Shawmut Valley Baptist Church," in Jim Obelkevich, Lyndal Roper, and Raphael Samuel, eds., *Disciplines of Faith: Studies in Religion, Politics and Patriarchy* (London: Routledge & Kegan Paul, 1987), pp. 13–36. See also Abraham Wolfensohn, *From the Bible to the Labor Movement* (Tel Aviv: Am Oved, 1975, Hebrew); and William Safire, *The First Dissident: The Book of Job in Today's Politics* (New York: Random House, 1992).

79. See "Selections from the Book of Moses," in *The Doctrine and Covenants of the Church of Jesus Christ of Latter-Day Saints and The Pearl of Great Price* (Salt Lake City: The Church of Jesus Christ of Latter-Day Saints, 1982), 1:6.

80. *Churches and Church Membership in the U.S. 1980* (Atlanta: Glenmary Research Center, 1982).

81. For a discussion of Mormon doctrine and practice, see Leonard J. Arrington and Davis Bitton, *The Mormon Experience: A History of the Latter-Day Saints* (New York: Vintage Books, 1979).

82. Wade Clark Roof and William McKinney, *American Mainline Religion: Its Changing Shape and Future* (New Brunswick, N.J.: Rutgers University Press, 1987), Table 4–2.

83. Herbal teas are used.

84. Thomas F. O'Dea, *The Mormons* (Chicago: University of Chicago Press, 1957), pp. 183–184.

85. Arrington and Bitton, *The Mormon Experience*, Chapter 14.

86. Stan L. Albrecht and Tim B. Heaton, "Secularization, Higher Education, and Religosity," *Review of Religious Research*, 26 (September 1984), 43–58.

87. James E. Smith, "Mortality," in Thomas K. Martin, Tim B. Heaton, and Stephen J. Bahr, eds., *Utah in Demographic Perspective* (Salt Lake City: Signature Books, 1986), pp. 59–70.

88. For a history of the Mormons that specifies the relevance of history and doctrine for contemporary activities, see Arrington and Bitton, *The Mormon Experience.*

89. Frank H. Jonas, "Utah: Crossroads of the West," in Jonas, ed., *Western Politics* (Salt Lake City: University of Utah Press, 1961), p. 273.

90. One example is *The Evangel*, published by Utah Missions, Inc., of Marlow, Oklahoma, which carries the banner, "Exposing Mormonism" above its masthead. Another example is the *Salt Lake City Messenger* (Salt Lake City: Utah Lighthouse).

91. The First Presidency includes the Prophet and two Counselors; below this group in the hierarchy is the Quorum of the Twelve Apostles.

92. M. Gerald Bradford and Armand L. Mauss, "Mormon Assimilation and Politics: Toward a Theory of Mormon Church Involvement in National U.S. Politics," paper delivered at the 1987 Annual Meeting of the American Political Science Association.

93. One question asked if they accept the *Book of Mormon* as "an actual historical record of ancient inhabitants of the American continent, . . . translated by the gift and power of God." Armand L. Mauss, John R. Trijan, and Marth D. Esplin, "The Unfettered Faithful: An Analysis of the *Dialogue* Subscribers Survey," *Dialogue: A Journal of Mormon Thought* 20 (April 1987), 27–53.

94. Q. Michael Croft, "The Influence of the L.D.S. Church on Utah Politics, 1945–1984," Ph.D. Dissertation, University of Utah, 1985, Chapter 3; David B. Magleby, "Religion and Voting Behavior in a Religiously Homogeneous State," paper delivered at the 1987 Annual Meeting of the American Political Science Association.

95. See, for example, J. D. Williams, "The Separation of Church and State in Mormon Theory and Practice," *Dialogue: A Journal of Mormon Thought*, Vol. 1, No. 2 (Summer 1966), 30–54.

96. Robert Gottlieb and Peter Wiley, *America's Saints: The Rise of Mormon Power* (New York: Harcourt Brace Jovanovich, 1986). This author has had similar experiences.

97. Roof and McKinney, *American*.

98. Croft, "The Influence."

99. Croft, "The Influence," p. 136.

100. *The Salt Lake Tribune*, February 25, 1989, p. B-1.

101. Croft, "The Influence," p. 129.

102. *Statistical Abstract of the United States, 1993,* CD-ROM edition (Washington, D.C.: U.S. Government Printing Office, 1993), Table 114.

103. *Statistical Abstract of the United States, 1993*, Table 741,

104. *Statistical Abstract of the United States, 1993*, Table 457.

105. *Statistical Abstract of the United States, 1993,* Tables 251, 325, 504.

106. They are 7 percent of the state's population, while the Catholics are 14 percent. Mormons are 8 percent of the population in Clark County (Las Vegas). See *Churches and Church Membership in the U.S. 1980.* On Mormon political activity in Nevada see James T. Richardson and Sandie Wightman Fox, "Religious Affiliation as a Predictor of Voting Behavior in Abortion Reform Legislation," *Journal for the Scientific Study of Religion*, 11, 1972, 347–359; James T. Richardson and Barend Van Driel, "Public Support for Anti-Cult Legislation," *Journal for the Scientific Study of Religion*, 23, 1984, 412–418; and James T. Richardson, "The 'Old Right' in Action: Mormon and Catholic Involvement in an Equal Rights Amendment Referendum," in David G. Bromley and Anson Shupe, eds., *New Christian Politics* (Macon, Ga.: Mercer University Press, 1984), pp. 214–233. For a history of Nevada, see Russell R. Elliott, *History of Nevada* (Lincoln: University of Nebraska Press, 1987).

107. Leonard J. Arrington, *The Mormons in Nevada* (Las Vegas: Las Vegas *Sun*, 1979).

108. Stefan Heym, *The King David Report: A Novel* (New York: G. P. Putnam's Sons, 1973); and Joseph Heller, *God Knows* (New York: Dell Publishing Company, 1984).

109. Such as Robert H. Moss's *The Covenant Coat* (Bountiful, Ut.: Horizon Publishers & Distributors, Inc., 1985); S. Dean Wakefield's *Elijah: a Novel of the Chosen Prophet* (Bountiful, Ut.: Horizon Publishers & Distributors, Inc., 1982); and Mark E. Petersen's *Three Kings in Israel* (Salt Lake City: Deseret Book Company, 1980).

110. *Ha'Aretz*, December 6, 1996, p. 6 (Hebrew).

111. See, for example, Louis Ginzberg, *Legends of the Jews* (Philadelphia: The Jewish Publication Society of America, 1911), and Lillian S. Freehof, *Stories of King David* (Philadelphia: Jewish Publication Society of America, 1952).

112. Genesis 38.

113. II Samuel 13.

114. Ehud Sprinzak, *The Ascendance of Israel's Radical Right* (New York: Oxford University Press, 1991).

115. See, for example, Pete Earley, *Prophet of Death: The Mormon Blood-Atonement Killings* (New York: Avon Books, 1991).

CHAPTER 4

1. This chapter draws heavily on "Ambiguities in Policymaking and Administration: A Typology," coauthored with Asher Friedberg, and published in *International Journal of Organization Theory and Behavior*, Vol. 1, No. 1, 1–17. A Hebrew version appears in *Iyunim*, 57, 1997, 50–62 (the journal of Israel's State Comptroller).

2. Harold D. Lasswell, *Politics: Who Gets What, When, How?* (New York: McGraw Hill, 1936).

3. A. Friedberg, B. Geist, N. Mizrahi, and I. Sharkansky, eds., *State Audit and Accountability: A Book of Readings* (Jerusalem: State Comptroller's Office, 1991); A. Friedberg, B. Geist, N. Mizrahi, and I. Sharkansky, eds., *Studies in State Audit* (Jerusalem: State Comptroller's Office, 1995).

4. Michael Lipsky, *Street Level Bureaucracy: Dilemmas of the Individual in Public Services* (New York: Russell Sage Foundation, 1980).

5. *Annual Report #35* (Jerusalem: State Comptroller, 1985), pp. 435–458 (Hebrew).

6. *Annual Report #34* (Jerusalem: State Comptroller, 1984), pp. 1–7 (Hebrew).

7. On the character and techniques of Israel's civil service, see Ya'acov Reuveni, *Public Administration in Israel: The Government System in Israel and Its Development During the Years 1948–73* (Ramat Gan: Massada, 1974, Hebrew). The incidence of appointments open to political considerations, noted here as between 20 percent and 40 percent of appointments, varies with the indicators and the time periods employed. Details appear in my "Israeli Civil Service Positions Open to Political Appointments," *International Journal of Public Administration*, Vol. 12, No. 5, (1989), 731–748. For further implications of the politicization of

Israel's public service, see David Dery, *Political Appointments in Israel* (Jerusalem: Israel Democracy Institute, 1993, Hebrew).

8. *Report on Statutory Authorities* (Jerusalem: State Comptroller, 1995, Hebrew); *Annual Report #37* (Jerusalem: State Comptroller, 1987), pp. 235–244 (Hebrew).

9. *Annual Report #45* (Jerusalem: State Comptroller, 1995), pp. 362–376 (Hebrew).

10. *Kal Ha'ir* January 17, 1992 (Hebrew).

11. Israel Radio, August 3, 1992.

12. *Kal Ha'ir*, September 13, 1991 (Hebrew).

13. *Kal Ha'ir*, September 6, 1991 (Hebrew).

14. *Kal Ha'ir*, June 7, 1991 (Hebrew).

15. For the estimate associated with the Interior Ministry, see *Kal Ha'ir*, January 17, 1992 (Hebrew). The lower estimate was provided by a senior official of the municipality.

16. Ehud Sprinzak, *The Ascendance of Israel's Radical Right* (New York: Oxford University Press, 1991); Sprinzak, "Fundamentalism, Terrorism, and Democracy: The Case of Gush Emunim Underground," occasional paper (Washington, D.C.: The Wilson Center, September 16, 1986, mimeo); and Sprinzak, *Every Man Whatsoever is Right in His Own Eyes: Illegalism in the Israeli Society* (Tel Aviv: Sifriat Poalim, 1986, Hebrew).

17. *Annual Report #37* (Jerusalem: State Comptroller, 1987), pp. 235–244 (Hebrew).

18. *Annual Report #42* (Jerusalem: State Comptroller, 1992), pp. 297–302 (Hebrew).

19. *Annual Report #39* (Jerusalem: State Comptroller, 1989), pp. 618–626 (Hebrew).

20. Chaim Kalchheim, "The Division of Functions and the Interrelationships between Local and State Authorities," in Daniel Elazar and Chaim Kalchheim, eds., *Local Government in Israel* (Lanham, Md.: University Press of America, 1988), pp. 41–82.

21. The State Comptroller's report that was a major step in the process of specifying details of the affair is *Report on the Bank Shares: the Crisis of October, 1983* (Jerusalem: State Comptroller, 1984, Hebrew).

22. *Audit Report on the Granting of Support to Institutions by Local Authorities* (Jerusalem: State Comptroller, 1991, Hebrew).

23. Peter Bachrach and Morton S. Baratz, *Power and Poverty* (New York: Oxford University Press, 1970).

24. *Annual Report #44* (Jerusalem: State Comptroller, 1994), Foreword (Hebrew); *Annual Report #45* (Jerusalem: State Comptroller, 1995), Foreword (Hebrew).

25. *Report on the Management of Water Resources* (Jerusalem: State Comptroller, 1990).

26. "Project Lavi: Decision-Making," *Annual Report #37* (Jerusalem: State Comptroller, 1987), p. 1291*ff.* (Hebrew).

27. *Report on the Bank Shares.*

28. *Annual Report #38* (Jerusalem: State Comptroller, 1988), pp. 188*ff.* (Hebrew).

29. *Annual Report #46* (Jerusalem: State Comptroller, 1996), pp. 78–95 (Hebrew).

30. James Scott develops this explanation with respect to some of the "corruption" that he describes. James C. Scott, *Comparative Political Corruption* (Englewood Cliffs, N.J.: Prentice-Hall, 1972).

CHAPTER 5

1. My thanks to Dr. Gedalia Auerbach who contributed substantially to the material in this chapter.

2. On the competing allegations about the contribution of holy sites to that war, see Norman Rich, *Why the Crimean War? A Cautionary Tale* (Hanover, N.H.: University Press of New England, 1985); and Brison D. Gooch, ed., *The Origins of the Crimean War* (Lexington, Mass.: D. C. Heath & Co., 1969). For various views as to the cause of the Crusades, see Aharon Ben-Ami, *Social Change in a Hostile Environment: The Crusader's Kingdom of Jerusalem* (Princeton: Princeton University Press, 1969); and Jean Richard, *The Latin Kingdom of Jerusalem*, translated by Janet Shirly (Amsterdam: North Holland Publishing Company, 1979).

3. U. O. Schmelz, "Jerusalem's Arab Population since the Mandatory Period (1918–1990)," in Aharon Layish, ed., *The Arabs in Jerusalem: From the Late Ottoman Period to the Beginning of the 1990's—Religious, Social and Cultural Distinctiveness* (Jerusalem: The Magnes Press, 1992), pp. 6–42 (Hebrew).

4. *Oxford English Dictionary*, CD-ROM edition (Oxford: Oxford University Press, 1992).

5. Meron Benvenisti, *Jerusalem: The Torn City* (Minneapolis: University of Minnesota Press, 1976), p. vii.

6. See, for example, I. William Zartman, ed., *International Multilateral Negotiation: Approaches to the Management of Complexity* (San Francisco: Jossey-Bass, 1994).

7. A classic discussion of the nature of cities appears in Louis Wirth, "Urbanism as a Way of Life," *American Journal of Sociology*, 44, 1938, 1–24.

8. M. A. Aamiry, *Jerusalem: Arab Origin and Heritage* (London: Longman, 1978). The quotations come from the Preface and pp. 1–12.

9. Islamic Council of Europe, *Jerusalem: The Key to World Peace* (London: Islamic Council of Europe, 1980), p. vii.

10. Terrence Prittie, *Whose Jerusalem?* (London: Frederick Muller Ltd, 1981), p. 1.

11. Quoted from Henry Near, ed., *The Seventh Day* (London: Andre Deutsch, 1970) by Ronald Segal, *Whose Jerusalem? The Conflicts of Israel* (London: Jonathan Cape, 1973), p. 135.

12. Saul B. Cohen, *Jerusalem: Bridging the Four Walls: A Geopolitical Perspective* (New York: Herzl Press, 1977), p. 23.

13. F. E. Peters, *Jerusalem: The Holy City in the Eyes of Chroniclers, Visitors, Pilgrims, and Prophets from the Days of Abraham to the Beginnings of Modern Times* (Princeton: Princeton University Press, 1985), pp. 285–286.

14. *The Jerusalem Post,* May 18, 1990, p. 7.

15. *Foreign Broadcast Information Service*, FBIS-NES-93–217, p. 47.

16. Quoted from Near by Segal, *Whose Jerusalem?* p. 136.

17. Yohanan Aharoni, *Carta's Atlas of the Bible* (Jerusalem: Carta, 1974), p. 115.

18. I. Kimche, "Jerusalem at a Crossroad," in Dan Soen, ed., *Environmental Planning* (Tel Aviv: The Israeli Association for Environmental Planning, 1996), pp. 11–25 (Hebrew).

19. Israel Kimchi, Shalom Reichman, and Joseph Schweid, "Arab Settlement in the Metropolitan Area of Jerusalem" (Jerusalem: The Jerusalem Institute for Israel Studies, 1986, Hebrew); "The Metropolitan Area of Jerusalem" (Jerusalem: The Jerusalem Institute for Israel Studies, 1984); *Ha'Aretz*, July 18, 1992 (Hebrew).

20. Dan Bahat, with Chaim T. Rubinstein, *The Illustrated Atlas of Jerusalem*, translated by Shlomo Ketko (Jerusalem: Carta, 1996), p. 28; for somewhat different estimates, see M. Broshi, "Numbering the Residents of Ancient Jerusalem," in Broshi, ed., *From Hermon to Sinai* (Jerusalem: Ronald, 1977), pp. 65–70 (Hebrew).

21. Yehoshua Ben-Arieh, *Jerusalem in the 19th Century: Emergence of the New City* (New York: St. Martin's Press, 1986).

22. *Ma'ariv*, February 14, 1992 (Hebrew).

23. Michael Dumper, *The Politics of Jerusalem Since 1967* (New York: Columbia University Press, 1997), Chapter 5.

24. David Kroyanker, *Jerusalem: Planning and Development 1982–1985: New Trends* (Jerusalem: The Jerusalem Committee and the Jerusalem Institute for Israel Studies, 1985).

25. Cohen, *Jerusalem: Bridging the Four Walls.*

26. Michael Romann and Alex Weingrod, *Living Together Separately: Arabs and Jews in Contemporary Jerusalem* (Princeton: Princeton University Press, 1991).

27. Abraham Ashkenasi, "Israeli Policies and Palestinian Fragmentation: Political and Social Impacts in Israel and Jerusalem" (Jerusalem: Hebrew University, Leonard Davis Institute, 1988); and Ashkenasi, "Opinion Trends Among Jerusalem Palestinians" (Jerusalem: Hebrew University, Leonard Davis Institute, 1990).

28. Ira Sharkansky, *Governing Jerusalem: Again on the World's Agenda* (Detroit: Wayne State University Press, 1996), Chapters 5–7.

29. *Ma'ariv*, July 25, 1997, Friday Magazine, pp. 1–3 (Hebrew).

30. Moshe Amirav, "East Jerusalem Is Palestinian," *Ha'Aretz*, July 31, 1991 (Hebrew); see also Benvenisti, *Jerusalem: The Torn City*; and Gerald Caplan with Ruth B. Caplan, *Arab and Jew in Jerusalem: Explorations in Community Mental Health* (Cambridge: Harvard University Press, 1980), Chapter 5.

31. *Kal Ha'ir*, August 7, 1998, p. 49 (Hebrew).

32. *Kal Ha'ir*, February 23, 1996, p. 23; May 22, 1998, p. 39 (Hebrew).

33. *Kal Ha'ir*, June 19, 1998, p. 82 (Hebrew).

34. *The Jerusalem Post*, May 22, 1996, p. 5.

35. Menachem Friedman, *Haredi Society: Sources, Goals, and Procedures* (Jerusalem: Jerusalem Institute for Israel Studies, 1991, Hebrew) and Tamar El-Or, *Educated and Ignorant: On Ultraorthodox Women and Their World* (Tel Aviv: Am Oved, 1992, Hebrew); Shlomo Hasson, *The Cultural Struggle Over Jerusalem: Accommodations, Scenarios and Lessons* (Jerusalem: The Floersheimer Institute for Policy Studies, November 1996); Ira Sharkansky, *Rituals of Conflict: Religion, Politics and Public Policy in Israel* (Boulder, Colo.: Lynne Rienner, 1996).

36. William Shakespeare, *Romeo and Juliet*, Act II, Scene ii, Line 43.

CHAPTER 6

1. Amos 5:22–24.

2. I Samuel 17.

3. *The Jerusalem Post*, December 19, 1993, p. 2.

4. Gregg Barak, "Toward a Criminology of State Criminality," in Barak, *Crimes by the Capitalist State: An Introduction to State Criminality* (Albany: State University of New York Press, 1991), pp. 3–16; and Daniel E. Georges-Abeyie, "Piracy, Air Piracy, and Recurrent U.S. and Israeli Civilian Aircraft Interceptions," in Barak, *Crimes*, pp. 129–144.

5. Avner Yaniv, ed., *National Security and Democracy in Israel* (Boulder, Colo.: Lynne Rienner Publishers, 1993); Michael Shalev, *Labour and the Political Economy in Israel* (New York: Oxford University Press, 1992); Baruch Kimmerling, ed., *The Israeli State and Society: Boundaries and Frontiers* (Albany: State University of New York Press, 1989); and Sammy Smooha, *Arabs and Jews in Israel: Conflicting and Shared Attitudes in a Divided Society* (Boulder, Colo.: Westview Press, 1989).

6. Shlomo Hasson, "The Cultural Struggle Over Jerusalem: Accommodations, Scenarios and Lessons" (Jerusalem: The Floersheimer Institute for Policy Studies, November 1996).

7. Ehud Sprinzak, *The Ascendance of Israel's Radical Right* (New York: Oxford University Press, 1991).

8. On Palestinian purchases of "Jewish land," see the liberal Israeli newspaper *Ha'Aretz*, July 9, 1997, p. 1.

9. Hillel Frisch, "State Ethnicization and the Crisis of Leadership Succession amongst Israel's Druze," manuscript, Department of Political Science, Hebrew University of Jerusalem.

10. John C. Green, "The Christian Right and the 1994 Elections: A View from the States," *PS: Political Scence & Politics*, Vol. 27, No. 1 (March 1995), 5–8.

11. Carol Meyers, "David as Temple Builder," in Patrick D. Miller, Jr., Paul D. Hanson, and S. Dean McBride, eds., *Ancient Israelite Religion* (Philadelphia: Fortress Press, 1987), pp. 357–376.

12. *Ha'Aretz*, October 11, 1995, p. 5 (Hebrew).

13. *Kal Ha'ir*, November 1, 1991 (Hebrew).

14. See the author's *Rituals of Conflict: Religion, Politics and Public Policy in Israel* (Boulder, Colo.: Lynne Rienner, 1996).

15. *The Jerusalem Post,* January 7, 1994, p. 4B. See also Charles S. Liebman and Elihu Katz, *The Jewishness of Israelis: Responses to the Guttman Report* (Albany: State University of New York Press, 1997). For a discussion of nuances among categories of Israeli Jews, see pp. 1–42. See also Eliezer Don-Yehiya, "Does Place Make a Difference? Jewish Orthodoxy in Israel and the Diaspora," in Chaim I. Waxman, ed., *Israel as a Religious Reality* (Northvale, N.J.: Jason Aronson Inc., 1994), pp. 43–74.

16. Robert A. Campbell and James E. Curtis, "Religious Involvement Across Societies: Analysis for Alternative Measures in National Surveys," *Journal for the Scientific Study of Religion*, Vol. 33, No. 3 (1994), 215–229.

17. The comparative figure for 1982 cannot be derived from the information available.

18. Ira Sharkansky, "Israeli Income Equality," *Israel Studies*, Vol. 1, No. 1 (Spring 1996), 306–314.

19. More recent data, to 1997, show continued decline in both Jewish and non-Jewish infant death rates, with similar declines for both groups.

CHAPTER 7

1. See, in particular, Gershon R. Kieval, *Party Politics in Israel and the Occupied Territories* (Westport, Conn.: Greenwood Press, 1983).

2. There is a lengthy list of credible surveys of the Israeli-Arab dispute, and no let-up of new publications. A reader might begin with several books that represent different emphases and approaches, such as Avi Shlaim, *Collusion Across the Jordan: King Abdullah, the Zionist Movement, and the Partition of Palestine* (New York: Columbia University Press, 1988); Robert F.Hunter, *The Palestinian Uprising: A War by Other Means* (Berkeley: University of California Press, 1993); Patrick Seale, *Asad: The Struggle for the Middle East* (Berkeley: Univer-

sity of California Press, 1988); and Conor Cruise O'Brien, *The Siege: The Saga of Israel and Zionism* (New York: Simon and Schuster, 1987).

3. Shlomo Gazit, *The Carrot and the Stick: The Israeli Government in Yehuda and Shomron* (Tel Aviv: Zmora, Bitan, 1985, Hebrew), p. 136.

4. Rafik Halabi, *The West Bank Story: An Israeli Arab's View of Both Sides of a Tangled Conflict*, translated by Ina Friedman (New York: Harcourt Brace Jovanovich, 1981).

5. *The Jerusalem Post*, December 19, 1993, p. 2.

6. For an expression of one Israeli's ambivalence, see Yaron Ezrahi, *Rubber Bullets: Power and Conscience in Modern Israel* (New York: Farrar, Straus, and Giroux, 1997).

7. The parties' allocation of seats were: Mapam, 3; Ratz, 5: Shinui, 2.

8. National Religious Party, 5; Tahiya, 3; Tsomet, 2.

9. *Ha'Aretz*, July 25, 1996, p. 3 (Hebrew).

10. Also at issue is the area of Gaza, for which the terminological options have been less contentious.

11. *Kal Ha'ir*, February 23, 1996, p. 23 (Hebrew).

12. *Ha'Aretz*, July 27, 1997, p. 3 (Hebrew).

13. *Ha'Aretz*, March 15, 1999, p. 6 (Hebrew).

14. *Washington Post*, October 24, 1998, p. A1.

15. *New York Times,* October 24, 1998, several articles; *Ha'Aretz*, October 25, 1998, several articles (Hebrew).

16. Aaron Wildavsky, *The Politics of the Budgetary Process* (Boston: Little, Brown, 1964).

17. *Washington Post*, October 13, 1998, p. 14A.

CHAPTER 8

1. Aaron Wildavsky, *Speaking Truth to Power: The Art and Craft of Policy Analysis* (Boston: Little, Brown, 1979), p. 2.

2. T. D. Cook, and W. R. Shadish, "Program Evaluation: The Worldly Science," *Annual Review of Psychology*, 37, 1986, 193–232.

3. Ecclesiastes 5:8.

4. Michael Kammen, *Empire and Interest: The American Colonies and the Politics of Mercantilism* (Philadelphia: J. B. Lippincott Company, 1970).

5. M. J. Cullen, *The Statistical Movement in Early Victorian Britain: The Foundations of Empirical Social Research* (New York: Barnes and Noble Books, 1975), p. 52.

6. Upton Sinclair, *The Jungle*, originally published in 1906 (Harmondsworth: Penguin, 1962), p. 214.

7. Ella Winter and Herbert Shapiro, *The World of Lincoln Steffens* (New York: Hill and Wang, 1962).

8. John Dinges, *Our Man in Panama: How General Noriega Used the United States—And Made Millions in Drugs and Arms* (New York: Random House, 1990), p. 270.

9. James S. Coleman, *Equality of Educational Opportunity* (Washington, D.C.: U.S. Government Printing Office, 1966).

10. Gerald Paul Grant, "The Politics of the Coleman Report," D.Ed. Dissertation, Graduate School of Education, Harvard University, 1972.

11. La Mar P. Miller and Edmund W. Gordon, eds. *Equality of Educational Opportunity* (New York: AMS Press, Inc., 1974); Donald M. Levine and Mary Jo Bane, eds., *The "Inequality" Controversy: Schooling and Distributive Justice* (New York: Basic Books, Inc., 1975); Christopher Jencks, *et al.*, *Inequality: A Reassessment of the Effects of Family and Schooling in America* (New York: Basic Books, Inc., 1972).

12. Glen G. Cain and Harold W. Watts, "Problems in Making Policy Inferences from the Coleman Report," *American Sociological Review*, Vol. 35, No. 2 (April 1970), 228–252.

13. James S. Coleman, "Reply," *American Sociological Review*, Vol. 35, No. 2 (April 1970), 253.

14. Joseph A. Pechman and P. Michael Timpane, eds., *Work Incentives and Income Guarantees: The New Jersey Negative Income Tax Experiment* (Washington, D.C.: Brookings Institution,1975).

15. Daniel P. Moynihan, *The Politics of a Guaranteed Income: The Nixon Administration and the Family Assistance Plan* (New York: Vintage Books, 1973).

16. Jencks, *et al.*, *Inequality;* and Levine and Bane, eds., *The "Inequality" Controversy.*

17. General Accounting Office, "Training and Education Catalog" (Washington, D.C.: U.S. General Accounting Office, 1991).

18. General Accounting Office, "Education Reform: Initial Effects in Four School Districts" (Washington, D.C.: U.S. General Accounting Office, 1989).

19. General Accounting Office, "Freight Trucking: Promising Approach for Predicting Carriers' Safety Risks" (Washington, D.C.: U.S. General Accounting Office, 1991).

20. General Accounting Office, "Enterprise Zones: Lessons from the Maryland Experience" (Washington, D.C.: U.S. General Accounting Office, 1988).

21. General Accounting Office, "Employee Stock Ownership Plans: Little Evidence of Effects on Corporate Performance" (Washington, D.C.: U.S. General Accounting Office, 1987).

22. General Accounting Office, "Highway Safety: Fatalities in Light Trucks and Vans" (Washington, D.C.: U.S. General Accounting Office, 1990) and General Accounting Office, "Freight Trucking."

23. General Accounting Office, "DOD Simulations: Improved Assessment Procedures Would Increase the Credibility of Results" (Washington, D.C.: U.S. General Accounting Office, 1987).

24. Ira Sharkansky, "Israel's Auditor as Policy-maker," *Public Administration* (London), Vol. 66, No. 1 (1988), 77–90.

25. *Annual Report #37* (Jerusalem: Office of the State Comptroller, 1987), pp. 1291–1325 (Hebrew).

26. Michel Foucault, *Discipline and Punish: The Birth of the Prison*, translated by Alan Sheridan (New York: Vintage Books, 1979).

27. David Dery, *Problem Definition in Policy Analysis* (Lawrence: University of Kansas Press, 1984); and Herbert Jacob, *The Frustration of Policy: Responses to Crime by American Cities* (Boston: Little, Brown, 1984).

28. T. H. Marshall, *Social Policy in the Twentieth Century* (London: Hutchinson University Library, 1967).

29. Kathi V. Friedman, *Legitimation of Social Rights and the Western Welfare State: A Weberian Perspective* (Chapel Hill: University of North Carolina Press, 1981).

30. Thomas Sowell, *The Economics and Politics of Race: An International Perspective* (New York: William Morrow, 1983); Moynihan, *The Politics*.

31. E. S. Savas, *Privatization: The Key to Better Government* (Chatham, N.J.: Chatham House, 1987); and David A. Stockman, *The Triumph of Politics: The Inside Story of the Reagan Revolution* (New York: Avon Books, 1987).

32. Tom Wolfe, *The Bonfire of the Vanities* (New York: Farrar, Straus, and Giroux, Inc., 1988).

33. Julian C. Stanley, "Introduction," in Sohan Modgil and Celia Modgil, eds., *Arthur Jensen: Consensus and Controversy* (New York: The Falmer Press, 1987), pp. 5–15.

34. Arthur R. Jensen, "Social Class, Race and Genetics: Implications for Education," *American Educational Research Journal*, 5, 1968, 1–42; Jensen, *Straight Talk About Mental Tests* (London: Methuen and Co., Ltd., 1981); James R. Flynn, *Race, IQ and Jensen* (London: Routledge and Kegan Paul, 1980); and Richard J. Herrnstein and Charles Murray, *The Bell Curve: Intelligence and Class Structure in American Life* (New York: Free Press, 1994).

35. Stephen Jay Gould, *The Mismeasure of Man* (New York: W. W. Norton and Company, 1981).

36. Martin Deutsch, Irwin Katz, and Arthur R. Jensen, *Social Class, Race, and Psychological Development* (New York: Holt, Rinehart and Winston, 1968).

37. Daniel A. Mazmanian and Paul A. Sabatier, *Implementation and Public Policy* (Glenview, Ill.: Scott, Foresman and Company, 1983); plus Irving L. Janis, *Groupthink: Psychological Studies of Policy Decisions and Fiascos* (Boston: Houghton Mifflin Company, 1983); and John W. Kingdon, *Agendas, Alternatives, and Public Policies* (Boston: Little, Brown, 1984).

38. *New Republic*, August 31, 1992, p. 18.

39. Patricia Davis and Leef Smith, "The Drive to Solve an Unproven Problem," *Washington Post*, Internet edition, November 29, 1998, p. B1.

40. David Brown, "In the Final Analysis," review of Edward Dolnick, *Madness on the Couch: Blaming the Victim in the Heyday of Psychoanalysis* (New York: Simon and Schuster, 1998); *Washington Post*, Internet edition, November 15, 1998, p. X01.

CHAPTER 9

1. Yehezkel Dror, *Public Policymaking Reexamined* (San Francisco: Chandler Publishing Company, 1968).

2. Dror, *Improving Policy and Administration in Israel* (Tel Aviv: Library of Management, 1978, Hebrew).

3. Dan E. Inbar, "Improvisation and Organizational Planning," in Robert V. Carlson and Gary Awkerman, eds., *Educational Planning: Concepts, Strategies, and Practices* (New York: Longman, 1991), pp. 65–80.

4. *Ha'Aretz*, October 10, 1996, p. 4 (Hebrew).

5. *Ha'Aretz*, October 30, 1996, p. 4 (Hebrew).

6. Gerd Theissen, *Sociology of Early Palestinian Christianity* (Philadelphia: Fortress Press, 1978).

7. Abraham Ashkenasi, *Israeli Policies and Palestinian Fragmentation: Political and Social Impacts in Israel and Jerusalem* (Jerusalem: Hebrew University, Leonard Davis Institute, 1988); and Ashkenasi, *Opinion Trends Among Jerusalem Palestinians* (Jerusalem: Hebrew University, Leonard Davis Institute, 1990).

8. Ilene R. Prusher, "Jerusalem's Future Not Found in Ballots," *The Christian Science Monitor*, Internet edition, November 12, 1998.

9. See the author's *Governing Jerusalem: Again on the World's Agenda* (Detroit: Wayne State University Press, 1996), Chapter 5.

10. *Al-Aalam Magazine*, June 1997, p. 27 (Arabic). My thanks to Dr. Hillel Frisch for translating the review.

11. See the author's *Rituals of Conflict: Religion, Politics, and Public Policy in Israel* (Boulder, Colo.: Lynne Rienner, 1996).

12. This list is abstracted from Richard E. Neustadt and Ernest R. May, *Thinking in Time: The Uses of History for Decision Makers* (New York: The Free Press, 1986).

13. See Ecclesiastes 3:1–8.

For Further Reading

Bachrach, Peter, and Morton S. Baratz. *Power and Poverty*. New York: Oxford University Press, 1970.

Benvenisti, Meron. *Jerusalem: The Torn City*. Minneapolis: University of Minnesota Press, 1976.

Berg, Robert J., and David G. Gordon, eds. *Cooperation for International Development: The United States and the Third World in the 1990s*. Boulder, Colo.: Lynne Rienner, 1989.

Bernstein, Peter L. *Against the Gods: The Remarkable Story of Risk*. New York: John Wiley & Sons, Inc., 1996.

Chelimsky, Eleanor. *Program Evaluation: Patterns and Directions*. Washington, D.C.: American Society of Public Administration, 1985.

Coelho, George V., David A. Hamburg, and John E. Adams, eds. *Coping and Adaptation*. New York: Basic Books, 1974.

Connolly, William E. *Politics and Ambiguity*. Madison: University of Wisconsin Press, 1987.

Dery, David. *Data and Policy Change*. Boston: Kluwer Academic Publishers, 1990.

———. *Problem Definition in Policy Analysis*. Lawrence: University of Kansas Press, 1984.

Dror, Yehezkel. *Policymaking Under Adversity*. New Brunswick, N.J.: Transaction Books, 1986.

———. *Public Policymaking Reexamined*. San Francisco: Chandler Publishing Company, 1968.

Elazar, Daniel, and Chaim Kalchheim, eds. *Local Government in Israel*. Lanham, Md.: University Press of America, 1988.

Foucault, Michel. *Discipline and Punish: The Birth of the Prison*, translated by Alan Sheridan. New York: Vintage Books, 1979.

Handler, Joel F. *Down from Bureaucracy: The Ambiguity of Privatization and Empowerment*. Princeton: Princeton University Press, 1996.

Heidenheimer, Arnold J., ed. *Political Corruption: Readings in Comparative Analysis*. New York: Holt, Rinehart & Winston, 1970.

Jacob, Herbert. *The Frustration of Policy: Responses to Crime by American Cities*. Boston: Little, Brown, 1984.

Johnson, Stephen D., and Joseph B. Tamney, eds. *The Political Role of Religion in the United States*. Boulder, Colo.: Westview Press, 1986.

Kimmerling, Baruch, ed. *The Israeli State and Society: Boundaries and Frontiers*. Albany: State University of New York Press, 1989.

Kingdon, John W. *Agendas, Alternatives, and Public Policies*. Boston: Little, Brown, 1984.

Kosko, Bart. *Fuzzy Thinking: The New Science of Fuzzy Logic*. New York: Hyperion, 1993.

Kramer, R., and L. M. Salamon, eds. *Government and the Third Sector*. San Francisco: Jossey Bass, 1992.

Lacey, Michael J., ed. *Religion and Twentieth-Century American Intellectual Life*. New York: Cambridge University Press, 1989.

Lasswell, Harold D. *Politics: Who Gets What, When, How?* New York: McGraw Hill, 1936.

Leege, David C., and Lyman A. Kellstedt, eds. *Rediscovering the Religious Factor in American Politics*. Armonk, N.Y.: M. E. Sharpe, 1993.

Lehman-Wilzig, Sam. *Stiff-necked People, Bottle-necked System: The Evolution and Roots of Israeli Public Protest, 1949–1986*. Bloomington: Indiana University Press, 1991.

Liebman, Charles S., and Eliezer Don-Yehiya. *Civil Religion in Israel: Traditional Judaism and Political Culture*. Berkeley: University of California Press, 1984.

Liebman, Charles S., and Elihu Katz, eds. *The Jewishness of Israelis: Responses to the Guttman Report*. Albany: State University of New York Press, 1997.

Light, Paul C. *Thickening Government: Federal Hierarchy and the Diffusion of Accountability*. Washington, D.C.: The Brookings Institution, 1995.

Lindblom, Charles E. *The Intelligence of Democracy: Decision-Making Through Mutual Adjustment*. New York: The Free Press, 1965.

Lindblom, Charles E. *The Policy-Making Process*. Englewood Cliffs, N.J.: Prentice-Hall, 1968.

Lindblom, Charles E., and David K. Cohen. *Usable Knowledge: Social Science and Social Problem Solving*. New Haven: Yale University Press, 1979.

Lipsky, Michael. *Street Level Bureaucracy: Dilemmas of the Individual in Public Services*. New York: Russell Sage Foundation, 1980.

Mazmanian, Daniel A., and Paul A. Sabatier. *Implementation and Public Policy.* Glenview, Ill.: Scott, Foresman and Company, 1983.

Moore, Laurence. *Selling God: American Religion in the Marketplace of Culture.* New York: Oxford University Press, 1994.

Moynihan, Daniel P. *Coping: On the Practice of Government.* New York: Vintage Books, 1975.

Nakamura, Robert T., and Frank Smallwood. *The Politics of Policy Implementation.* New York: St. Martin's, 1980.

Neusner, Jacob. *Death and Birth of Judaism: The Impact of Christianity, Secularism, and the Holocaust on Jewish Faith.* New York: Basic Books, 1987.

Neustadt, Richard E., and Ernest R. May. *Thinking in Time: The Uses of History for Decision Makers.* New York: The Free Press, 1986.

Obelkevich, Jim, Lyndal Roper, and Raphael Samuel, eds. *Disciplines of Faith: Studies in Religion, Politics and Patriarchy.* London: Routledge & Kegan Paul, 1987.

Quade, E. S., and Grace M. Carter. *Analysis for Public Decisions.* New York: North-Holland, 1989.

Romann, Michael, and Alex Weingrod. *Living Together Separately: Arabs and Jews in Contemporary Jerusalem.* Princeton: Princeton University Press, 1991.

Rose, Richard, and Guy Peters. *Can Government Go Bankrupt?* New York: Basic Books, 1978.

Satire, William. *The First Dissident: The Book of Job in Today's Politics.* New York: Random House, 1992.

Salamon, L. M., *Partners in Public Service: Government-Non-Profit Relations in the Modern Welfare State.* Baltimore: Johns Hopkins University Press, 1995.

Scott, James C. *Comparative Political Corruption.* Englewood Cliffs, N.J.: Prentice-Hall, 1972.

Shalev, Michael. *Labour and the Political Economy in Israel.* New York: Oxford University Press, 1992.

Sharkansky, Ira. *Governing Jerusalem: Again on the World's Agenda.* Detroit: Wayne State University Press, 1996.

———. *Rituals of Conflict: Religion, Politics and Public Policy in Israel.* Boulder, Colo.: Lynne Rienner, 1996.

Simon, Herbert. *Administrative Behavior.* New York: Free Press, 1976.

Smith, Rathgreb, and Michael Lipsky. *NonProfits for Hire: The Welfare State in an Age of Contracting.* Cambridge: Harvard University Press, 1993.

Smooha, Sammy. *Arabs and Jews in Israel: Conflicting and Shared Attitudes in a Divided Society.* Boulder, Colo.: Westview Press, 1989.

Sprinzak, Ehud. *The Ascendance of Israel's Radical Right.* New York: Oxford University Press, 1991.

Stone, Deborah A. *Policy Paradox and Political Reason.* Glenview, Ill.: Scott, Foresman and Little, Brown, 1988.

Thaler, Richard H. *The Winner's Curse: Paradoxes and Anomalies of Economic Life*. Princeton: Princeton University Press, 1992.

Wald, Kenneth D. *Religion and Politics in the United States*. Washington, D.C.: CQ Press, 1992.

Waxman, Chaim I., ed. *Israel as a Religious Reality*. Northvale, N.J.: Jason Aronson Inc., 1994.

Weiss, Thomas J. *Humanitarian Challenges and Intervention: World Politics and the Dilemmas of Help*. Boulder, Colo.: Westview Press, 1996.

Wolfsfeld, Gadi. *The Politics of Provocation*. Albany: State University of New York Press, 1988.

Wuthnow, Robert. *The Restructuring of American Religion*. Princeton: Princeton University Press, 1988.

Yaniv, Avner, ed. *National Security and Democracy in Israel*. Boulder, Colo.: Lynne Rienner Publishers, 1993.

Index

Abraham, 58
Accommodation, ix, 3, 6–7, 10, 19, 139, 140, 149, 163; as a component in democratic politics, 25; definition, 6; distinguished from other coping mechanisms, 19; during Roman rule, 166; effects of, 7, 25; in election campaign, 140; and fear of voter backlash, 106; frustrations of, 167; in Jerusalem, 6; missed opportunities for, 113; in U. S. policy, 7
Accountability, 37, 39–40, 90
Al Quds, 104
al-Majali, Dr. Abd-al-Salam, 97
Aloni, Shulamit, 64–65
Ambiguity, 9; and assessment, 111; and coping, 19; definition of, 6, 19; effects of, 89; how it occurs, 85; limitations of, ix; and limited war, 15; perceptions of, 138; and politics, 20; and President Bill Clinton, 144; in private activities, 17; problems of, 60; and quasi-governmental organizations, 37; and religion, 53, 54; when it oc-

curs, 84; where it occurs, 82; why it occurs, 87
American, 131, 135
Arabs. *See* Palestinians
Arafat, Yassir, 106, 107, 135–36
Assessment: and allegations, 115; and ambiguity, 112; and comparison, 116; and emotion, 113; technical problems, 111
Avoidance, 3, 8–9, 12, 19

Baker, James, 136
Bank shares, 88
Bathsheba, 58
Beit Jalla, 100
Bethlehem, 98, 100, 136
Bible, 62
Borders, 133
Bosnia, 15
Boundaries, 82, 100
Brigham Young University, 68, 72, 74
British mandate, 100
Budget, 22, 23, 37, 87; and indirection, 9
Bureaucratic politics, 23
Burial, 44, 45, 64, 133

Burke, Edmund, 152
Bush, President George, 14

Capital, 137
Catholic, 2, 53, 67, 70
Cave of Patriarchs, 134
Census, 98, 119
Central Bureau of Statistics, 119
Centralization, 35
China, 13, 131, 145, 166
Christians, 38, 167
Clinton, President Bill, 13, 15, 144
Coalition, 31, 34, 43; and ambiguity,
   35; ambiguous membership in,
   117; implications for minor par-
   ties, 113; inevitability of, 36; Ra-
   bin's, 136; and religious tension,
   121
Coleman, James S., 154–56, 162
Conservative Judaism, 46, 62
Coping, 5, 20, 141, 168, 175; and am-
   biguity, 19, 35; the costs of, 170;
   definition, 5; disadvantages, 163;
   as the essence of governance, 21;
   as humane, 23; in Jerusalem, 107;
   the judgement of, 166; the stress
   produced by, 168
Corruption, 11, 24, 32, 117–18, 150
Crime, 3, 67
Crimean War, 93
Crusaders, 95, 101, 103

David, 55, 57–58, 83, 119
Declaration of Independence, 113,
   126
Definition, 19
Democracy, 116, 122
Deri, Ariyeh, 37
Deseret News, 72
Diaspora, 30; ancient, 38; Diaspora
   Jews and Israeli leadership, 62; Di-
   aspora Jews and Israeli politics,
   122; and the nature of the Israeli
   state, 32, 37, 43; Orthodox Jews

in, 31; and religious tensions in Is-
   rael, 43
Difficult problems, 3
Diplomacy, 12, 28
Disinformation, 13, 170
Divorce, 44, 45, 63, 64, 66, 76, 121,
   123

East Jerusalem, 7, 83, 95, 103; desig-
   nation of, 96; Israeli annexation of,
   133; Palestine Authority activity
   in, 145; possible scenarios, 106
Ecclesiastes, 55–56, 75, 151, 170
Edah Ha-Haredit, 119
Egypt, 131, 133, 134
Ethnicity, 123

Family incomes, 70, 123, 125, 127
Fictitious fringe benefits, 80, 85
Final solution, 24, 141, 149, 170
Flag, 105, 117, 118, 122
Foucault, Michel, 158, 162

Gaza, 132, 134
General Accounting Office, 12, 43,
   79, 112, 154, 157
Germany, 13, 24, 104, 126
God, 64, 122
Golan Heights, 132, 137
Governance, 20, 22–23, 149
Greek Orthodox, 67, 95–96
Greeks, 67
Guaranteed income, 154, 155–56

Haram Esh Sharif, 63, 103, 105, 108,
   165
Hebrew Bible, 55–59, 75–76, 112,
   126, 151
Hebron, 64, 98, 131, 133–34, 141
Herrnstein, Richard J., 159
Holocaust, 66
Holy sites, 7, 67, 93, 95, 96, 101
Homilies, 169
Housing, 82, 100, 136

Illegal building, 82
Immigration, 29, 89; and the power of the state, 32; recent wave of, 46, 89
Implementation, 10, 65, 79, 90, 165
Improvisation, 6, 7–8, 19, 20, 23, 149, 163, 164
Indirection, 9, 19
Infant mortality, 126
Informal rules of the game, 11, 142
Insoluble problems, 29
Intafada, 28, 64, 84, 112, 134, 136, 142
Interior Ministry, 36, 82, 83
Investors, 17
Iraq, 14, 131
Islamic Council of Europe, 94
Israel distinguished from other countries, 28

Jensen, Arthur, 159–60
Jeremiah, 55
Jesus Christ, 57, 68
Jewish settlements, 41, 98, 113, 131, 133, 136, 139, 141, 144, 164
Jewish-Arab relations, 38, 114
Jordan, 25, 38, 51, 63, 93, 129, 133, 134, 136
Josephus, 30, 31, 151
Judaism, 45, 59, 61–62, 69, 74

Khartoum Declaration, 133
Kiryat Arba, 134
Knesset, 35, 42, 63, 66, 79, 83, 89, 105, 107, 136
Kollek, Teddy, 39, 82, 101

Labor, 134, 135, 136
Labor Federation, 38, 105
Labor Party, ix, 24, 25, 38, 45–46, 65, 106, 136
Land of Israel, 133
Lasswell, Harold, 79

Lebanon, 25, 28, 33, 84, 128, 129, 130, 133, 134, 135, 136, 140, 141, 142
Likud, 134, 135, 136
Limited war, 13, 15, 28

Machiavelli, 10, 151
Mandates, 11
Marriage, 44, 45, 46, 63, 64, 66, 70, 76, 103, 121, 152
Meretz, 136
Metropolitan Jerusalem, 98, 103
Middle East, 131
Military engagements, 28
Minister of Religious Affairs, 46
Ministries, 36
Ministry of Construction and Housing, 120
Ministry of Education, 42, 46, 120
Ministry of Housing and Construction, 136
Ministry of Religions, 46, 120
Ministry of Welfare, 120
Monarchy, 55
Montesquieu, 152
Mormons, 68
Moslem, 38, 101, 167
Moynihan, Daniel Patrick, 5
Murray, Charles, 159
Muslim, 7, 38, 94, 101, 131, 134, 165, 167

Nathan, 55
National holiday, 45, 122
National Religious Party, 65
Nationalism, 131
Neighborhoods, 82, 100, 103, 133–34
Netanyahu, Benjamin, 61, 98, 107, 112, 136–37, 139, 140–41, 143, 144
Neusner, Jacob, 62
New Testament, 58–59, 68
New York, 135

Non-Orthodox Jews, 29, 38, 44, 45, 63, 65–66, 113, 114, 118, 120, 121–22
Nonprofit organizations, 12, 41–43
Noriega, Manuel, 153

Office of Economic Opportunity, 156
Old City, 95, 97, 100
Orient House, ix, 105, 106, 108, 142
Oz, Amos, 97

Palestine Liberation Organization (PLO), 135–36
Palestinian Authority, 4, 84, 103, 114, 130, 137, 164; and authoritarian-ism, 138; and East Jerusalem, 145; and economic hardship, 140; and Hebron, 141; on its way to becom-ing a state, 25, 47
Palestinian State, 25, 47, 103
Palestinians, 83, 94, 95, 103, 134–36, 167
Partisanship, 22
Patronage, 22
Peace process, ix, 46, 84, 90, 113, 126, 129, 135, 164; and uncer-tainty, 129; and violence, 4
Peres, Shimon, ix, 45, 106, 117, 135, 136, 140–41
Perspective, 136
Philippine Commission on Audit, 158
Philistines, 57–58
Pilgrims, 38
Planning, 38, 83
Policy analysis, 150–62
Politics, 19–20, 22–23, 53, 61, 67, 149
Pollard, Jonathan, 144
Post-Zionism, 112
Privatization, 18, 32, 47
Prohibition, 2
Protestant, 2, 53, 70, 72
Public policy, 63

Quasi-governmental, 12, 32, 37–43, 80, 82

Rabbinate, 45
Rabin, Yitzhak, 25, 30, 34, 76, 106, 117, 136, 140, 164
Ramallah, 98, 100
Rational Decision-making, 21, 149
Reform Judaism, 45–46, 62
Religion, 28, 29, 131; and politics, 17, 26, 54, 61
Religious doctrine, 2, 17, 76–77, 109–10, 117
Religious law, 46, 62, 63, 67, 119, 168
Responsibility, 8, 12, 37, 39, 40, 43, 82, 85, 86, 159, 164
Romans, 4, 38, 59, 67, 83, 94, 99, 101, 103, 123, 166

Sabbath, 29, 63, 66–67
Salt Lake Tribune, 71
Saul, 55
Schach, Rabbi Eliezer, 65
settlements, 131, 133, 136
Shamir, Yitzhak, 135
SHAS, 37, 65, 136
Six-Day war, 41, 131
Smith, Adam, 152
Smith, Joseph, 68–69, 74
Society for the Protection of Nature, 42
Solomon, 56, 58
South Africa, 18, 104, 175
Soviet Union, 4, 29, 66, 82, 131
St. Augustine, 151
State Comptroller, 36, 42–43, 79–80, 81, 82, 84–85, 86–87 88, 89, 91, 112, 120, 158
Status of women, 44
Steffens, Lincoln, 153
Stress, 5, 6, 18, 163
Subtlety, 17
Syria, 133, 136

Tax concessions, 41, 42
Taxes, 3, 6, 20, 31, 32, 36, 106, 116, 119, 121
Tel Aviv, 134
Temple, 38, 83, 101, 119
Temple Mount, 96, 103, 108, 165
Ten Commandments, 56
Theocracy, 76
Torah, 57, 58, 60, 62, 65, 75, 136
Traditional Israeli Jews, 44, 122

Ultra-Orthodox, 44, 63, 64, 119, 122
Uncertainty, 6, 17, 129, 175
Unemployment, 29, 47
United Nations, 135
United States, ix, 2, 3, 11, 12, 13, 14, 18, 30, 35, 38, 43, 45, 47, 53, 62, 63, 69–70, 79, 96, 106, 109, 112, 113, 122, 123, 125–26, 127, 128, 129, 135, 136, 143, 145, 153, 154, 155, 157, 158, 159, 165, 168
University of Utah, 68, 71

Vietnam, 28
Von Clausewitz, Carl, 14

War of Independence, 30, 96, 129, 131
West Bank, 132–33, 134, 137
Western Wall, 44, 63, 83, 93, 94, 107, 133
World Bank, 32

Yugoslavia, 2, 7, 165

About the Author

IRA SHARKANSKY is Professor of Political Science and Public Administration at the Hebrew University of Jerusalem. Earlier he taught at the University of Wisconsin-Madison. He has published articles and books on policy making, public administration, politics and religion, American and Israeli politics, including most recently, *Policymaking in Israel* and *Rituals of Conflict*.

ISBN 0-275-96718-2

HARDCOVER BAR CODE